THEY CALL HEROES MISTER:

THE JESSE WHITE STORY

BY RICK DAVIS

Jesse White

Published by
Lumen-us Publications©
Bringing Light to the Mind
4129 West Sauk Trail
Richton Park, Illinois 60471
Business Phone (708) 679-1255
Fax Phone (708) 679-0437
E-mail: Lumenuspubl@aol.com

They Call Heroes Mister: The Jesse White Story
By Rick Davis

Editor: Wayne Brown

Library of Congress Cataloging-in Publication Data
Davis, Rick

Library of Congress Control Number: 2005936262

They Call Heroes Mister: The Jesse White Story/by Rick Davis

Includes bibliographical references and indexes.
ISBN: 0-9703611-7-3

Barcode: 9780970361172

Printed in the United States of America

For

Julia and Jesse C. White Sr.,
– and –
Lorry and Dick Davis

A house is only as strong as its foundation.

Foreword

I thought I marked the December day in my 1997 date book, but it must have escaped my attention. Important things sometimes do because they don't seem so important at the time.

But I remember the episode, if not the date. Fred Lebed and I were stepping off an elevator in the Cook County Building en route to a meeting with the recorder of deeds, Jesse White. As the elevator doors parted, I could see a gentleman dressed in a white shirt and necktie, buzzing around a table like a hummingbird, picking off empty soft drink cans with one hand, sweeping plates with the other. Few of the people in the hallway were assisting him as he cleaned off the holiday office party buffet table; most were watching him.

"That's him, isn't it?" I asked Fred.

"Yep. That's him."

"Don't these guys have it backwards? Isn't he supposed to be the guy standing there with his arms folded, watching everyone else clean off tables?"

"You don't know Jesse White," Lebed offered.

Eight years and a thousand stories later, I still don't know Jesse White.

Oh, make no mistake. I know him better than some and not nearly as well as others. I hope that I know him well enough to have written the story of his life.

After working shoulder to shoulder with him in the pivotal political campaign of his career, I think I know him. After talking with hundreds of people who know him and who confess to loving him probably less than he loves them, but who love him fiercely nonetheless, I hope I know him. And after sitting in life's press box these past eight years, sometimes watching, sometimes helping, sometimes just wondering, yes, I sometimes think I don't know Jesse White at all.

Bill Clinton knew everything about the fellow whose biography he wrote. He had advantages, though, that I didn't. He grew up with the guy. Me, I've known Jesse White for about 18 percent of my life, about 10 percent of his. Take it from me – I'm the luckier of the two for the experience.

First impressions are lasting ones and my first impression of Jesse White lasts to this day. He won't ask you to do something that he won't do for himself. Just ask the thousands of young men and women whose lives he's saved by guiding them through the Jesse White Tumbling Team adventure. Even when the pain was so severe that he could barely walk with knees that screamed for replacements, the team's namesake still carried the tumbling mats and the trampolettes. He may have grimaced a bit, but he still took his stand as gymnast after gymnast vaulted over, under and around him at the front of the line.

He didn't offer to write the story of his life. He's letting me do it. It's not that he wouldn't, it's just that he was never trained to. But I never played for the Cubs (not that I ever wanted to), and he's never written a book.

In knowing Jesse White and in talking with so many others who do, I find myself knowing much more about him, but still not always knowing what's in him. He is either a very complex man reduced to simplicity or a very simple man wrapped in complexity. Maybe he's both. It wouldn't surprise me.

After all, he's successfully and simultaneously balanced at least four careers over a half century – athletics, teaching, politics and humanitarianism. If, after you've read his story, you can figure out which one he most cherishes, please let me know. I asked him once to make a choice:

Here's your dilemma, Jesse. God comes to you and says, "Jesse White, you can be one of these, but only one. And the one you choose? I'll make you the best one there is. You can be a major league baseball player, or you can be the Illinois secretary of state, or you can be coach and founder of the Jesse White Tumbling Team."

And he thought for a moment. Then he said:

*Well, I was a pretty good basketball player, too, you k*now.

In talking with some of the people in Jesse White's life, I will admit to becoming bored. Not that his life has been boring; it's been anything but. It's just that so many people said so many good things about him that in transcribing some of the interviews I found myself typing, blah, blah, blah.

But you know what? All those blah-blahs actually are the stories of people whose lives have been saved and preserved so that another life can produce more good things. And it's been a good thing for me that I have been assigned the task of encapsulating a life of so many good things.

In reviewing with him the text of this manuscript, I suggested that he was awfully forthright in his recollections of the spankings he dealt out to boys who'd misbehaved in school or who violated the principles established for his youth programs. And he just as forthrightly explained that times have changed, but that parents still want their children to understand the standards of discipline and good behavior. If you find yourself a little judgmental when you read about his approach to corporal punishment, remind yourself that most of these young men were children of mothers without husbands. And trust in the knowledge that, without exception, the men who as boys were spanked by Jesse White will tell you that without his stern hand, many of them might not even draw a breath today. It's quite probable that yesterday's corporal punishment spared today's capital crime.

I have a tattered copy of Webster's New World Dictionary of the American Language perched upright in my credenza. It's old, so its gender preference is masculine. On page 657, this is what it says about a hero:

... any man admired for his qualities or achievements and regarded as an ideal or a model ...

See, you don't have to be famous to be a hero. You don't have to achieve physical feats of magnificence or scale the heights of political fame. In fact, Webster's says you don't even have to save a life to be a hero.

In the books of thousands of people scattered all over this planet, Jesse White is defined as a hero. So if you ever see him on the street or at one of his hundreds of tumbling shows each year or at a political rally, or if you see him delivering a Christmas turkey to a disadvantaged family, you'll be within your rights to call him Jesse.

But just to be safe, call him Mister White.

When it comes to Jesse White, well, they call this hero *mister.*

Rick Davis
Winter 2006

Acknowledgments Researching the life of a man like Jesse White is like holding a mirror up to its own reflection and watching the images shrink into infinity.

For every door that opens, several new doors appear. The research could trail on forever. A biography of a life is the compilation of stories, tales that wouldn't exist without the life itself.

But as the years drift over the stories of the past, it becomes harder to sweep the grit and the cobwebs from those anecdotes. It takes the help of others to pick them up, dust them off and make them presentable.

Therefore, here's a heartfelt *thank you* to those who provided a few of the feather dusters:

To all those who gave their time to talk about their contributions to Jesse White's life and about his impact on theirs. Many of their names are printed in this book; some are not. To so many people who picked up the phone and didn't know the man on the other end of the line, yet who were so gracious to give time and assistance to a cold-call author, you not only provided some of the cement between the bricks, you renewed faith in humankind.

To Steve Densa, who provided minor league statistics and proper name spellings and to Gene Callahan for his referral. To Fred Whitteds, another of the many strangers who helped track college statistics and tried to exhume numbers that sadly belong only to the ages. To Paulette for helping transcribe some of those long, long interviews. To Lillian Jenkins for getting me through when it mattered. To Al Gore for inventing the Internet; research is sure a lot easier than it was thirteen years ago, the last time I tried something like this.

Thanks to Ted Randall for enduring an author's frustrations as well as his exhilarations. Doug Graham and Jim Spence share fireman of the year honors.

To our publisher, Marilyn Foster, for your patience; understanding the difference between encouragement and nagging is a gift. To Wayne S. Brown, our editor. You are the manifestation of "The Elements of Style."

Finally, to My Three Suns – Gloria, Carrie and Kelly — and our Fab Four – Veronica, Olivia, Kira and Joe.

Even for the
reluctant gladiator
there is **glory**
to be **won.**

— Dick Johnson

Chapter One His rich, brown eyes seeped with melancholy, hardly the preferred game face of a gladiator preparing for blood sport. He sat with a handful of friends and advisers in a holding area in the corner of the WLS newsroom on State Street, a few feet from the studio where he would soon face the lions.

This man was an athlete, a baseball player who once stood in front of fastballs that buzzed past his ears like so many mosquitoes on a July Chicago night. This man – the same one, mind you – was trained among the world's fiercest fighters and defenders of freedom as a member of the US Army's 101st Airborne Division. Fear? The first time he rode in an airplane, he was ready to jump out the back of it. And this man was a mentor, a spike of a man who drove home the message of responsibility, commitment and respect in the Cabrini-Green neighborhood that sorely lacked father figures, not to mention law-abiders.

This man had faced some of the nastiest gangsters the neighborhood could thrust at him. Cabrini-Green has produced some of the most violent, calculating and manipulative criminals grown in the Midwest. The gang members long ago were anesthetized to feel nothing when they pulled a trigger or flashed a blade. Still, these worst of the worst never, ever, made the mistake of messing with the man.

Hello, Mr. White. How are you today? Mister White. Never Jesse. Mister White to you, Jesse to your mother.

But on this cold March night, just six days before the Illinois statewide primary election of 1998, Jesse White sat across from an adviser and gloom smeared his chocolate-colored face. He looked woefully less like a warrior than a slaughterhouse guest.

As he spent the final minutes before his televised debate with Timothy J. McCarthy, Jesse White looked as if he had just struck out in the bottom of the ninth, with the bases loaded and the tying and winning runs on base. His campaign advisers gamely attempted to prop him up, to encourage him, to make him understand that a million dollar smile can buy an awful lot of votes.

The man has a million dollar smile, no doubt about that.

But this evening, as a cold drizzle coated the elevated tracks to the north, the only smile Jesse White could muster was meek and submissive. His eyes hovered over his lips in sadness, not sparkle.

"Man, I sure wish it was *you* going out there instead of me," said the candidate.

"Jesse, you'll be fine. This is a home game. He's playing in your park. We got the fans – we've got maybe even the umpire – with us tonight. You'll be fine."

The campaign adviser reached across the table and gripped Jesse White's thick forearm. Even at 64 years of age, the man had forearms as thick and hard as the barrel of a Louisville Slugger.

"And whatever you do, don't forget to flash that million dollar smile. You've got a million dollar smile. Use it."

For the first time, Jesse White, one of two remaining candidates for the Democratic nomination for Illinois secretary of state, smiled more than a timid, apologetic smile.

There have been a million smiles in the man's lifetime. More important, his work has spread the smiles of countless people who would have little to smile about were it not for Jesse White. Life is a game of dominoes. Push the first domino and watch the rest of them tumble, one into the next, until they've all run their course and collapsed from the push by the dominoes before them. Dominoes are black and white. Life is eighteen shades of gray, the eighteen shades of gray that form the perfect photographic negative.

Life is also black and white — and when it is, it can be ugly.

Blessed is the man who endures the ugliness of life and who emerges stronger, wiser and more tolerant because of or in spite of the experience. For that man, for the one who understands strength, wisdom and tolerance, debate is a discussion and not an argument. For that man, for the fortunate man who understands black and white and eighteen shades of gray, life is meaningful.

When he provides the energy that causes the dominoes to tumble in the right direction, he provides meaning to life.

My brother is not the type of person to hold grudges and he forgives anybody.

The old motto is : "do unto others . . . " I don't ; my motto is "do it first."

— Doris Ivy

Chapter Two Since the beginning of time on this rock we call Earth, someone preceded someone else. Before someone there was always someone else, at least so far back to the point there wasn't anybody. Most often, the succeeding person is a genetic copy of the ancestor. Genes determine height, weight, longevity and, to a degree, intelligence. Genes determine *what* you are in terms of matter.

But social scientists in recent centuries have also looked at environment as a dominant factor in determining *who* you are. Environment helps determine so many of those other things that really matter.

Before there was a Jesse Clark White Jr. there had to be a Jesse Clark White Sr.

The Senior White was born February 12, 1911, in Caruthersville, deep in the boot heel of Missouri and separated from Tennessee by the Mississippi River. The woman who would one day be Mrs. Jesse White Sr., Julia Chapman, was born in Earle, Arkansas, thirty-five miles west of Memphis.

They met a few months after Julia's first husband died and they were more than satisfied to relocate to Illinois.

Together they raised seven children. Julia's three children from her previous marriage to Edward Shaw, who died of typhoid fever, were Doris, Edward and Charles. Jesse and Julia White also had four of their own, including Dorothy, Cora and George. Of the White children, Jesse was the eldest, born in Alton, Illinois, on June 23, 1934. Seven years later, the family moved to Chicago to pursue brighter economic opportunities in the nation's second city.

"My family roots are in the South but as a child I always lived in

Illinois," the younger Jesse White explains. "I think they just wanted to get away. They wanted to get away from the deplorable conditions of the South, all of the segregation and discrimination."

The very reasons they relocated to Illinois would be the same ones that caused considerable anxiety for Julia White when her son was ready for college.

"When my mother and father moved us from Alton to Chicago, my father left without having a job waiting for him."

But Julia and Jesse White lived the belief that any life in Chicago was preferable to a life in the South, where their parents and grandparents felt the sting of racial discrimination and witnessed mindless violence. For several years on and off after they moved to Chicago, the White family was forced to accept public aid, although it clearly was not the first choice of Jesse White Sr.

"My father didn't have a job. He'd sell wood, he'd sell ice, he'd sell coal. He did whatever he could to put food on the table. Finally, he got a job during the war at the American Aircraft Corporation and was involved in making planes.

"He worked for American Aircraft for a few years and then went to work in a pottery factory in Chicago, making sinks, bowls and toilet seats. After that, he decided to go into a business of his own and he started a janitorial company. So for a while, he would go to work at the pottery company during the day and come home, get something to eat and go back out and run his janitorial business at night.

"I can't remember exactly, but he probably had the janitorial business for maybe twenty-five or thirty years before he passed away in 1977."

The custodial company was called, appropriately, Mr. White's Janitorial Service and Jesse White Sr. ran the business out of the family's home on the Near North side.

"He started out on his own but then it grew like so many small businesses and then he was able to hire a few people to work for him. He had customers like Prudential Insurance, General Finance Company, some of the larger companies in Chicago."

And like so many other small businesses, Mr. White's Janitorial Service was a child of necessity.

"He just wanted some extra income because he had a large family and it took some extra money to make sure that we all had what we needed to get by. He was a gentleman in every way. He was well liked and respected by all. He taught us the meaning of respect and how to work with his fellow man."

Physical strength helped Jesse White Sr. put in the hours it took to grow a business. But the mental toughness – one of those intangible environmental traits – helped him grow his son.

"He worked with a lot of white people and most of his friends were white and he had established a good working relationship with the people who worked with him and the people he worked around. He seemed to get along well with everyone, everywhere he worked."

As a boy, Jesse White Jr. attended Schiller Elementary School, a place where he'd one day earn a living. School was a place to learn the basic academic foundations of literacy and arithmetic. But life was to be learned on the extracurricular turf of the city's parks and assorted recreational facilities. During and after World War II, the parks and youth centers in Chicago played a major role in sculpting young men's minds as well as their bodies. The best student-athletes of the era came out of the programs offered by the Chicago Park District.

One celebrated Chicagoan who evolved his amateur sports experiences into a legendary political career is Edmund L. Kelly. It's an overcast Saturday morning and a chilly February wind is making a feeble attempt to breathe life back into the death of yet another winter. But there's a flame burning in the octogenarian heart of Ed Kelly and he's bursting with pride as he shows a visitor the surfeit of pictures on the walls of his outer office. A walk through the modest Ed Kelly Youth Foundation office at 2224 W. Lawrence Avenue is a stroll through the second half of the twentieth century's history of Chicago politics and sports. Scores of black-and-white photographs plaster the walls. Pictures of Ed Kelly and famous athletes. Pictures of Ed Kelly and nightclub and movie stars. Pictures of Ed Kelly and the most powerful politicians of his era.

Many of the photos are signed. There are pictures of household Americana like Sinatra and Ali and Clinton. There are Chicago icons like Veeck and Caray, Butkus and Skowron. Perhaps the most poignant photograph is the one of Ed Kelly, then superintendent of the Chicago Park District, bending over and whispering to a smiling Richard J. Daley during a dedication ceremony at Mann Park on the city's East Side. Daley appears tired in the photo. It is the last photograph ever taken of the legendary Chicago mayor, who died three hours after the shutter was snapped.

Ed Kelly was born August 19, 1924, and raised in the same neighborhood that produced the young Jesse White.

"We've called it a lot of different names," Kelly says. "Little Italy, Smoky Hollow, Hell's Kitchen. When we came back from the war, a lot of the families were moving out of the area and a lot of African Americans were coming into the area."

After returning from the war, Kelly was working as a physical instructor at Welles Park. In 1948, one of his supervisors downtown called and asked him to drive to the Near North neighborhood and see what he could do with a potentially explosive racial situation percolating at Seward Park at Sedgwick and Division streets.

"This supervisor asked me to go down there and talk with my buddies," Kelly explains. "These were the guys who I used to play ball with when we were kids. My supervisor asked me to go down to the park and straighten them out, to tell them to leave this man alone because he was such a wonderful young man."

The "wonderful young man" to whom Ed Kelly refers was Claude Walton, the new hire at Seward Park. Claude Walton wasn't your ordinary new employee at the park; he was the first African American to work at Seward Park.

"Claude Walton was a track star with Ralph Metcalfe," Kelly recalls. Metcalfe, who later would serve in the United States House of Representatives, was one of Jesse Owens' mates on the four-man 400-meter relay team that won the gold medal at the Berlin Olympic Games in 1936. "Claude was a great runner and a wonderful, wonderful person.

He had problems down there at Seward Park because he was an African American in a park where they had never had an African American working there before.

"So I went down there and I knew who the trouble guys were. I got a hold of them and I backed them off, and within three months they fell in love with Claude Walton down there. These guys were Irish and Italian and some German — a mixture. There was a black element living there but until then they weren't much involved in the park.

"I think the white guys who were down there were threatened and felt the park was going to be taken over by blacks. I think that was their first reaction. Then when they found out what kind of a man Claude was, it evaporated."

That year, a young man from Waller High School enrolled in the Seward Park gym classes. He was 14, barely a teenager, but something inside him was beginning to click.

"Back then, there were row houses on Oak Street and Hudson," Claude Walton remembers. "And Jesse White was a student at Waller High School. The line that tied most of the kids at Waller was the gym program we had at Seward Park.

"That's where Jesse got his first exposure to tumbling, which is one of the activities I conducted at the park. Jesse was a nice kid, low-key and easy. He was not brash or imposing. He was a likeable individual and all of the kids respected him.

"I do not think that Jesse himself tumbled because he was too old. The tumblers were midgets and juniors between the ages of 10 and 14. Jesse was already in high school, but he saw the kids tumbling and that probably impressed and inspired him."

Perhaps it did. If the seed was planted in Seward Park, it would take more than a decade for it to sprout new life. There were other sports in which a young man could excel. But the discipline that was required of Claude Walton's kids most certainly reinforced the lessons being taught at home by Jesse Sr. and Julia White.

"The joke was, if you were bad or not maintaining your grades, you could not come to the park. That was a tough type of punishment for those kids," Walton offers. "But back then the parents were very supportive and they understood the principles that were being instilled. During that time the community was different. There was neither gang influence nor the element of fear."

Like so many kids of his generation, the parks sustained Jesse White. There were no electronic devices to pollute a child's mind and atrophy his muscles. A pod and a mouse still were names for a vegetable shell and a rodent. In the summer Jesse White played baseball. In the winter he played basketball. And as one season melted into the next and then froze again, he got better and better in each sport. As a young Jesse White hopscotched from one sport to another, he bounced into men who would refine his skills and shape his attitude.

Warren Chapman was one of the men who helped chisel Jesse White's proficiency as an athlete.

"I've never forgotten the way that young man carried himself," Chapman remembers. "Back in those days the guys back in the neighborhood called him 'Buck' because that's what he was – a young buck. Even today, the guys who knew him back then call him Buck because he's the same guy to them now as he was back where they were just kids."

Chapman, who in 1939 was the first African American to play basketball for DePaul University, was counselor and physical education instructor at the Lower North Center, which was one of the neighborhood hangouts where kids could focus on sports. Now a part of the Chicago Youth Centers, it served kids of all ages and complemented the park district programs. In addition to Jesse White, two other notable protégés of Warren Chapman were musicians Ramsey (The In Crowd) Lewis and Curtis (Superfly) Mayfield.

"Everybody in there was an outstanding athlete," Chapman contends. "But there were a lot of athletes from the city who just didn't make it. I had a feeling Jesse would be different though. He was special and you could see that he was special not just because he was an athlete, but because of the way he carried himself.

"I remember he came to me one day when he was playing baseball for Waller and he told me he couldn't get a hit. I told him to move up on the plate. The next day he got a hit and he never looked back. He started hitting the ball all over the place."

Indeed, he did. For most boys growing up in Chicago after World War II, sport was life and life was sport. There may have been a few bullies and derelicts among Jesse White's classmates, but there certainly was not the threat of gangs that permeates so many Chicago neighborhoods of the twenty-first century. And as he matured, Jesse White's dream continued to come into focus. Major league baseball was a white man's fortress until Jesse White became a teenager. But when the color barrier started to wobble at the behest of a white man named Branch Rickey, black kids like Jesse White could dream. There just might be a chance ...

As a sophomore, Jesse White began to blossom in the infield dirt of the Waller High School baseball team. Testament came from this spring 1950 story in the Chicago Tribune:

Waller May Be Strong in 1951

By Edward Jensen

Waller High School, which is having a lean year in baseball, will have five of this year's regulars back for the 1951 season.

Coach Tom Roberts hopes the five veterans will give him the nucleus for a winning team in 1951.

Basket Star at Third

Jesse White, the sophomore who was on the Tribune all-north section basketball team this winter, plays third base and may develop into one of the best players in the section in 1951. He was handicapped most of this season by a sprained ankle.

White also may have been handicapped by playing out of position. The greatest of third basemen possess quick feet but are not necessarily blessed with speed. Brooks Robinson, the Baltimore Oriole who arguably was the greatest defensive third baseman of his time, looked on the base paths as if his feet were cast in concrete. But at the hot corner he was a cat. Paul Blair, on the other hand, patrolled centerfield for the same Orioles teams. He had quickness but he also had speed. Quickness can be harnessed; velocity implores to be unleashed.

By his junior year, Jesse White was moved to centerfield where his blazing speed and quickness off the ball worked to the Wolves' advantage. The switch enabled him to blossom and White was voted to the *Chicago Tribune's* All-North city baseball team.

Seasons may not change much in California, Arizona and Florida. But in Chicago, that little village hugging the western shores of Lake Michigan, summers are short and winters are bitter. The only winter leagues in the Chicago of the 1940s were staged on basketball courts. Jesse White's exploits on the hardwood were legendary. In his day, the Chicago Public League divided its teams according to height – the seniors (taller than 5 feet 9) and the juniors. At 5 feet 8, White played on the Waller Wolves junior squad. Because he was one of the taller players on the junior team, White was moved to center by the time he was in his final year of high school.

But position didn't matter. Throughout his basketball career at Waller, now known as Lincoln Park Academy, Jesse White was a running, gunning, scoring machine.

"I could shoot the ball," he says today without a trace of modesty. He's not cocky about it. He's just matter-of-fact. Paging through the crispy old pages of newspaper sports pages provides corroboration. Aged to a smoky sepia, the crusty, light brown pages from the *Chicago Tribune* and *Chicago Sun-Times* supply evidence that Jesse White could indeed put the ball in the hole.

At Waller, he was given a proper platform to demonstrate his basketball aptitude. Waller was a basketball powerhouse before and during White's years at the school. The *Chicago Daily News* reported:

Waller Poised to Give Junior Cage Foes 1-2

Aim to Repeat 1946 Title Sweep

By Bud Nangle

A good left with an equally good right is a terrific asset to any sport.

That's the way coach Russ Chappel figures it and he ought to know because he has one of the most prolific one-two scoring punches in junior ball he's ever had at Waller.

"The '46 team (which won the title) had a little more depth in scoring,"

he observed.

"This year Mogan and White have done most of it, but I'm sure some of the other kids could score if they'd only shoot."

Of course Dan Mogan and Jesse White, both forwards, compiled the most brilliant scoring record at the school, finishing virtually under a blanket with 227 and 231 points respectively.

A year later, White caught the attention of *Tribune* sportswriter Jerry Le Donne:

Mainstay of the Waller attack is sharp-shooting Jesse White, who led the Wolves to the section title last year and was named to The Tribune's all-league team.

White is regarded by Coach Russ Chappel, who has developed and seen many outstanding junior players in his 32-year coaching career, as one of the finest players to come out of the City league.

"Jesse is only 5 feet 8, but he gets about three feet off the floor when he lets loose with his one hander and is next to impossible to stop.

Last year White finished fourth in the scoring parade with 231 points as Waller had a 9-0 league record. He is expected to top that total this season. Despite his height several colleges have shown interest in him.

As Le Donne projected, White surpassed his 231-point third year total with 301 in his final year at Waller, finishing second overall in the Public League behind Frank Stryczek of Washburne Trade School.

After putting the finishing touches to an outstanding high school basketball career, White summarized the experience for the *Chicago Sun-Times:*

Jesse White, star of the Waller Junior basketball team, says the thing of which he is most proud is having been able to play with the Waller Juniors for three years ...

White has among his accomplishments a total of 1,410 points for 60 games in the three years. He has a total of 674 points in 27 league games, an average of 25 points per game. He has made the All-North Section for three years and the All-City team for the past two years.

As a politician, Jesse White has never been on the losing side of a recount. But a sports writing recount erased the 24-hour glory of what would have been an incredible 68-point night:

Because of a schoolboy prank played on the City News Bureau, Jesse White of Waller was credited with scoring 68 points in a Public League basketball game Wednesday against Tuley.

The City News Bureau *said Thursday that its regular school correspondent did not report the game, but instead an outsider telephoned with the box score.*

The correct box score shows White actually scored 51 points as Waller won the game 102-67.

Only 51 points?

"Everything I touched went in the basket that night. I could have shot from half court and it would have gone in. I was a ball of fire that night."

With all-city credentials in both basketball and baseball, Jesse White found himself facing a choice as he gripped his Waller High School diploma in the spring of 1952. Forty-three years later those credentials would be strong enough to prompt his election to the Chicago Public League Basketball Coaches Hall of Fame.

Major league baseball scouts had seen his ability and were impressed enough that the old St. Louis Browns offered him a contract. The big leagues had at long last been integrated five years earlier, and the Negro Leagues were no longer the only choice for a talented black baseball player. Opportunity was peeking through the clouds and African American players were beginning to feel the warm rays of hope.

Jesse White Sr. was most certainly proud of his namesake's athletic abilities and accomplishments. Junior's future was ablaze with promise and hope. But Jesse White Sr. knew how hard life can be, how work can drain a man's energies and prey on his soul. A graduate of nothing higher than sixth grade, Jesse White Sr. nonetheless understood the value of education.

"It was my decision," the younger White says today. "I had an offer to play professional baseball and I had a scholarship offer to continue on to college. But my father told me to take the scholarship. He told me that no one can take your education away from you. Once you are educated, no one can take it away from you. The day comes when everyone loses the ability to hit a baseball, when we no longer can run. My father only had a sixth-grade education, but he was wise enough to understand that an education can sustain you."

It was Junior's decision, but he was smart enough to respect the opinion of the man who preceded him to the planet.

I get **up** and

nothing gets me down . . .

Might as well **jump.**

— Van Halen

Chapter Three "So I'm standing in line, waiting to go see the registrar so I can get signed up for classes."

It's September 1952, and, that's right, Jesse White heeded his father's advice and accepted the scholarship.

"I had a friend by the name of Otho Anthony, who was a basketball player at Alabama State College and he knew what I had been up to back in Chicago. He had already graduated from Alabama State but he knew that I could shoot the ball and he said that's what they needed down at Alabama State."

Between Otho Anthony's referrals and some networking by his old friend Warren Chapman, Jesse White secured the financial support necessary to choose college over professional baseball.

"So I'm standing in line, waiting to see the registrar and these fellows in front of me are talking about how they're getting a big-time basketball player from Chicago."

He remembers what he heard as he eavesdropped:

"Man, we've got a real player coming down here, some guy who knocked the lights out up in Chicago. His name is something like Green or Brown or White. That's it – White – his name's Jesse White. That's the guy's name.

"People have been talking about him and saying the guy can really shoot the ball. Yeah, he's a big guy, something like six-four or six-five. Man, is that cat gonna give us a strong basketball team this year!"

White pauses and chuckles at the recollection.

"Well, the registrar calls out the name Jesse White. I said, 'This is he.' Then I hear some guy behind me say, 'That little, short son of a bitch. He can't play ball. I thought we had some star player coming down here from Chicago."

He may not have been six-four or six-five, but Jesse White brought something with him other than size from Chicago. Until the winter of 1953, no one at Alabama State College or anyone else in the Southern Intercollegiate Athletic Conference had seen a modern jump shot. Not until Jesse White showed 'em how it was done in Chicago.

Ask four former students who saw him play what set White apart from any other southern player of his era.

"Jump shot," says Dr. Emmit Horne.

"He brought the jump shot," remembers Eddie Poole.

"No one ever saw a jump shot until Jesse came to Alabama State," Richard Jordan contends.

"The jump shot got to be the thing here because of Jesse White," asserts Robert E. James.

James was still a student at Booker T. Washington High School when he first saw White play for Alabama State.

"The thing that was so unique about him was that jump shot," says James. "We had guys like Sweetwater Clifton come through here but they didn't stay long." It's interesting James would remember Nathaniel "Sweetwater" Clifton, the first African American to play in the National Basketball Association when he signed with the New York Knickerbockers out of Xavier College in 1950. Clifton, who also hailed from Chicago and who earned his nickname because of his love for soft drinks, played seven years in the NBA and two with the Harlem Globetrotters. But Sweetwater Clifton was 6 feet 7, nearly a full foot taller than Jesse White. "I was just in high school when I saw Jesse White play, but I can't forget how he shot that jump shot and the way people watched in awe at the new play he brought to this area."

James, now 65, worked as an executive at the Montgomery YMCA for thirty years before taking a position with the local job corps center. He is an avid sports enthusiast and since childhood has closely followed Alabama State athletics.

"Man, Jesse was a wizard," James asserts. "You've heard of Michael Jordan? Think of Michael Jordan when you think of Jesse operating on the floor. Jesse was smooth. He wasn't a talker on the floor. He would just do what he had to do. Jesse White was as good as any basketball player I've seen come through these parts."

During White's college career, Alabama State was a member of the Southern Intercollegiate Athletic Conference (SIAC). The conference was composed of all-African American colleges and produced some of the nation's best athletic talent. The SIAC, founded in 1913, today is a Division II member of the National Collegiate Athletic Association. Now Alabama State University, it since has moved to the Southwestern Athletic Conference (SWAC), whose membership includes such traditional black college sports powers as Grambling State University and Southern University.

When traditional white universities in the South began to first accept and later recruit black athletes, the SIAC and SWAC began to lose their appeal to outstanding African American players. In the playing days of Jesse White, however, a black player's route to the major leagues, the NBA or the National Football League was not through Tuscaloosa, it was by way of Montgomery. Today's preeminent black athletes go on recruiting visits to Baton Rouge and visit the campus of LSU. In the collegiate salad days of Lou Brock and Bob Love, the only Baton Rouge campus with an open door to a black athlete was Southern University.

As a result of the segregated admissions policies of southern colleges and universities, the SWAC produced dozens of star athletes who later flourished in professional sports. The Southwestern Athletic Conference Hall of Fame is packed with the names of athletes who went on to notable professional sports careers:

- Lou Brock, Southern University, Baton Rouge. Brock, who played in the Chicago Cubs organization before he was traded to the St. Louis Cardinals, holds the National League record for career stolen bases with 938 and has been eclipsed only by the American League's Rickey Henderson. Brock was elected to the Baseball Hall of Fame in 1985.

- Eddie Robinson, Grambling State University, Grambling, Louisiana. Robinson, who coached at Grambling from 1941 to 1997, is the winningest head football coach in national collegiate history. He compiled a 408-165-15 record as head coach of the Tigers.
- Doug Williams, Grambling State. In 1988, Williams became the first African American quarterback to play in the Super Bowl as he led the Washington Redskins to a 42-10 thrashing of the Denver Broncos.
- Walter Payton, Jackson State University, Jackson, Mississippi. The man they called Sweetness won the hearts of Chicago Bears fans from 1975 to 1987 and broke Jim Brown's career rushing record of 12,312 yards.
- Zelmo Beaty, Prairie View, A&M, Prairie View, Texas. Twice an NBA all-star, Beaty jumped to the maverick American Basketball Association in 1971 and helped the new conference gain credibility as a basketball major league.
- David "Deacon" Jones, Mississippi Valley State University, Itta Bena, Mississippi. Jones, who attended the school when it was known as Mississippi Vocational, was an eight-time Pro Bowler for the Los Angeles Rams in the National Football League.
- Bob Love, Southern University. Love was a three-time NBA all-star with the Chicago Bulls during the 1970s.

Other SWAC Hall of Famers include former NFL stars Buck Buchanan, Lem Barney and Charlie Joiner; NBA all-star Willis Reed, and Tommy Agee, who created his own memorable moments as a member of the New York Mets in the 1969 World Series. It is a very impressive list of student-athletes. It is a list that includes Jesse White, who was inducted in 1995 as a member of the SWAC's fourth Hall of Fame class.

Regrettably, most of the records and statistics forged prior to 1970 by thousands of black collegiate athletes in the South have been lost or purged from their institutions' files. Alabama State University has virtually no records to support the wonder of Jesse White's basketball or baseball feats and it is not alone. Neither the sports information office nor the university's Levi Watkins Library and Resources Learning Center has any records of their sports teams before 1965 and the earliest statistics from the mid-1960s can be found sprinkled only sporadically in cabinets in the library.

However, at least one independent source of African American collegiate sports information confirms Jesse White is worthy of his election to the SWAC Hall of Fame. Fred Whitteds, whose *Black College Sports Encyclopedia* has begun to comb through hundreds of newspaper articles in an effort to re-create past athletic achievements, found a couple references to Jesse White's basketball career at Alabama State. According to Whitteds' research, White was named to the all-Southern Intercollegiate Athletic Conference basketball team for the 1953-54 season and to the conference all-tournament team in 1954.

In the SIAC postseason conference tournament, Alabama State beat Benedict College of Columbia, South Carolina, 92-73 in the first round. White paced the Hornets' attack with 21 points. In the second round Florida A&M eliminated Alabama State, 74-72, and White scored 28. Alabama State lost the consolation game to Xavier College of New Orleans, 74-72 and White ended his season with 19 points.

"Unfortunately, a lot of that history has been purged from those schools," Whitteds said. The SIAC didn't join the National Association of Intercollegiate Athletics until 1955, so there was no uniform reporting system required of its member schools prior to that era. In the case of Alabama State, the statistics have simply disappeared. "Much of what we have today, which isn't a lot, has been re-created from combing through newspaper stories and oral histories."

Whitteds said the brand of basketball played by the black colleges in the South was a "fast-paced, run-and-gun kind of a game." He confirms that although the game was faster paced than white players were accustomed to, the set shot was still standard fare until Jesse White arrived in Montgomery.

Fortunately, there are survivors among the people who witnessed Jesse White's collegiate career.

Richard Jordan is president of the I Support the Athletic Program (ISTAP), a student-athlete sponsor group at Alabama State. He earned his bachelor's and master's degrees from Alabama State and was two years behind Jesse White at the Montgomery campus. With or without the printed numbers, Richard Jordan is able to re-create White's athletic prowess.

"He was a super athlete. In fact, he was ahead of his time," contends Jordan. "Coming to Alabama State he brought what you call the jump shot. That was something new for this area and I guess he brought it with him from Illinois. We weren't used to it in this area and it took a couple years for the coaches around here to figure out a defense for it.

"For his style he was better than any other, other than John Chaney, who was playing for Bethune-Cookman. At the time they were the two hottest basketball players that I could think of. They were really rivals at the time."

Chaney, who has earned national acclaim as head basketball coach at Temple University, was voted National Association of Intercollegiate Athletics all-America in 1953. The same year, he was named most valuable player in the NAIA championship tournament. Chaney was elected to the National Basketball Hall of Fame in 2001.

Eddie Poole, a Montgomery native and fraternity brother of Jesse White's, said his friend, the Chicago Public League import, stunned Alabama State fans.

"The first time I saw Jesse play, I had just returned from the Air Force," Poole remembers. "Jesse brought with him from Chicago the jump shot and most of the people in the South had not seen that kind of play before. They were accustomed to the set shot."

To this day, admiration pours over Eddie Poole's lips as he speaks of his friend's athletic ability.

"Jesse would be on the fast break or a steal – I can still see it in my mind – and instead of going all the way and laying it in, he would pull up at the free throw line and shoot the ball. And it would go in. He was a remarkable athlete."

Because baseball is far less a spectator sport than is basketball at the college level, White's contemporaries didn't see much of him on the diamond. Richard Jordan, however, echoes the sentiments of the major league scouts who saw Jesse White play.

"He was a good hitter and had an unusually strong arm," Jordan says. "And he could fly."

Eddie Poole concurs:

"Jesse was very popular because he was such a good guy, but also because he was such an outstanding athlete. He was so fast, so quick and he was a terrific baseball player. Any time he'd get on first base you knew he was going to steal second. Without a doubt."

Today, Jesse White freely admits that he was so consumed with the fire to succeed on the court, in the field and in the classroom that he had little time for social issues. Sometimes, however, change sucks you into the whirlpool without asking if you mind getting wet.

For the student who is fortunate enough to attend a college or university away from home, higher education is an exposure to the future. The classroom serves as an incubator for knowledge, but day-to-day experience is a laboratory for life. Jesse White earned his bachelor's degree in education from Alabama State, a certification that would open doors to employment and a career as a schoolteacher.

You can use some of what you learn in the classroom when you enter the real world. But more of what you learn outside the classroom becomes your foundation, your blueprint for the streets. At Alabama State, Jesse White drank from the trophy cup of athletic success and glory. He learned how to instruct and to pass that instruction on to future generations.

But whether he wanted to encounter it or not, change was about to explode across the nation. What Jesse White was learning outside the classroom was unique to his generation of Americans. And the lesson would change the course of this nation.

Oh, **be swift, my soul,**
to answer Him. **Be jubilant,**
my feet. Our God
is marching on.

— Dr. Martin Luther King Jr.,
Montgomery, Alabama,
March 25, 1965

Chapter Four Ghosts seem to walk the earth forever, which is a lot longer than their mortal carcasses.

They carry the chains of their past lives and they rattle about at the most inopportune times. Just about the time you think they've finally evaporated into the ether, they slip through a crack in the floorboards and scare the crap out of you.

Ghosts must like heat and humidity because Montgomery, Alabama, is as steamy as a wok on Chinese New Year. And ghosts are everywhere in Montgomery. If you can't see them, you most certainly can feel them. And if you learn to listen with your eyes, you can hear much of what they trumpeted in life. These ghosts, the spirits of Montgomery's rich and historic roots, they hang over the town like moss from a bayou cypress tree.

In Montgomery, the ghost of Jefferson Davis is ubiquitous. He stands atop the last marble step in front of the hulking wooden double doors of the milky white capitol, his right hand raised in fealty as he forever pledges his faith and honor to the Confederacy he has just created.

At the throat of the old senate chambers, the ghost of Jefferson Davis presides over his secessionist brothers-in-arms as they craft a constitution to free them from the chains of the Union and Abraham Lincoln's commitment to stitch together two divergent philosophies that never shall meet.

Surely the ghost of Jefferson Davis darts back and forth between the statue of his living likeness on the capitol lawn and the Confederate memorial less than a hundred yards to the northeast, where replicas of each of the Confederacy's flags hang limp in a summer swelter. For a nation with a legitimate life of only four years, the Confederate States of America sure had a lot of flags.

Across Bainbridge Street, the ghost of the Confederacy's only president can take respite in a parlor or in the president's own bedroom. Jefferson Davis's Confederate White House surely receives the ghost of its late owner, especially on June 3, the president's birthday and a state holiday in Alabama.

And outside the old Alabama supreme court chamber, the ghost of Jefferson Davis most certainly stops to visit the spot where his catafalque rested in state just days before his mortal remains were planted beneath the Virginia topsoil.

The ghost of Jefferson Davis hangs over Montgomery like the heat and humidity of a July morning. But his ghost is not alone. The ghosts of the Confederacy have been fused forever in this southern town with the spirits of peaceful revolution and a fight for equality under the law of a Union that ultimately prevailed.

Just a block west of where Jefferson Davis began his inaugural parade on February 18, 1861, the spirit of a Baptist minister lives on as a small wedding party descends the stairs of the nineteenth century brick church at 454 Dexter Avenue. Surely the ghost of this simple minister, the man whose birthday today is a national holiday, accompanies the bride and groom down the stairs and to their waiting car.

The ghost of Dr. Martin Luther King Jr. hovers a couple dozen stairs below the statue of Jefferson Davis. Most assuredly, you can hear this spirit as his declaration pours forth the words from his speech of March 25, 1965:

Segregation is on its deathbed …

Several blocks to the north, the ghost of Martin Luther King drifts above the front porch at 309 S. Jackson Street, where dynamite rocked his mortal residence just a few weeks after a diminutive black woman launched a protest that would mark the beginning of the end of legalized segregation in the United States.

And Dr. King's spirit must also come to visit the corner of Montgomery and Molton streets, where Montgomery police led Rosa

Parks from the city transit bus after she refused to give up her seat to a white passenger who had moments earlier embarked onto the bus.

It is impossible not to feel the spirits of Jefferson Davis and Martin Luther King as the heat rises from the pavement. Ghosts of two centuries brought together by a culture of separatism and the movement to defeat it.

Montgomery is home to ghosts of disparate and contradictory movements, two pivot points in America's history. It's not the place where a black Chicago teenager would likely seek refuge in 1952. Still, educational opportunity was painfully limited when Jesse White graduated from high school and agonized over his college choices. For the black athlete, the best places to study and play were the all-black colleges and universities in the deep South, the ones born of reconstruction, when children of slaves began to reap the benefits of education.

The irony of Jesse White's choices is painfully obvious. His best opportunity to succeed as an athlete existed where he was least likely to perform as an American citizen. On the athletic fields and courts, he had the unlimited ability and prospects to excel. In the classroom he had the ability to blossom and grow.

But the streets of Montgomery, Alabama, where the ghosts of separatism and segregation haunt us even today, are the avenues where the parades of inequality and justice collided a century apart. Jesse White was availing himself of a culture he had not expected. A son of tolerance and peaceful coexistence, Jesse White was about to enter a world where skin rivaled only concrete in the strength of its walls.

With apologies to L. Frank Baum: *Jesse White, I have a feeling you're not in Chicago anymore.*

I am a **historian**

and I

respect history

— Aroine Irby, Alabama state capitol docent

Chapter Five Two of American history's most significant parades snaked their way up Montgomery, Alabama's Dexter Avenue.

The first marched up Goat Hill, the site of the Alabama state capitol, on February 18, 1861. A bronze star today marks the spot where the parade culminated on the top step of the capitol; it is where Jefferson Davis took the oath as president of the Confederate States of America.

Like the parades that its Dexter Avenue hosted, the City of Montgomery has a great seal emblazoned with contradictory mottoes. One inscription, set inside a six-pointed star, pronounces Montgomery the *Cradle of the Confederacy*. A second motto encircles the star and proclaims *Birthplace of the Civil Rights Movement*.

Perhaps Aroine Irby best explains the contradiction when he says:

"If you were raised behind a blind, you would never see the light."

Irby's muscular frame belies his 59 years. He has lived most of his life in Alabama and today works as a docent at the Alabama state capitol in Montgomery. Aroine Irby personifies a docent; anywhere else he might be titled a tour guide. He is articulate and holds a doctorate degree in world history. It is a background that has instilled in him a deep and abiding respect in the past as a crystal ball for the future. Aroine Irby is a docent of metaphysical as well as material history.

Irby chooses his words carefully as he describes in intricate detail the circumstances surrounding the planting of Montgomery's "moon tree," a loblolly pine whose seed orbited the moon as part of the *Apollo 14* mission in 1971. As he methodically describes the rich history of the Alabama state capitol, he stops from time to time to inject an editorial comment.

For example, he claims to be a fishing buddy of Governor Bob Riley but refuses to hide the fact he would never vote for the man. He confides he would never vote for a Republican because of the Grand Old Party's refusal as a party to embrace the 1965 Voting Rights Act. A friend can only do so much, you see.

The Voting Rights Act holds a special place in Aroine Irby's heart. He was one of thousands of demonstrators to march from Selma across the Edmund Pettus Bridge and on to Montgomery in March of 1965, a prelude to the Reverend Dr. Martin Luther King Jr.'s declaration that "segregation is on its deathbed."

"It was a moving time," Irby recalls. "There are some things I remember about it more than anything else."

In 1965, Irby was a student at Alabama State University in Montgomery, the school that eight years earlier produced Jesse White. As he, relatives and friends prepared to march from Selma to Montgomery, they were faced with a very real possibility that some of them might not finish the trip.

"When we left home to do this march, I remember my mother telling us that she was not *ready* for us to die, but she was *prepared* for us to die because we needed change in the country. At the time I was a student at Alabama State, and this march was loaded with students from all over the United States, from all over the world for that matter. We had limited medical support, at best, so I think for the most part that all of us – black, white, old and young – everybody in that march was prepared to die.

"We were prepared to die not because we wanted to, but because we were there for a cause. I like pointing out to people that this was not a civil rights march. This was a voters' rights march. We were marching simply for the rights of African Americans to vote. And in doing so we were marching for the rights of all Americans to vote."

Aroine Irby has made the Alabama capitol his passion. He becomes animated when he tells the tale of the murder that took place in the nineteenth century inside the Alabama state treasurer's office. Beneath her second-floor color portrait, he tenderly describes the short reign of Governor Lurleen Burns Wallace, the only American woman to serve both as first lady and governor. He meticulously draws attention to Confederate government securities bonds and Alabama Civil War currency as they hang on the walls of an office replete with nineteenth century appointments.

But he takes special pains to be certain that a visitor understands the significance of the role the Confederacy played in the history of Alabama and vice versa. Alabama is what it is because of yesterday and the yesterday before that. It's the only day that gives us a glimpse of tomorrow. Irby paints a colorful portrait of the past as he stands below a life-size statue of Jefferson Davis. The pedestal supporting Davis's statue is inscribed with the names of the states that comprised the Confederacy. Fewer than a hundred yards northeast of Davis' statue sits a colossal column that supports a statue of Aunt Sophy, who tended to thousands of wounded and dying Confederate soldiers in her hospital. The monument stands eighty-five feet tall and Davis himself laid its cornerstone in 1886. The column is surrounded by the various Confederate flags that flew over Civil War battlefields from 1861 to 1865.

The afternoon sunlight pours through a matrix of windows into the old Alabama senate chambers just a few feet behind Davis's statue. Within the walls of the chambers, in February 1861, Davis crafted the constitution of the Confederate States of America. The same chair in which he sat is empty today; symbolically, however, it looms larger than any other furniture in the room, perhaps in the entire building. Just outside the windows to the old senate chambers stands a giant sycamore tree. As a sapling, the tree was transplanted to the capitol grounds in 1870 from a Civil War battlefield in Virginia.

The Confederacy swallows Aroine Irby and his guests whenever he escorts them on a tour of the capitol grounds. His shaved, chocolate-colored scalp glistens in the morning sun as he stands beneath the Davis statue. Until a few years ago, the specter of the Confederacy loomed even higher above Montgomery; the Stars and Bars flew above the capitol dome until it was ordered off the flagpole and assigned to its designated place within the Confederate Memorial Monument.

The United States has been living with the ghosts of its first century since Lincoln was assassinated. With his emancipation proclamation of

September 22, 1863, President Abraham Lincoln issued slavery's death certificate. But the soul of slavery, the ghost of human bondage, has walked the earth of the Union for too many years since.

Between December 20, 1860, and January 26, 1861, six states seceded from the United States of America. On February 4, 1861, the six – South Carolina, Mississippi, Florida, Alabama, Georgia and Louisiana – admitted themselves as the founding members of the Confederate States of America.

The Confederacy rooted itself in the basic constitutional philosophy that states' rights held superiority over federal dictates. The cornerstone privilege of the Confederate states was the right to buy and hold human beings and deny them their freedom.

By the time the Union defeated the Confederacy in the bloodiest of all American wars, eleven southern states had declared their independence from the North. On April 12, 1861, the Civil War commenced with the Confederate army's charge on Ft. Sumter, South Carolina. In fact, the telegram that essentially launched the attack on Ft. Sumter was sent from a building on Dexter Avenue, just a few blocks west of the Alabama state capitol. Exactly four years later, the Union flag – the one that today we call the *American* flag – was hoisted above the Alabama capitol dome.

The Civil War officially ended with the surrender of General Robert E. Lee's Confederate troops at Appomattox Courthouse in Virginia on April 9, 1865. But its ghosts have haunted the nation forever since.

All of the memories of the reasons for the war between the states serve as a reminder, not a threat, to Aroine Irby.

"I am a historian," Irby explains, "and I know that to reject history is to open the door for history to repeat itself. I see all of this as history. I think the memorial is in an appropriate place. If this history were put to a vote to move it from its place on the capitol grounds, I would vote for it to stay here. It is in its appropriate place.

"I believe in my heritage; I believe in my history. I would hate the thought of anybody saying that we couldn't talk about the voters' rights march from Selma to Montgomery or that we couldn't maintain the historical sites that deal with that event. Certainly the Confederacy has its place and I support it being here.

"After all, this is where it was formed. Jefferson Davis was sworn here. And I enjoy telling this history so that people will understand its importance in the history of our nation."

Irby is proud to have performed a supporting role in another major chapter in the history of this nation. On March 25, 1965, 104 years and a month after Jefferson Davis's inaugural parade, several thousand demonstrators marched up to Goat Hill and demanded their rights to vote in free American elections.

A century after the end of the Civil War and the emancipation of slaves, not all citizens enjoyed the rights of free people. Throughout the South, blacks were prohibited by technicalities in state statutes from participating in the electoral process. Separate, but equal thrived in the hearts of millions of men and women of the South. Reconstruction began in 1865, but by 1965 there were some loose floorboards in a drafty old house called the United States.

Almost immediately after the Civil War ended, southern blacks began to reconstruct their opportunities as free people. Before the outbreak of the war between the states, education in the South was the private reserve of white people. The abolition of slavery gave Negroes the green light to open educational opportunities to people too long denied the right to read and cipher numbers. The opportunities, however, faced considerable resistance.

In a perfect example of the golden rule, the sons and daughters of slaves found it difficult to attend schools because those with the gold, rule. In the late nineteenth century there wasn't much gold in the pockets of Negroes.

"A major change on their behalf," states a passage from the mission statement of Alabama State University, "came in 1887 when the legislature authorized the establishment of the Alabama Colored People's University. The Act allocated $10,000 for the purchase of land and the construction of buildings and set aside $7,500 annually for operating expenses."

During the two decades prior to the Alabama legislature's $10,000 appropriation, a black college offered classes in Marion, 80 miles northwest of the first capital of the Confederacy. For the first time in Alabama history, black people were given the opportunity of higher education in Montgomery. But the spirit of freedom's denial was still alive and fresh in Alabama.

"Opponents to state support of education for blacks remained hostile to the new university," reads the ASU mission statement history. "Indeed, such opponents filed suit in state court and won a ruling in 1887 from the Alabama Supreme Court that declared unconstitutional certain sections of the legislation that established the university for African Americans."

The spirit of slavery's denial of freedom was very much alive in Alabama two decades after all men and women were declared by the federal government to be free. The irony is that in the belly of the beast there began to sprout a slow-growing movement that ultimately would turn this nation on its collective ear. Where the Confederacy began its last stand to defend the right to enslave human beings, there would be an event that would forever repel that defense. As a young college student-athlete named Jesse White went about his business dazzling basketball and baseball fans throughout the South, a soul was about to free itself from the chains of segregation and bias. Amidst the mist of slavery's ghost, the spirit of freedom would burst forth from one of the most unlikely of souls.

On Thursday, December 1, 1955, a black woman boarded a municipal bus and headed for home after a day's work as a seamstress. Perhaps she was ready to die. Perhaps she was prepared to die. Only she knew. But what she let the rest of the nation know that late autumn evening was that she was tired. She was tired from yet another tedious day stitching and basting. Mostly, however, this soul was tired of a system that treated African Americans as citizens of a second class. The day would be forever remembered as a day of celebration and the beginning of liberation. It is a day that would appropriately be marked fifty years later if someone held a parade.

But the only parade that day fifty years ago happened when the cops marched Rosa Parks off to a Montgomery jail cell.

. . . it shall be **unlawful**

for any passenger to

refuse **or fail to take**

a seat among **those assigned**

to the race **to**

which he belongs . . .

—Montgomery, Alabama, Municipal Code, 1955

Chapter Six There's a new mayor in town and his name is Richard J. Daley. The calendar says it's 1955, but the 52-year-old mayor's victory is proof that the Democratic machine is alive and well in Chicago.

There's a story in the sports section that talks about a 16-year-old kid playing for St. Catharine's, Ontario, who may be ready to make the jump to the National Hockey League. Lord knows the Blackhawks need some scoring punch. Maybe this kid – didja say his name is Bobby Hall or *Hull?* – maybe he can help.

A dozen large eggs down at the Jewel cost 59 cents, 24 cents more than a six-pack of Pepsi-Cola in returnable bottles. And don't forget to take those bottles back. You can buy twelve penny packs of baseball cards with the money you get back on the deposit.

There's a new hamburger joint way out in the suburbs in Des Plaines. They say you can buy a hamburger for 15 cents, an order of French fries for a dime and wash it down with a soft drink for another dime. Supposedly they cook the stuff pretty quick over at that McDonald's joint. The winking mascot on the sign outside is named *Speedee* because he supposedly cooks food fast. Or is it fast food?

Some 750 miles to the south, it's Thursday, December 1, same as it is in Chicago. On this day the population of Chicago is 3,620,000, second only to that of New York City. Montgomery's population is a fraction of that. But no one in Chicago – not Mayor Daley, not Bobby Hull, not even McDonald's restaurants – will influence future lives the way a 42-year-old seamstress will. Rosa Parks would flex muscle in a way to make even Richard J. Daley envious. She would demonstrate her resolve to be harder than a Bobby Hull slap shot. And while it is arguable that her influence might not reach the international proportions of McDonald's fast-food empire, her courage would nourish the soul of a people starving for equal treatment and opportunity.

On December 1, 1955, Rosa Parks stepped into history in a most unlikely way. Within minutes after she boarded the Cleveland Avenue bus at 5 p.m., she refused to give up her seat on a crowded Montgomery city bus.

Parks worked as a seamstress in Montgomery, where she lived with her husband Raymond, an activist in the National Association for the Advancement of Colored People. In addition to their work with the NAACP, both Raymond and Rosa Parks had been activists in the campaign to save the Scottsboro Boys, nine young black men who were accused of raping two white teenagers in 1931.

Then aged 42, Parks was too familiar with the segregationist policies of the South. A dozen years earlier as she tried to board a Montgomery bus, the driver ordered her to walk around the side of the vehicle and board through the rear door so that she would not come into contact with white passengers in the front of the bus. As she walked outside toward the rear door, the bus drove away and left her at the stop. The driver and jilted passenger would meet again one day in the distant future.

Parks is not the simple seamstress some historians portrayed her to have been. It's true that she was a seamstress and it's true that her arrest in 1955 came at the end of her day at work. But Rosa Parks was an educated woman. As a high school student, she attended a lab school at Alabama State College because there was no high school for blacks at the time. Prior to her arrest in 1955, she had completed a workshop on race relations at the Highlander Folk School in Monteagle, Tennessee. Most important, she was respected within the Montgomery African American community and her record as a citizen was above reproach.

Around 5 p.m. on December 1, 1955, Rosa Parks boarded the bus and took a seat with three other black passengers in the fifth row, the first row designated for black occupancy. As the bus proceeded along its route, it began to fill with passengers. By the time it reached the Empire Theater on Montgomery Street, the seats reserved for white passengers were filled. The driver ordered the four black passengers in row 5 to forfeit their seats and proceed to the rear of the bus. This driver was not new to Mrs. Parks; he'd left her behind before. Three of the passengers complied with the order. Rosa Parks remained in her seat.

After unsuccessfully ordering Parks to vacate her seat, the driver left the bus for a pay phone and called for help. Within minutes, two Montgomery city police officers arrived at the scene, placed Parks under arrest, handcuffed her and escorted her off the bus.

It's doubtful anyone in Chicago noticed. But in Montgomery, Alabama, a 42-year-old woman had just fired the first volley in a peaceful revolution for civil rights in the United States. Mayor Daley didn't know it. Bobby Hull certainly didn't know it. The people munching on 19-cent cheeseburgers in Des Plaines didn't know it, but a revolution had begun.

Jesse White didn't know it either. Not right away. But he was able to understand the frustration of people like Rosa Parks because he was a victim of the segregation of the South. That night, on the Alabama State College campus where Jesse White was a student, a college employee named Jo Ann Robinson mimeographed a couple hundred pamphlets that she and a handful of students passed out on Friday. The pamphlets called for a one-day boycott of the bus system. That one-day boycott would grow by 343 more days before a federal judge would proclaim once and forever that segregated buses were not lawful in the United States.

Jesse White already was a junior at Alabama State when the Montgomery bus boycott began. Three years earlier, however, choosing Alabama State for his college education was not an easy chore.

"After I graduated from Waller High School I was searching for a college or university to attend," White remembers. "I had received some interest from Ripon College, Beloit College and Northwestern, but I was rejected by Northwestern because I didn't have the sufficient sequence in mathematics.

"Keep in mind that while I was at Waller High School, it was one of the most diverse institutions of learning in Chicago. I was captain of the baseball team. I was captain of the basketball team. I had white teammates and black teammates and we all socialized together. These people were my friends. We ate together, played together, socialized together and didn't think anything of it."

Warren Chapman was White's counselor and physical education instructor at the Lower North Center when Jesse was starting high school. He saw potential in his young protégé and encouraged White to play sports. Chapman, now 85, was instrumental in guiding hundreds of kids out of the projects in the 1940s and 1950s. Among them were renowned musicians Ramsey Lewis and the late Curtis Mayfield.

"Jesse White was one of my favorite kids," says Chapman, "and I took an interest in him. He was enthusiastic. He was a hustler. He always had a job, worked in a grocery store. He did everything – football, basketball, track. Baseball was really his specialty. So Jesse was one of the boys that I sent to college."

Jesse White and Warren Chapman talked over White's options for higher education.

"When I told my mother," White explains, "that I was looking at some possibilities for college – Wisconsin at Beloit or Ripon – she said that was fine. I told her that I might stay, maybe go to Northwestern. She said that was okay with her, too. But when I mentioned Tennessee as a possibility, she said no way. My father was raised in Tennessee and she knew how he had been treated in the South."

As a child, Jesse White spent time in Tennessee, too, at the home of an uncle, William Palmer. According to White, his uncle had stashed a considerable amount of money in his apartment above a bar and restaurant he owned in Humboldt in west Tennessee.

"He owned the whole block," White explains, "but he didn't want the white people in town to know how wealthy he was so he never put his money in a bank. Instead, he kept all his money in his home. One night, there was a fire and it destroyed everything, including him and all his money."

Chapman said he mentioned to White the possibility of Alabama State because Chapman had already made a connection there.

"One of my teammates in the Air Force was the track coach at

Alabama State," Chapman explains. "Dr. Johnny Jones. So I wrote him and told him that I had a kid who needed a chance. And he responded."

Chapman says he understands the culture shock experienced by the 18-year-old Jesse White upon entering Alabama State.

"He was always in an integrated neighborhood, the Near North side. Not too many black kids living up there. All the kids who went down to Alabama State from Chicago had some culture shock."

But before he would experience the culture of the South, White had to face the shock of his mother.

"When I told her that I was going to Alabama, well, that was the living end. She didn't want to debate the issue with me, but she let me know that she was not happy about me attending school in the South because both she and my father had lived in the South and they knew how badly they were treated and they didn't want me to experience that kind of treatment.

"They were afraid for my health. They feared for my safety, for my well-being."

Indeed, those fears were well founded. The summer before Rosa Parks launched the celebrated Montgomery bus boycott, 14-year-old Emmett Till traveled from Chicago to Money, Mississippi, to visit relatives at the home of his uncle, Mose Wright.

On August 24, 1955, Till was showing pictures of his white friends from Chicago to a group of local boys outside Bryant's Grocery Store in Money. The boys dared Till to say something to Carolyn Bryant, the store clerk. On his way out of the store after buying some candy, Emmett Till either said something or whistled at Bryant. The details are not clear.

Four nights later, two men came to Wright's home. One of them was armed with a pistol. They abducted Emmett Till and threatened his uncle with death if he contacted authorities. Three days later, Till's body was found in the Tallahatchie River. Till's killers used barbed wire to tie a 75-pound cotton gin fan around his neck. The boy's face was so disfigured his grieving mother ordered his casket open for viewing so the world could see his grotesque disfigurement and the brutality of his murder.

(Although no one was convicted of Till's murder, the investigation was reopened in 2005. The Federal Bureau of Investigation has treated the murder as an open investigation and in June 2005 exhumed Till's body to conduct tests for forensic evidence and DNA.)

The world where Jesse White pursued a college degree was in a different solar system from where he was raised.

"All of a sudden, when I decided to go to Alabama, my life was turned upside down. So here I am, my first day in Montgomery," he says. "I had just gotten registered and I wanted to go downtown to buy some supplies. The campus is a couple miles from downtown Montgomery. So I got on the bus and I sat right behind the driver and I looked toward the back of the bus and there were these black people, and they were beckoning me to come to where they were in the back of the bus.

"Well, I really didn't know anybody so I just sat there. But with all of the noise that these people were making in the back, the bus driver decided to look around and see what the problem was. When he saw me sitting there he said, 'Oh my God! What are you doing here?'

"I said, 'I paid my fare. I can sit anywhere I want. Is there a problem?'" As Jesse White relates the incident, he does so with an air of innocence, not defiance. He did not, plain-and-simply, know that he was not allowed to sit in that seat.

"He told me that, yes, there was a problem."

"Can't you read?"

"Yes, I can read."

"Look over there. Look at those signs."

The driver pointed to portable signs, affixed to the handrails along the top of two seats that read *Colored Seating Behind This Sign.*

"So he and I had an exchange and he said something about putting me off the bus. I told him that his job was to drive the bus. I had paid my fare and it wasn't his place to be concerned about where I was sitting. I was standing up to this white bus driver, big time."

But the driver wasn't about to be stood up by an 18-year-old black kid.

"As we're going down the hill, toward the hospital and past a Texaco station, there sat across the street a squad car on the northeast corner. So the driver got off the bus and ran over to the police car and was trying to get the police officer to arrest me, I guess. But right about the same time a car ran through a red light and the squad car took after it.

"When we got off the bus, the people from the back of the bus gathered around me and asked me where I was from. I told them I was from Chicago."

"Don't you know you're supposed to obey those signs? Otherwise they'll lock you up and throw away the key. Down here, they're serious about their seating arrangement and don't you understand that *segregation is all centered around sitting down?"*

"You gotta be kidding me," White told the group. "You mean you can't just sit anywhere you want? I don't understand it."

That was it. The kid from Chicago *didn't understand it.* He'd ridden the bus hundreds of times in the city, sat where he wanted to sit and never heard a disparaging word. But this was a different world. Down in Montgomery, the ghosts of the Confederacy wanted their seats on the bus reserved.

"After the bus incident, when I refused to move to the back of the bus, it kinda went through campus. Here was a guy from Chicago who refused to go to the back of the bus. People would see me and say, 'Hey, you can't do that down here.' And they warned me about how terrible things could have been for me if that police car had not gone elsewhere."

Alabama wasn't the only place in Jesse White's world where bus drivers behaved differently from those who worked for the Chicago Transit Authority.

"One day, I'm on the bus coming from Chicago to Montgomery," he recalls. "On the bus to Evansville, Indiana, is a northern bus driver and at Evansville they would change over to the southern bus driver and they would actually change the way people were arranged in the seats.

"If you were sitting in the front of the bus from Chicago to Evansville and you were black, that was fine. When the southern driver came on, the black people would have to go to the rear of the bus. I happened to be sitting maybe five or six seats from the front, and I'm sitting with an executive from Pittsburgh and we were having a nice conversation all the way from Chicago to Evansville. I had established a good relationship with the guy.

"At Evansville the bus driver walked back and said, 'You have to sit back there.' I said, 'I beg your pardon.' and he told me that I was going to have to go to the back of the bus."

As the driver ordered Jesse White to move to the back of the bus, the white Pittsburgh businessman spoke up.

"I would suggest that you drive the bus," White quotes the businessman as saying. "This is my friend and we're having a nice conversation. He isn't bothering you and he isn't bothering me. Just do your job."

White says the driver's "face turned red and he didn't bother us anymore. It was highly impressive that a black would sit near the front of a Greyhound Bus on the way to the South."

In Montgomery, however, it would take additional time and a little more clout than a white businessman from Pittsburgh.

"As it turned out, the next time I got on the bus in Montgomery, I went straight to the back because I didn't want any problems."

White was able to fully appreciate the fortitude Rosa Parks exhibited.

"I thought she was a very brave woman," he says, "especially after what happened to me. I knew what the code of conduct was down there. You weren't supposed to step on anyone's toes or step out of line. They had a way of dealing with you."

Retrospective analysis is a tricky endeavor. Much of Montgomery, Alabama, in 1955 was enveloped in a primitive culture of the nineteenth century. The laws there made it nearly impossible for blacks to vote. By 1955, a full ninety years after the end of the Civil War, only 2,000 of the county's 30,000 black residents were registered to vote. Not only was seating on public buses segregated, there were separate taxi systems for blacks and whites.

The Montgomery bus boycott was pivotal because it marked the first time in American history that African Americans used economics to earn rights. The bus boycott hurt the black community to be sure. A majority of black households depended on the buses to get to and from their jobs. When the black taxi company tried to charge the same fare as the bus, a dime, the city threatened to shut it down. African American residents formed car pools to move each other around town.

But although the boycott was a major inconvenience for the city's black population, it was an economic disaster for white merchants

Eddie Poole is a native of Montgomery and was one of Jesse White's Kappa Alpha Psi fraternity brothers at Alabama State.

When White pledged the fraternity as an underclassman, the pledge director was Ralph Abernathy, a young minister born and raised in Linden, Alabama. Abernathy, who would go on to become president of the Southern Christian Leadership Council, required that the new Kappa Alpha Psi pledges attend his church during pledge period.

"Reverend Abernathy, one of our fraternity brothers, insisted that we go to this church," White recalls. "We arrived there the first time and there were ten or twelve people in the church. The next week, there may have been a couple dozen or so people at the church. By the third week there were probably 150 people there. Every time we went back to this church there were more and more people. The next thing you knew, this church was bursting at the seams. And it was all because the people down there kept hearing about this minister who gave such beautiful sermons.

"His name was Reverend Martin Luther King."

King was just a 24-year-old preacher when he arrived in Montgomery. By the end of his service there he would be an international figure, beloved by multitudes, defiled by legions.

Eddie Poole has no trouble remembering the atmosphere of the Montgomery bus boycott of 1955-56.

"I grew up in a part of the city that was totally segregated so far as housing was concerned," Poole says. "There were some white merchants who owned grocery stores in the neighborhood. Other than that, we didn't have any direct contact with whites unless you went downtown or decided to walk to school and walked through their neighborhood.

"I remember when Rosa Parks was arrested. Of course, many of us didn't know it until it appeared on the pages of the *Montgomery Advertiser.* So that night there was a meeting at the Holt Street Baptist Church. We were all hanging from the rafters.

"So we jammed the place, hung from the rafters, and they explained to us what had happened. A bus boycott was called for. Most of us had never even heard the word *boycott* before. But they didn't want us to ride the buses.

"Prior to that, when you would ride the bus if you were a Negro, you'd just automatically go to the back of the bus. Sometimes if there were whites standing at the front of the bus, you'd hand your money to the driver and then walk around to the rear of the bus."

As happened to Rosa Parks twelve years earlier, Eddie Poole remembers paying his fare and being left in the dust by a white driver who most likely chortled as he drove away.

"Sometimes he would take off without even opening the door. I am quite clear about that because it happened to me. If you were a Negro, you couldn't get on through the front door because there were whites standing in the aisle. They didn't want us brushing against the white guys. So you had to pay them your fare and walk around to the rear of the bus."

In 1955, Eddie Poole was 22 years old and had returned to Montgomery after a hitch in the Air Force. By then, he had saved enough money to buy a car and was no longer dependent on the Montgomery bus system for transportation. But once you're dehumanized, you tend not to forget. Eddie Poole wasn't about to let the boycott leave the station without him.

"I didn't like the way people were treated," he explains. "I remembered how it was when I was a kid and when the bus was my only mode of transportation, or I walked because I didn't have enough money to take a cab."

The concept of a bus boycott was novel. African Americans had not yet dared to defend their constitutional rights on a national scale and they did not yet understand their collective economic power. But Eddie Poole and his fellow black citizens were about to find out how powerful they really were.

"I guess you could say that we had been brainwashed to a degree to accept the system as it was. We accepted that we had to get up and surrender our seat on the bus so a white could sit down, whether it was a man or a woman. But after I had been in the Air Force and seen another side of life, I decided that enough was enough.

"We supported the bus boycott 100 percent. Those of us who had cars, we'd stop and pick up and take people as far as we could in whatever direction they needed to go. I would stop and pick up kids on my side of town who were on their way to the college."

The white city administration issued a stern warning that car pooling was unlawful.

"They said it was illegal," Poole explains, "but we continued to give rides and sometimes people would just drop a fare in the cigarette ash tray or just leave it on the seat."

Eddie Poole vividly remembers the night of January 30, 1956. In retrospect, it should have come as no surprise that the bus boycott would spawn violence, as evidenced by a letter to the editor of the *Montgomery Advertiser:*

Preview of the "Declaration of Segregation"

When in the course of human events it becomes necessary to abolish the Negro race, proper methods should be used. Among these are guns, bows and arrows, slingshots and knives.

We hold these truths to be self-evident that all whites are created equal with certain human rights; among these are life, liberty and the pursuit of niggers.

In every stage of the bus boycott we have been oppressed and degraded because of black, slimy, juicy, unbearably stinking niggers. The conduct should not be dwelt upon because of dead niggers. The conduct should not be dwelt upon because behind them they have an ancestral background of Pigmies (sic) head hunters and snot suckers.

My friends it is time we wised up to these black devils. I tell you they are a group of two legged agitators who persist in walking up and down our streets protruding their black lips. If we don't stop helping these African flesh eaters, we will soon wake up and find Rev. King in the White House. LET'S GET ON THE BALL WHITE CITIZENS.

Such correspondence was emblematic of an undercurrent of hatred and venom that coursed through the community. It was no surprise that the hatred spewed from certain corners of the community would bubble over and spill into violence.

At 9:15 p.m. on January 30, 1956, the simple wood frame house at 309 S. Jackson Street was rocked by a bomb, planted on the front porch. No one was injured in the blast at the home of the Reverend Dr. Martin Luther King Jr.

"I remember the night they bombed his house," says Eddie Poole, "and word spread throughout the campus that Dr. King's house had been bombed. He lived a few blocks away from the campus. So we all went down there with bats and clubs and sticks and knives, whatever we had or could find. We all surrounded Dr. King's house because we didn't know at the time if he or his family were injured."

"The police were there. They tried to break up the crowd and threatened to use tear gas to break us up. But we wouldn't move. Dr. King came out and assured us that he and his family were fine, told us to go home and that we would talk about it tomorrow. So the people left, and that really upset the police chief because he had been trying for hours to disperse us and we wouldn't leave.

"There was civil unrest, for sure, but we were always peaceful because that's what Dr. King preached."

Jesse White vividly remembers the charged atmosphere during the days following the bombing of Dr. King's residence.

"We talked about the bombing and it scared some of the guys who came from that area," he says. "The guys who were born and raised in the South knew a little bit about the mentality of the people down there. They knew how violent they could be.

"They knew about the lynchings, the hangings, the way people had been tied and dragged behind horses, cars and pickup trucks. They knew how violent these people were. Many of my friends came from small towns in the South where the Klan was alive and well. They had experienced a lot of terrible acts of violence.

"But for those of us who came from the North, I guess we didn't believe that such acts of violence could or would be tolerated. We came from people who didn't do that kind of thing. Those who did engage in violence were punished accordingly.

"I remember being very upset about that whole incident. I could not believe that here we are in a country like this and we would treat each other so differently in different parts of the country. When I was up North, I could sit anywhere I wanted to sit on the bus. I could eat anywhere I wanted to eat and talk with anyone I chose to talk with. I had freedom of movement, integrated schools, theaters, churches, bathrooms and water fountains."

Richard Jordan is another Montgomery native who found himself in the middle of the civil rights movement while a student at Alabama State. In fact, he was with Eddie Poole in the aftermath of the explosion that blew out the front of Dr. King's home.

Racial separatism and inequality were staples of the South as Jordan was growing up.

"I lived in a professional family," Jordan explains. "My parents were schoolteachers. I knew that discrimination was a way of life because we had white water fountains and black water fountains. We had to go to the back of the bus. That was accepted procedure whether we liked it or not.

"Dr. King was my pastor at Dexter Avenue Baptist and my church has always been a church of social change. The preachers that Dexter has had have always been well-educated ministers."

Jordan vividly recalls the atmosphere that night and how quickly the black community responded to the King residence as word of the explosion raced through the neighborhood.

"In the neighborhood at that time there were a number of cafes and nightclubs. There were hundreds and hundreds of people in those nightclubs and cafes. So the night the house was bombed, everybody emptied out of those places. Quite naturally, there were people coming out of those places who had handguns on their persons for no particular reason. Some had pocketknives and they gathered and they wanted to get a little rowdy."

As the crowd gathered in size and in its potential for violence, Dr. King arrived at the residence, as Jordan recalls.

"By that time Dr. King came over from the Holt Street Baptist Church and immediately ran into the house to check on his daughter, Yolanda, and Mrs. King. After he found out that they were all right, he came back out on the front porch and raised his hands and told everyone that Yolanda and Coretta were doing just fine, that they had not been injured but that this was a nonviolent movement and that we were not going to become violent.

"He had both hands in the air and he expressed his appreciation for their concern and he asked everyone not to use any weapons, to go back home and that we were going to continue in a nonviolent manner. And the crowd dispersed.

"I was right in the middle of it."

Jordan said Dr. King's message to the community was clear.

"He was very specific. He made it very clear that we have some good white folks and we have some bad white folks, just like we have some good black folks and some bad. If the movement was going to be successful, it was going to be successful because we have more good folks than we had bad. And that was so true. And all of us – the good white folks and the good black folks – were ready to do whatever we could to make a better life for everyone, regardless of race. And we were determined to do it non-violently."

Eddie Poole was ready for a taste of a better life, too. After graduating with a biology degree from Alabama State in 1958, Poole moved to Chicago and took a job teaching biology and chemistry at South Shore High School. Ironically, he was the first black teacher at South Shore, whose student body at the time was predominantly Jewish. He finished off his career in education by serving as assistant principal at South Shore until his retirement in 1989.

Another of Jesse White's fraternity brothers, Dr. Emmit Horne, was accustomed to the way he'd been treated while growing up in the South. A native of Florence, Alabama, Horne says he understands how difficult it must have been for a northern black like Jesse White to adjust to his new surroundings.

"It had to be hard to make the transition," says Horne, a former dean of vocational education for Chicago city colleges. "We had separate water fountains for blacks and whites. I was quite accustomed to the way we were treated down there. Being from Florence, Alabama, about 200 miles from Montgomery, I knew what it was like. My mother warned me when I left for college, 'Don't you be starting anything down there or you'll get yourself hurt bad.'"

Horne said it was tough maintaining a peaceful approach to the civil disobedience of the day because the police department commonly harassed the bus boycotters.

"During the bus boycott, would you believe that you had some of the policemen harassing people who were walking down the street? There were times when we walked down the street and we ducked into doorways because we saw a policeman heading our way and we knew that he would do what he could to break us up.

"We had white taxi drivers and black taxi drivers. The black taxi drivers would load up their taxis and take as many people as they could to wherever they were going. The policemen would stop them if they had more than two or three in their car and they'd give them a ticket.

"There were times when the domestic workers would get sent home from the houses of white people where they worked because they were late getting to work because they were forced to walk across town to get there. The bus boycott was rough on everybody. The white storekeepers lost a lot of business but black people who didn't know anyone with a car and couldn't afford a taxi suffered hardships, too.

"I rode the buses before the bus boycott but I wasn't about to ride them after we decided to boycott. I just did the best I could and got where I had to go as best as I could."

As a young man, Horne was accustomed to taking a place at the back of the bus. As odd as it may sound a half century later, knowing your place was a fact of life and had become ingrained in the culture of many African-Americans.

"Being from Florence, Alabama, it's something that I had become accustomed to," Horne says. "But once I began to understand that it was part of our rights and once Rosa Parks stood up to show us that we had the same rights as everyone else, I felt obligated to support the cause. I realized that there are times when you have to jeopardize yourself and accept the consequences. Sometimes you may have to suffer."

The established white city government invoked legal technicalities in efforts to break the strike. On February 21, 1956, eighty-nine people – all black – were indicted under an old Alabama law that prohibited boycotts. Dr. King was among those arrested. His conviction carried a $500 fine and $500 in court costs. But the boycott supporters held fast.

On November 13, 1956, the United States Supreme Court upheld an earlier federal court ruling that declared segregation on buses to be unconstitutional. The bus boycott was over. The end of the Montgomery bus boycott, however, marked the beginning of an awareness that African Americans could win rights through solidarity. The Montgomery bus boycott propelled a movement that would ultimately win voting rights for all Americans as well as the right of all people to dine in all public restaurants.

By the time Jesse White received his degree from Alabama State in 1957, black people could sit anywhere there was an empty seat on the bus. Progress was slow but it was becoming certain. Civil rights leaders like Martin Luther King and Ralph Abernathy continued to push forward and African Americans began to understand their place in America was to be a better one.

Eddie Poole admits the South today is radically different from the South of his youth.

"When I go to visit in the South now – I used to go two, three times a year – it's totally different," he contends. "You can go anywhere you want to go. They have blacks and whites going to all the schools."

Richard Jordan sees the change, too.

"Basically, we have a generation of people who just don't pay any attention to what happened in the past, with the history of the Confederacy and all," he says. "The blacks certainly ignore it and the white community's generation now kind of wants to forget about it. There are some diehards who try to carry it on, but they are few and far between. But it's an experience we need to remember to protect us from it ever happening again."

His own experience in Montgomery could have radicalized Jesse White. After all, another side of American life was not the life to which he was accustomed in Chicago. Certainly, the experience produced changes in the young man's life, but they were changes for the better.

"I could have been a bitter guy," he says today, "but for some reason I chose to go the other way. My father never let me carry a grudge. He saw no upside, no benefit to anything like that."

Despite the disrespect accorded to him in some sectors, Jesse White considers his time in Montgomery to have been well spent.

"It was a great experience down there, an experience I'll always remember."

And remember is what the history books help us do. History jars our collective memory and enables us to recall the historic parades of Montgomery, Alabama. The parades down Dexter Avenue today are more of the garden variety. It's doubtful Montgomery will ever host another presidential inaugural; and the birthplace of the civil rights movement has seen its progeny achieve the rights to vote, hold office and sit elbow to elbow with fellow lunch counter diners, regardless of race. Few American thoroughfares outside the nation's capital have borne so many footsteps marching in passionate pursuit of such divergent principles as the Confederacy and the civil rights movement.

Today, a mustard-and-green transit bus chugs away from the Montgomery Area Visitors Center twice an hour. You pay your 25 cents and you sit wherever you want. Except for the handicapped access door, the bus is an exact replica of the bus from which Rosa Parks stepped into history. The sign emblazoned over the windshield proclaims Cleveland Avenue. It's a misnomer, actually. *Cleveland Avenue* is now Rosa Parks Boulevard.

After you drop your quarter into the fare box, you can sit anywhere you want.

No matter who you are.

No matter where you're headed.

The tour bus driver jokes that his job is "an aerobics workout every day" because the bus is built exactly the way General Motors manufactured its buses in 1955. There may be no power steering, but there's a power of another dimension on that bus.

It's not a ghostly power. It's a spiritual one.

The **Screaming Eagle**
is a fitting emblem for a division
that will **crush its enemies**
like a thunderbolt falling
from the skies.

— Major General William C. Lee, August 19, 1942

Chapter Seven Historians define the Cold War as a forty-five-year hangover that began two years after the end of World War II and ended with the fall of the Soviet Union in 1991. The term *Cold War* is attributed to Bernard Baruch, an American financier, statesman, and adviser to a range of presidents from Woodrow Wilson to John F. Kennedy.

Baruch was not around to advise Richard M. Nixon, who arguably got some very bad advice as he revved up his reelection campaign in 1972. But sometimes lost in Nixon's dubious legacy of the Watergate break-in and subsequent coverup was the conversion in 1973 from a system of military conscription to the all-volunteer armed forces. As the ravages of the Vietnam War began to subside and Americans retreated from Southeast Asia, the United States ended the military draft and began to stock its military forces with young men and women who were not required under law to register for the draft.

The concept of the all-volunteer military was as foreign to young American men in 1957 as Red Square and borscht. So when Jesse White signed a contract in 1957 to play for the Chicago Cubs, he knew there was a very real possibility that he'd be required to wear another sort of uniform before his playing days were over. And it wasn't the uniform of the Cardinals, the Yankees or the Dodgers.

"In 1956, after I signed a contract to play for the Cubs, I was scheduled to report to spring training in March of 1957." Jesse White has told this story a thousand times and the details never change. "Four days before I was supposed to go to spring training, I ended up in basic training. I was drafted into the military."

There's never a good time to be drafted into the military, unless you consider peacetime to be better than war. For Jesse White the timing was particularly inconvenient.

"I was a little disappointed," he admits. "It meant that I wasn't going to be able to start doing what I always wanted to do since I was a kid — and that was to play professional baseball. A lot of guys had qualified for deferments and I was hoping that I could get a deferment, too. But it didn't work out, so I reported for duty."

The draft was not the political hot potato in 1957 that it was to become as the Vietnam War revved up a decade later. American men (women were not draft eligible then) often took advantage of their military duty and traveled to Europe or the Pacific, places they'd never seen and might never see again. Then again, most of them would never see the inside of a professional baseball park without buying a ticket.

"I guess it was like having to report for jury duty," he says today. "No one ever wants to get called for jury duty, but when you are, you go about your business and accept the responsibility. For me, this was like reporting for jury duty, reporting for a very long case."

After receiving his orders, Jesse White reported to Ft. Leonard Wood, Missouri. Because of a paperwork snag, he had not been able to receive his Alabama State diploma until after he was inducted into the Army.

"So there was a point during my training when I received permission to return to Montgomery, Alabama, to walk across the stage to receive my degree, to get my diploma. So I took the bus from Ft. Leonard Wood to St. Louis and I took a train to Montgomery. I got my degree and afterward I was scheduled to fly back to Illinois out of Maxwell Air Force Base in Montgomery to Wright-Patterson Air Force Base in Dayton, Ohio.

"A storm developed over Birmingham, about 100 miles north of Montgomery. It was so violent that it shook the plane up really hard. At one point the captain – these were reservists flying the plane – came on the speaker and said, 'Put a 'chute on.'"

During Army basic training at Ft. Leonard Wood, Jesse White learned the rudiments of being a soldier. He learned survival techniques, weapons operation and discipline. He didn't learn how to strap on a parachute.

"They gave me a parachute and I got strapped in and I started talking to the crew chief. He told me there were about twenty ways to get out of the aircraft. I asked him if he'd ever jumped out of an airplane. He told me he never had: 'I've never jumped and I won't ever jump.'"

Not exactly the kind of inspirational words you'd like to hear when your airplane is in trouble.

"But he gave me the 'chute."

The aircraft continued to bounce and tumble through the thunderstorm cell.

"When both of the pilots put their 'chutes on, I realized this was serious business." Jesse White laughs as he recalls the adventure. "Everyone on the airplane was white. Including me.

"They climbed eastward toward Memphis, and as they climbed the sun broke through the clouds. 'Jesus,' I thought. 'This is beautiful.' This was my first airplane ride."

After the plane set down at Wright-Patterson Air Force Base, a sergeant approached White with his itinerary back to Ft. Leonard Wood. Jesse White reconstructs their conversation:

"Private White, your plane is ready for Scott Air Force Base."

"I'm sorry. I'm not getting on a plane again. Do me a favor, where's the bus station?"

White jumped on a Greyhound Bus pointed west and meandered back toward Ft. Leonard Wood.

"I was late getting back to my base, but when I told my lieutenant what had happened, he ended up giving me some favorable consideration."

If you were to guess that the near-death experience was the end of Jesse White's military aircraft adventures, you would guess wrong.

"A few days later, I was walking on the base and I saw these guys with these spit-shined boots, bloused pants – tailor-made pants – nicely starched and ironed uniforms. My uniform was just, well, you washed it and that was it. No ironing. Forget about that.

"I asked who those fellows were and I was told they were paratroopers and that they were recruiting people to go to Ft. Campbell, Kentucky, to become part of the 101st Airborne Division. I decided that was the army I wanted to be in. I talked with the recruiter and told him I'd very much like to be part of the unit. He asked me what I had to offer and I told him I was a college graduate and that I was a professional baseball player."

"Who do you play for?"

"Well, I haven't played for anyone yet but I have a contract to play for the Chicago Cubs."

"Is there any way you can get me a copy of your contract?"

"Sure. I just happen to have a copy of it with me."

White rustled through his belongings, retrieved the contract and the next day presented it to the recruiter for the 101st Airborne.

"As it turned out, I had to take a physical fitness test and there were about a couple hundred people who took the physical fitness test. I think there were about a dozen of us who passed. After I finished basic training I went back to Chicago and after that I caught a bus to Ft. Campbell, Kentucky."

Located between Hopkinsville and Clarksville, construction had started on Camp Campbell three months after the Japanese bombed Pearl Harbor. When it opened in the summer of 1942, Camp Campbell became the home of the Army's 12th, 14th and 20th armored divisions.

During World War II, the Pathfinders of the 101st Airborne Division inserted itself during the night drop prior to the invasion of Normandy on June 6, 1944. Nicknamed *The Screaming Eagles*, the 101st Airborne specializes in air assault. In 2005, the 101st Airborne was among the primary wings of the United States military stationed in Iraq.

Despite that harrowing experience of his first flight in a raging thunderstorm, Jesse White was excited by the opportunity to train as an elite member of the 101st Airborne Division. At Ft. Campbell, he enrolled in jump school "where they prepared us to jump out of a perfectly good airplane." Nearly a half century later, his memory is crystal clear about the jump techniques drilled into him by the Army.

"You have to leave the aircraft in a good body position," he explains with the precision of the schoolteacher he still is. "They slow the aircraft down because, otherwise, the prop blast and the speed of the aircraft will keep you in the plane. You have to jump up and out with vigor. And you have to maintain a good body position. Your knees and feet are together and your hands are on your reserve in case there's a malfunction."

The sun blazed bright over the green Kentucky hills on the day in 1958 when Jesse While made his first parachute jump from a C130 Hercules.

"We were lined up with eighteen men going out each door," he recalls. "The light is red when the aircraft is flying. It goes amber when it's time to stand up, hook up and stand in the door. We were sitting facing inward in the plane when they told us to stand up, hook up. Then, once you got hooked up, they called out for the equipment check. The person behind you checks your equipment and you check the equipment of the person in front of you.

"Then the light turns green and it means you're over the drop zone. When you jump out of the plane, your chin is on your chest because when the risers come out of the main part of the 'chute, they come out with such force that you can injure your neck. There were a few times after jumps that I had a stiff neck and realized that it was because I wasn't burying my chin deep enough into my chest the way I should have.

"As I exited the airplane on that first jump, I remember counting, *one thousand, two thousand, three thousand, four thousand,* with my chin tucked into my chest. Then I looked up and pushed my risers out to make sure the canopy was fully inflated."

In combat, there's no backup for a faulty main parachute because paratroopers carry no reserve. During training, White and his fellow paratroopers jumped from a training altitude of 1,250 feet. During his first five jumps leading up to earning his paratrooper's wings, he carried only his main and reserve 'chutes. But in combat, bailing out at an altitude of just 500 feet, the paratrooper's reserve 'chute pack space is loaded instead with survival equipment: mess kit, tent, tools and weaponry.

"I weighed about 165 back then and it felt like the equipment weighed as much as I did."

White admits he spent a sleepless night before his first jump.

"I was scared. I came out of the airplane and the wind was blowing in my face and I was being tossed around in the air. I remember the 'chute opening and I began oscillating under the canopy. You're swaying back and forth under the 'chute and you're being tossed around.

"And there's a sinister whine – I can still hear it in my ears now – an out-of-this-world kind of a sound you hear when you jump. There's a calmness up there that's hard to explain.

"As you're coming down, the ground is coming up. When you're coming down, there's a tendency to look down at the ground as the ground is coming toward you. And if you do that, you tend to brace your legs for the impact and that's the worst thing you can do. You look to the horizon and learn how to feel for the ground in a relaxed mode."

During his attachment to the Strategic Army Corps, Jesse White completed thirty-five jumps as a Screaming Eagles paratrooper. He was trained hard and combat-ready for rapid deployment anywhere in the world. His time of military service was sandwiched between the end of the Korean War and the escalation of an American presence in Vietnam. He came closest to combat deployment in 1958 when then-Vice President Richard M. Nixon's motorcade was attacked during a visit to Caracas, Venezuela.

"Our unit was airborne but by the time it got halfway down, the First Marine Division had come in to quell the unrest," he remembers.

Jesse White's peacetime military service added an element of strict discipline to his life. Following his two-year hitch of active service in the Army, he completed another four-year commitment as a member of the reserves. And from 1970 until he was elected in 1974 to the Illinois General Assembly, he served as a member of the Illinois National Guard.

"I enjoyed my military experience. It was a good experience for me. Some of the other guys I knew were able to get deferments, and I thought I had a legitimate reason. I wanted to play baseball." He laughs as the recollection. "I thought that was a legitimate enough reason for me to be granted a deferment. Now that I look back, I understand that was poor logic at the time.

"I really feel good that I was able to serve not once, not twice, but three times. I'll tell you something. When you say you've served in the military, it's an honorable thing to do, to serve your country. At the time

I was drafted, I felt I was dealt a bad hand. I may have looked at it as a negative at the time, but I've grown to understand it was a positive.

"A lot of the experiences that I gained from the military have become part of my life's philosophy. It's helped me move forward in my life and I've tried to share that experience with others."

Even today, he uses military terms in his everyday language, including directives to members of his tumbling team.

"As a matter of fact, when I taught school and we said the Pledge of Allegiance, I made the kids stand up straight, heels together, feet at a 45-degree angle. I made sure their thumbs were placed along the seams of their trousers, that their head was held high and that they placed their hand over their heart."

Today, there are more than a fair share of politicians who feign patriotism, who use the flag as a cloak of fear rather than a symbol of freedom. But after you get to know Jesse White, you begin to understand he's not one of them. When he talks about a love of country, he means the mechanics of freedom, not just its symbols.

"I love this country. It's the greatest country on the face of the earth. It bothered me an awful lot back in the '60s and '70s when there were problems with African American students who refused to stand up for the National Anthem, who protested things by showing disrespect. That bothered me. Whatever your problem is, you should address it in another way. When you show disrespect for the flag and show disrespect for our country, you rub me the wrong way."

So Jesse White fulfilled his military obligation and to this day is proud of his service.

But in 1959, there was a life to live and a dream to pursue. There comes a time in a man's life when he discards the sobering responsibilities of an adult and gets down to chasing the dreams that kids dare to dream.

By the spring of 1959, Specialist Fourth Class Jesse C. White was ready to report to another camp.

A-roundin' third, and
headed for home,
it's a brown-eyed
handsome man;
anyone can understand the way
I feel.

— John Fogerty, Centerfield

Chapter Eight Joe Hardy sold his soul to the devil. Even after he met Lola, Joe Hardy's only lust was for a chance to wear Washington Senators' pinstripes and do something – anything – to beat those damned Yankees.

His dream was the dream of millions of American boys.

Some say the American dream is to own a home and raise a family. That's a canard, probably the fiction of housing contractors and mortgage bankers.

Others say the American dream is to make a million dollars before age 30, retire to an island in the Caribbean and sip pina coladas under a palm tree. Not true. For every Donald Trump there are a million Walter Mittys, but they don't dream about making money.

The real American dream, the one played out on every little boy's pillow from the time he's old enough to lift a mitt that's too big for his arm, much less for his tiny fingers, is to play major league baseball.

Where's the romance in owning a house? A house is just wood, nails and a little bit of brick. Money? Money is just green paper.

Green? You want green? Roy Hobbs told Pop Fisher the greenest green he ever saw was winter wheat.

Go suit up.

Green? Have you ever seen the green of a swath of major league outfield just after twilight, in the bottom of the fifth just as the full effect of a thousand artificial lights bathes the grass in the glow of a midsummer's evening?

That's green. You can see it, you can smell it and you can taste it. You really can taste it, you know. Step inside a major league ballpark for the first time and the taste will never leave your tongue. On millions of American pillows over billions of American summer nights, little boys dream the same dream. But so few of them will ever live it. To play professional baseball is to fulfill a lifetime of hard work and fun. To play in the major leagues is simply a dream come true.

"I always wanted to be a ballplayer," says Jesse White. "From the first time I put on a glove, it felt like it was just the perfect fit."

Jesse Clark White Sr. played a little ball during his time in Chicago. A little fast-pitch softball, a little 16-inch slow-pitch, the kind of softball unique to Chicago, where a *Clincher* isn't the end to a business deal. In the twilight of a hundred sandlot evenings, Jesse White Sr. played and Jesse White Jr. watched. And on his pillow the little boy dreamed.

Daylight gave the son an opportunity to work on the kind of skills required of a baseball prospect – hitting, fielding. But he was gifted from above with a pair of lightning-fast legs that took him from here to there faster than most mortals. The kid could run like a deer.

Warren Chapman, one of Jesse White's early mentors, remembers a specific instance when he understood how fast his young protégé really was. The summer after White graduated from Waller High School, the St. Louis Browns invited him to St. Louis for a look-see. More than a half-century later Chapman's memory of the event is vivid.

"When he first tried out for the major leagues, before he went off to college, he had a tryout with the St. Louis Browns, Bill Veeck's old team," Chapman recalls. "They were playing a game during the tryout and Jesse comes to the plate and the pitcher walks him. Jesse White stole second.

"Then the pitcher went into his motion and Jesse White stole third. And before the pitcher could look around again, Jesse White stole home. I never will forget that."

Jesse White remembers the tryout, too. After all, when a dream begins its transformation from fantasy to authenticity, you have a tendency to remember the details.

"I was asked to come down to St. Louis to try out for the St. Louis Browns," White explains. "They told me that I would stay at the Pine Street YMCA. I didn't realize then that the reason for my staying there was because the hotels were segregated in St. Louis."

Jesse White also tried out for the Pittsburgh Pirates in Brunswick, Georgia. Ultimately, the Browns offered him a minor league contract, but the 18-year-old turned it down.

"I told my father that I had an offer from the Browns, but he told me he didn't want me to take the contract. He wanted me to go to college. No one else in our family had ever gone to college and this was a chance my father thought I should not let pass me by. He never went far in school but he realized the value of an education."

In retrospect, that decision may have been the one that cost Jesse White a career in the major leagues. By the time he completed his studies at Alabama State College in the spring of 1956, he was nearly 22 years old. But the four years at the college level provided him with additional experience and, although it may not have been professional experience at the knee of coaches at the organized level, Jesse White's natural athletic ability was the kind of gift that had the knack of transcending instruction.

"In May of 1956, I signed a contract to play for the Cubs. I tried out at Wrigley Field and they had about 300 players. They selected six players out of the 300 and they offered those players contracts. I happened to be one of the six."

This time, Jesse White didn't have to ask permission to sign. He took the contract and got himself ready to report to spring training the following March. He never did get there because a few days before he was scheduled to report to spring training, his draft board sent him a love note and ordered him to a different camp.

But the United States Army couldn't stifle the little boy's dream; it only would postpone it. By the summer of 1959, Jesse White was getting paid – not a lot, but getting paid nonetheless – to live the dream of so many millions of American boys. Today, he nonchalantly describes his experience in reporting to the Cubs' training camp in Arizona. But it must have been just a little intimidating. It usually is for a rookie.

"I just took it in stride because I knew I had a job to do," he says. "I was a little bit in awe because here I was, right in the middle of everything. These were the Cubs. We were in different locker rooms – the major leaguers were separated from the minor league guys – but we were using the same practice fields.

"We'd see the major leaguers practice and we would rub elbows with them in the hotels and on the ball fields."

In the summer of 1959, Jesse White pulled on the uniform shirt of the Potashers of Carlsbad, New Mexico, in the Class D Sophomore League.

As center fielder and leadoff man for the Potashers, White hit .312 with two homers and 52 runs batted in. Under manager Walter Dixon, Carlsbad posted a 72-54 record on its way to the North Division championship. Jesse White burst out of the chute.

After his rookie year in organized ball, the Cubs assigned White to their Class A affiliate in the Eastern League, the Lancaster Red Roses. In a short stay under manager Phil Cavaretta, White batted .243 with a homer and 17 RBI until he hurt his leg.

"I pulled a hamstring there, but while I was at Lancaster I enjoyed playing for Cavaretta," White remembers. "We had a knack for losing ball games by one run that year. And Phil was the kind of guy who loved his ballplayers. He always treated us with respect.

"But he had a foul mouth, especially with umpires."

Now, when little boys dream about the colors of playing in organized baseball, they may dream of the green grass and the blue skies that hang over a Sunday afternoon doubleheader. But it's unlikely they dream of the colorful language that flows from the mouths of minor league managers.

"If he didn't like a call, he'd go out and grab between his legs and yell something like, 'Take my Italian sausage,' or 'Kiss my ass' and rake his hand up the seat of his pants. He could get pretty foul from time to time.

"But after the game was over he'd come into the locker room and tell us, 'Hey, don't worry about it, fellas. Nice try. We'll go get 'em tomorrow.' Then he'd go into his office and tear the phone off the wall. He'd break the chairs. He'd turn over his desk and he'd break the mirror. He'd wreck the joint.

"And then he'd come back out, as calm as can be, and say, 'Okay, fellas, take care. See you tomorrow.' He was like Dr. Jeckyl and Mr. Hyde."

Cavaretta, eighteen years older than Jesse White, would be a rarity were he playing in this era of free agency. Twenty of his twenty-two years in the major leagues were spent with the Chicago Cubs; he finished his career in 1955 after little more than a season with the crosstown White Sox. A native of Chicago, Cavaretta was an all-star caliber first baseman who in 1945, the last year the Cubs appeared in a World Series, led the National League with a sizzling .355 batting average.

For a first baseman he didn't supply much power; his biggest year for home runs was 1950, when he hit ten. It was the only time in his big league career that he reached double figures in homers. His ability to make contact, however, enabled Cavaretta to compile a lifetime .293 batting average. During three World Series appearances with the Cubs – 1935, 1938 and 1945 – Cavaretta hit .317.

After his playing days were over, Cavaretta returned to the Cubs and managed them to a 169-213 record from the end of 1951 through 1953.

"Phil had a little trouble seeing over the infield," White remembers. "I was playing centerfield and the wall in Lancaster was like the Green Monster in Boston, probably thirty feet high. One night a guy hit one over the wall for a home run. When I came back to the dugout after the inning was over, Cavaretta says, 'You should have caught that ball.'

"I said, 'Phil, the ball went over the wall. It was a home run.' But he couldn't see past the infield. But he was a nice guy and he was good to his players. I was just a little embarrassed for him, the way he handled himself around other people."

After suffering the injury to his hamstring, the Cubs dispatched White to the St. Cloud (Minnesota) Rox, the Cubs' Class C affiliate in the Northern League. White bounced back from his injury and hit a blistering .353 with a homer and twenty-three runs batted in under manager Freddie Martin. But the Rox were a reflection of the major league club, which had posted only one winning season since its 1945 pennant-winning season and which would not begin to establish respectability until some of Jesse White's contemporaries were old enough to make a run at the National League flag in 1969. During the 1960 season, the only one Jesse White spent in St. Cloud, the Rox finished in the Northern League basement with an anemic 49-74 record.

But the Rox' won-loss record wasn't the only statistic that begged attention from the parent club's front office. In 1960, Jesse White's second season in organized baseball, African American players still struggled to win their rightful place among the nation's elite baseball players. It had been thirteen seasons since Brooklyn Dodgers owner Branch Rickey broke major league baseball's color line by putting Jackie Robinson inside uniform jersey No. 42. In doing so, Rickey by no means shattered the racial barriers that kept black men from playing in the major leagues. He cracked it a little bit, and as years went by that crack began to spider-web. But it took a full dozen years before Elijah "Pumpsie" Green of Oakland, California, became the first African American player to suit up for the Boston Red Sox. The Red Sox thus became the last of the sixteen franchises to integrate their major league roster.

The new black stars — Willie Mays, Henry Aaron, Frank Robinson and the Cubs' own Ernie Banks among them – burst across the game's horizon like asteroids ablaze in an ebony night sky. But the effort to integrate all of major league baseball didn't burn as brightly or as quickly as the men who carried the torch. As the black stars began to shake the white establishment to its core, the marginal African American players continued to face the same slights and prejudices endured by their pioneer brethren in all other walks of American life.

In his second year of organized ball, Jesse White was on his way to his second season of batting better than .300. Moreover, the scouts who recommended signing him in 1958 were quick to note that the kid could fly.

Ned Cuthbert of the Philadelphia Keystones is credited with baseball's first stolen base in 1863, when he ran from first to second before the ball had been hit. Fans and the opposing players derisively laughed at him until Cuthbert persuaded everyone that there was no rule against it.

In the century since Ned Cuthbert's accidental innovation, baseball has warmed to the value of larceny. Players steal bases and coaches steal signs. You've got to be a bit of a thief to succeed in the game of baseball.

As speedy Latin American and black players began to penetrate major league rosters, managers began to take advantage of their quickness. The stolen base became a creative offensive weapon and players like Luis Aparicio of the Chicago White Sox began to alter the dynamic of run cre- [illegible]yers like Jesse White were fast becoming a hot commodity. Defensively, White was a slick-fielding outfielder with a pretty good arm. Offensively, he was able to get to first base and terrorize opposing pitchers with his speed.

But the guy on the mound isn't always the only guy throwing curves and playing chin music. In the era of the emerging black baseball player, there was too often an enemy from within, an organization mentality that held fast to the notion that black players were stupid and unworthy and encroaching. They may even have been bad for business, so one theory advanced.

One morning after a night game, Jesse White sat down for breakfast with a female journalist in St. Cloud. That in and of itself wasn't rank-and-file ordinary in 1960. The newspaper business was still a spiderweb network of good old boys, chomping cigars and swapping dirty jokes with the players they covered. More often than not, Max Mercy was alive and living in the American bush leagues of the early 1960s; Linda Cohn was barely a year old.

That this female reporter was white raised some eyebrows in the restaurant. The wrong pair of eyebrows.

"I was sitting in a restaurant with a white female reporter. We were talking about the team, my background and my military service and how I got into baseball. The whole bit."

Jesse White stifles emotion as he talks of the encounter through the mist of a half-century of yesterdays. He's as dispassionate discussing the breakfast in St. Cloud, Minnesota, as he is about the one he ate in Chicago today. He measures his words carefully and precisely.

"Afterward my manager, Fred Martin, called me into his office and he told me this: 'As long as you play baseball in the Cubs organization, you will never make it to the major leagues. Talking to a white woman like that is way off limits.'"

Martin spent three seasons after World War II as a pitcher for the St. Louis Cardinals and compiled a respectable 12-3 lifetime record.

Jesse White remains unemotional as he describes the encounter, but he knows which words to emphasize.

"That was ugly. I thought at the time that he was just speaking for himself, but I found out later on that he had sent a report to Chicago that, in effect, put me on a list. That was ugly. I really, really feel badly about that."

The year after Martin managed the Rox to a last-place finish, twenty-three games behind the Winnepeg Goldeyes, the Cubs promoted him as their major league pitching instructor. Martin held the Cubs' position as pitching coach from 1961 until 1965.

Jesse White is quick to say that, like much of the nation itself, major league baseball has moved beyond racial barriers. Today's Chicago Cubs, he notes, are among his biggest supporters in such efforts as literacy and life-saving organ donor programs.

But the franchise was forced to cope with the growing pains of American society as it moved away from the prejudices that dominated the first century and a half of the republic's life.

"For the most part I really loved my experience in minor league baseball," he says, this time with a drop of melancholy. "But there were some ugly, ugly incidents along the way. When we'd go into towns in Texas like Midland and Odessa, Plainview, we'd have to sleep in private homes while the white guys were sleeping in hotels and motels.

"Let me tell you about Plainview, Texas."

The Plainview Athletics was the Kansas City franchise in the Class D Sophomore League during White's rookie season at Carlsbad, New Mexico.

"One day, I was playing third base because our third baseman was hurt, so they moved me from centerfield to third base. I'm standing out there and my head is down between pitches.

"My manager, Walt Dixon, yells out to me, 'Hey Whitey, wake up!'

"And some heckler pipes up from the bleachers, 'Whitey? Whitey! Where the hell did you get the suntan, Whitey? What the hell kind of a name is that for a nigger?'

"All during that season – I was there three times – they called me everything under the sun. But I'd just go five for five and steal second third and home. Let me tell you; I'd be in the major leagues today if I played all my games in Plainview, Texas. The way I played in Plainview, I pinch myself when I think about it. I would run faster, I would throw farther and I hit the ball farther. I stole more bases there than anywhere else. I was fired up because they used the racial piece on me. And they used it big time."

Even though Jesse White was witness to the inequalities of the law in Montgomery during his days as a student at Alabama State, he enjoyed the buffer of athletics and was able to keep a safe distance from the worst of it. But in the minor leagues, he found himself face-to-face, black-to-white, with the most despicable and mindless of racial hatred. The irony is that the object of the racial taunts and venom was better educated than the hecklers. Moreover, he carried with him an honorable discharge from one of the nation's fiercest and most courageous branches of military service, yet he was being forced to defend his honor before gaggles of nitwits because his skin pigmentation was darker than pink.

"I actually grabbed a bat and went after a guy in the parking lot after one of the games down there. This guy was heckling me, getting really personal and ugly and I actually started after him with a baseball bat. A couple of my teammates grabbed me before I could hurt somebody. I never experienced that kind of personal hatred up to that time. In Montgomery it was the system. That didn't make it right, but it was systemic. Down there in Texas? That was personal and it was hatred. I've just never been able to understand that at all."

Walt Dixon, Jesse White's manager at Carlsbad, was also his skipper in 1962 when White played for the Class AA San Antonio Missions of the Texas League. Dixon, who hailed from South Carolina, was a good old boy in almost every sense of the word. But he possessed a high degree of compassion and loyalty for his players, as evidenced by this story told by Jesse White:

"We were on our way out of spring training in Arizona, on our way to Texas in 1962. We were riding on the bus and a bunch of us were on the back of the bus, playing cards. We arrived someplace in Amarillo or El

Paso, I can't remember exactly which town it was. The rest of the guys got off the bus and walked into a restaurant and I came in later after I took care of some business with my equipment on the bus.

"When I arrived at the door of the restaurant, the manager of the place was waiting at the front door. When I started to walk in, he said to me, 'Sorry, but you can't come in.' I could see that the other players were already seated at their tables, looking at menus, getting ready to order their meals."

"Sorry," the restaurant owner told Jesse White, "you can't come in here. We'll hang you. We don't serve coloreds and you can't come in here."

"So Walt Dixon could see that I was talking to the manager of the restaurant and that I wasn't having any luck getting in the door. So Walt comes up to the guy and asks him what the problem was.

"And the guy just looks at Walt. Walt says, 'This guy is one of my ballplayers. Why aren't you letting him in?' Now, Walt's from South Carolina, a redneck guy. And the guy tells Walt, 'Sorry. We don't let colored people eat in here.'

"So Walt looks at the guy and never hesitates. 'Look, I've got twenty-five ballplayers who are going to eat in here. If you don't serve this guy here, then I have twenty-five ballplayers who are not going to eat in here. You're either going to serve all of us or you're not going to serve any of us.'

"And the guy looks at Walk and says, 'We're not going to serve any of you.'"

True to his word, Walt Dixon ordered his players up from their tables and back onto the bus.

"So we all got back on the bus and drove down the road a little bit to a supermarket, and Walt sends us in to get baloney, cheese, pop, juice, milk and cookies. And we ate on the bus. That really elevated my feelings toward the guy."

Four of the six Texas League teams were based in the Lone Star State – Amarillo, El Paso, San Antonio and Austin. The other two clubs were Albuquerque, New Mexico and Tulsa, Oklahoma. For Jesse White, Texas proved to be the hardest place to wear dark skin.

One afternoon, White and teammate Paul Casanova, a hulking catcher and future major leaguer, walked into a restaurant in Amarillo. Casanova was tall for a catcher of that era; he stood 6 feet 4 inches and weighed 180 pounds, larger than most of his contemporaries. By comparison, the Cardinals' Tim McCarver was listed at 6 feet and 183 pounds; Dick Bertell of the Cubs played at 6 feet one-half inch and 200 pounds.

Born on New Year's Eve 1941 in Colon Matanzas, Cuba, Casanova played in 859 big league games from 1965 to 1974. He came up with the Washington Senators and finished his career with the Atlanta Braves, compiling a lifetime batting average of .225. Casanova's best year was 1966 when he hit .254 with 13 home runs in 122 games for the Senators.

"Paul Casanova was a black cat," Jesse White recalls. "I mean a *real* black cat, the color of my shoes. Paul and I decided we were going to go out and eat. We were the only blacks on that team that year and we decided we'd go out and have lunch.

"So we sat in this restaurant. And we sat. And we sat. And finally a Mexican waiter passed by and I stopped him."

"Sir, we'd like to have a menu, some silverware, some water."

"Sorry, amigo, we don't serve colored people here."

"What?"

"We don't serve colored people here."

"So I turned to Paul and in my broken Spanish I said, '*Vamanos, andale. No servido.*' And he agrees that we should go somewhere else.

"So I get up and get ready to leave and I'm walking ahead of Paul. I get to the door and I turn to say something to him and he's not there. I look back toward our table and Paul's sitting there, at the table, with a menu in his hands.

"Now, at this point I'm a few years out of the Army and so I go back to the table and get ready to sit down again with Paul. The waiter comes back and says, 'No, you cannot sit here. You cannot eat here. We don't serve colored people here.'

"I said, 'What do you think that guy is?' As it turned out I walked away and Paul stayed there and ate. But that upset me a little bit.

"Here I am, an American, a former military serviceman, a taxpayer, and this restaurant is serving a foreigner, a guy from a country we won't even recognize because our leaders won't even talk to each other, but you won't serve one of your own. Even after all these years, I haven't been able to reconcile that one."

Jesse White left more than one restaurant hungry. Once in Midland, Texas, while playing for the Carlsbad Potashers, the white players stayed in a local hotel while their three black teammates stayed in private homes.

"The guys told us to come over to the hotel in the morning so we could all have breakfast together. So the black guys get to the hotel and the man there tells us, 'Sure, you can eat here. But you can't eat out *there,'* and he pointed to the dining room. 'You have to eat in the kitchen.'

"I said, 'Wait a minute. Are you telling me that we have to eat in the kitchen but pay you the same price for our food as the people who get to eat in the dining room?'"

When the hotel manager told him that, yes, that would be the case, Jesse White and his African American teammates left the hotel.

"That didn't seem to make much sense to us, so we walked out."

White's bizarre interracial encounters didn't all occur south of the Mason-Dixon line. During his days as a St. Cloud Rox he wound up in an unexpected scrape following a rainout.

"I'm in St. Cloud and we got rained out one afternoon, so I decided to go out by myself, have a nice meal, maybe go to the show and just take it easy, chill out. I'd just bought a nice suit that cost me a couple hundred dollars in Minneapolis. I decided to put on the suit and head to a restaurant.

"The restaurant had a horseshoe-shaped type of a counter and I'm sitting at this counter with this new suit on, looking pretty dapper. This guy comes in and he must have been about 225 pounds, about 6 feet tall. He had a friend with him and the guy must have been 6 feet 5 and looked like he weighed 250, 260 pounds, a giant of a guy. And they had two beautiful ladies with them.

"So I'm sitting and eating, and I just happened to look up across the counter and the smaller guy got up and started toward me. The big guy said, 'No, no, take it easy,' but his friend told him to leave him alone, that he just wanted to talk to me.

"I put another bite in my mouth when I looked up and this guy is standing over me, with fire in his eyes like I had done something to him. He looked like he wanted to kill me."

At that point White decided he was finished eating and asked the waitress for his check.

"I didn't even take the check to the cash register. I left everything at the counter, tip and all. By that time I could see some of my teammates had come by and were standing outside the door of the restaurant. So I went outside to get alongside them, figuring if this guy knew I had some friends with me he'd decide to leave me alone.

"So by now I'm outside the restaurant, standing with a couple of my teammates when the guy comes outside and taps me on the shoulder. I said, 'Sir, I don't know you and you don't know me and I haven't done anything to you and you haven't done anything to me. Why don't you go back inside and finish eating your supper with that nice young lady you have with you.'

"He just kept glaring at me, so I asked him what the problem was. He still didn't say anything so I turned away from him and just as I did, he grabbed me and threw me down and I tore the knees out of my pants. As I got up, I could see he was still coming at me and I managed to get in a swing and caught him on the mouth, dazing him a little bit.

"Then I lunged for him, knocked him to the ground and grabbed his hair and started hitting his head against the pavement. I was half his size, but I had to protect myself.

"I knew I must have been pretty upset because I don't bother other people. I looked up and his friend was coming out of the restaurant – this was the big guy. I figured this was it. The big guy was going to tear me up.

"But when the big guy got to me, he touched me on the shoulder and asked me to please stop knocking his friend's head against the pavement. And I was glad to stop because this gave me a chance to get out of this mess.

"Within a few minutes the police arrived and the guy's head was bleeding and he's telling the cops that I provoked him. But the ballplayers told the police that it was the other guy who provoked me."

After the police calmed the storm, the aggressor approached Jesse White and asked if they could talk.

"I tried to talk to you. I tried to reason with you," White told the man. "But you were beyond reason."

"Okay. Here. Let me tell you what happened."

"I'd like to hear what happened."

"See, I saw you sitting there in the restaurant, eating your food, acting proper and you looked very nice with your suit and tie. A colored person is not supposed to look better than a white person."

"Go ahead ..."

"Well, you look like a successful person and I didn't like that a colored guy like you would look better than a white guy like me. Here I am, a white guy, and I'm out cutting wood, a lumberjack, and you make more money than me and that's not the way it's supposed to be. But I'll tell you that I'm really sorry. I was wrong and I want to apologize to you. Will you please accept my hand?"

"I was ready to give him my hand, but not the way he wanted it. I was ready to pound him some more. My knees were bleeding and my suit was all torn up. But I shook the man's hand and went upstairs to my room, which was just down the street so I could clean up. While I was in there I heard an ambulance and the next thing I know, one of my teammates is knocking on my door and telling me that the guy was so upset that I beat him up that he punched his fist through a window at the Greyhound Bus station.

"Sometimes I wonder if he wouldn't have cleaned me up big time had I not been able to get back on my feet as fast as I did."

In spite of the racial and cultural obstacles that blocked his path, Jesse White assembled a respectable record over seven years at six different levels of the minor leagues. Here are his career statistics, provided by Steve Densa, assistant director of media relations for the National Association of Professional Baseball Leagues:

Year	Club	Level	Average	HR	RBI
1959	Carlsbad	D	.312	2	52
1960	Lancaster	A	.243	1	17
	St. Cloud	C	.353	1	23
1961	Wenatchee	B	.320	0	41
1962	San Antonio	AA	.294	1	36
1963	Salt Lake City	AAA	.287	1	37
1964	Salt Lake City	AAA	.250	0	27
1965	(Inactive List)				
1966	Dallas-Ft. Worth	AA	.293	0	26

Missed the 1965 season because of kidney infection and accident in which he lost the tip of a finger. Submitted his retirement and was released September 8, 1966.

Comparing eras in any sport is difficult, if not impossible. But there are unavoidable facts that need to be considered when analyzing Jesse White's professional baseball career and what might have been.

First, there were twenty major league teams during the latter stages of White's minor league career. That means that at any given time, there were no more than 500 roster spots available at the major league level. Today, with thirty franchises in operation, there are 250 more players on major league rosters than there were during the Jesse White era.

Second, with his offensive numbers and based on the opinion of those who played with him and who saw him play, White probably had the tools to play baseball in the major leagues. His abilities have been compared to those of contemporary players who enjoyed success at the major league level.

By the time Jesse White decided to retire and the Cubs granted him his release, he was already 32 years old. Did he start his professional baseball career too late? By pursuing a college degree and losing two years to military service, he was six years behind some of the other rookies who reported to spring training in 1960.

At 32, he was ready to make a career decision and says today that the Cubs had assured him they would bring him up to the major league team. It never happened. Moreover, as was common in those days, White and the Cubs had differences over compensation.

Everyone grows up. At some point dreams become fantasy and are no longer viable pursuits. Jesse White's little boy dream of playing major league baseball came *this close* to coming true. He distinguished himself as a quality outfielder at every level of the minor leagues. He could hit a little bit and he could run a lot. His arm was better than average for a centerfielder, and he was acknowledged by those who played with him to have been a good and loyal teammate. Sure there were scrapes and bumps along the way. That's how life is meant to be. You bandage the scrapes and you ice the bumps and you learn from mistakes and you remember what made you what you are. There's always the opportunity to look back, but you can't change what's already passed.

History teaches the most important lessons of a life and only a fool disregards the lessons of the past. But another fool is the man who lives in that past.

At a point in everyone's life, the time comes to move on. Turn around and look ahead, see what's over the next hill and on the horizon. After the summer of 1966, Jesse White's time at the fork in the road had come. It was time to put baseball in the rear-view mirror.

"Sure I was a little disappointed," he says. "But some promises had been made and those promises weren't kept, so I decided it was time to move on.

"I felt badly about how I walked away from the game. I was promised something that never happened. I was promised more money and a raise when I got to Triple A. They promised they would double my money and that eventually they would bring me up to the majors."

There is a hint of wistfulness in his voice as he talks about leaving a game he loved.

"Certainly I would have liked to play major league ball. It's what I wanted from the time I was a kid. I probably would have played more for the pride than the money. I could have done anything for money. You can always get a job. If I had a job mopping this floor or emptying the garbage, washing dishes or cleaning tables, that would get me money to live on. Even in the job I have today, I work seven days a week and I never complain about it.

"But I would have liked to have played in the major leagues. That would have been the dream come true. But when dreams don't come true you move on."

Had he been able to break the glass ceiling and crack the Cubs' major league roster, he may never have pursued other career options. Politics may never have opened its doors. Moreover, what of the thousands of kids who have modeled their lives after his? Hypothetical questions.

But there's one question that should gnaw at the psyche of every middle-aged fan of the Chicago Cubs: What if Jesse White had been playing centerfield in 1969?

Nice guys
finish
last.

— Leo Durocher

Chapter Nine Never in the history of Chicago sports has a team received so much attention for accomplishing so little.

Millions of Bears fans are still living in the backwash of the 1985 Super Bowl victory over the New England Patriots. Bulls fans rocked the old barn on Madison Street through six NBA championships between 1991 and 1998. A few graybeards recall September 22, 1959, as the night Chicago Fire Commissioner Robert Quinn set off the air raid sirens to celebrate the Sox' first American League Pennant in forty years. The Stanley Cup? It stopped in Chicago, but that was forty-two years ago.

True, it doesn't happen often, but when a championship falls in the laps of rabid Chicago sports fans, they savor the glory for years because it will be years more before it happens again.

But Cubs fans? Those born during or before the Kennedy administration are prone to celebrate not a pennant or World Series Champion; rather, they regale one another with tales of one of the classic sports collapses in history. In 1969, the summer that Neil Armstrong and Edwin Aldrin stepped on the moon, the Chicago Cubs fiddled away an eight-game lead over the seven-year-old New York Mets.

On Wednesday, August 6, the Cubs behind right-hander Rich Nye beat the Houston Astros 5-4 to extend their league lead over the Mets to eight and a half games and run their record to 71-40. They would remain in first place for thirty-five more days before Gil Hodges' Mets would overtake them and build an eight-game cushion of their own en route to a 100-62 record and the franchise's first National League Pennant.

The Cubs, meanwhile, nosedived over the last seven weeks of the season, losing thirty of their last fifty-one games.

Theories abounded for the Cubs' collapse. Manager Leo Durocher, some said, refused to rest his regulars. Wrigley Field in 1969 was still without lights, the only major league park that wouldn't give players a chance to perform past the predusk heat of the day, and critics accused Durocher of allowing his players to melt in the Friendly Confines during the summer of '69's dog days. The fact is, the Mets played out of their minds over the last seven weeks of the season. Led by Tom Seaver's 25 wins and 2.21 earned run average, the Mets blistered their way to a 41-15 record – a .732 pace – during the Cubs' seven-week collapse.

But the beginning of the end began the afternoon of July 8 in Shea Stadium.

In his book *The Cubs of '69: Recollections of the Team That Should Have Been*, the late sports writer Rick Talley recapped the nightmare that would forever be Don Young's legacy:

Much has happened to Don Young following that fateful afternoon in Shea Stadium, July 8, 1969 – that bright but hazy day when Don Young misplayed two fly balls and the Mets beat the Cubs 4-3 …

Young completed the season a forgotten man, batting only 69 times in August and September yet batting a respectable-for-his-role-average of .239 with six home runs and 27 RBI. Young had been hired to catch fly balls and hit eighth …

Talley quotes Young:

"But I wasn't being a major league ballplayer in 1969. I couldn't throw a lick because I'd injured my arm and I never was much better than a .235 hitter. And in that big game I dropped two fly balls … Hell, that incident didn't end my career. I just wasn't good enough."

Under a microscope of national media attention, albeit nothing like it is today, Young wilted and never emerged from his shell.

Six of the Cubs' regular position players today remain household names and fan favorites: first baseman and Hall of Famer Ernie Banks; left fielder and Hall of Famer Billy Williams; third baseman and Cubs broadcaster Ron Santo; second baseman Glenn Beckert; shortstop Don

Kessinger; and catcher and sometimes fill-in broadcaster Randy Hundley. Flanking Young in right field was journeyman outfielder Jim Hickman.

With the trio of Kessinger, Beckert and Hundley, the Cubs' defense was 75 percent superb up the middle, where it counts. As for Young, his .975 fielding average was better than only two regular National League center fielders – Clarence "Cito" Gaston and Bobby Tolan, and Tolan made up for his stone fingers with a rock-solid .305 batting average.

Of the players on the Cubs' 1969 roster, Glenn Beckert is probably among Jesse White's best friends. Beckert and White played together at Triple-A Salt Lake City in 1964, the year before he made his debut in a Cubs' uniform.

A native of Pittsburgh, Pennsylvania, Beckert earned a degree in political science from Allegheny College in 1962.

"When I graduated from Allegheny College, I ended up signing as a shortstop with the Boston Red Sox," Beckert explains. "That first year I was playing at Waterloo, Iowa. I believe I showed up there in June.

"When I graduated from college, the folks in the neighborhood chipped in and bought me a couple of suits. So when I showed up in Waterloo, I was dressed in a suit and a tie and I walked into the clubhouse right before the game started.

"Matt Sczesny was the manager and he's got a big cigar in his mouth and his feet are up on the desk. I walked in and said, 'Mr. Sczesny, your shortstop prayers have been answered.' He looked at me, kind of laughing in a way and he said, 'How much money are they paying you to play for me?'

"I told him that I signed for $2,500 and if I make the major leagues, I'll make a total of $7,500. He looked at me for a few seconds and said, 'Well, we have a fella named Petrocelli from Boston and they're paying him $125,000 to play shortstop for me. Do you play any other position?'

"And right then and there I told Mr. Sczesny that I'd play anywhere that he wanted me to play."

Smart kid, that young man with the political science degree from Allegheny College. Petrocelli, with the Christian name of Rico, was called up a year later to the parent Red Sox club and stayed for thirteen years, piecing together a .251 career batting average with 210 homers, a considerable number for a shortstop of his era, although the second half of his career was spent at third base. Ironically, his best year was 1969 when the Red Sox finished third to the Baltimore Orioles. The year Gil Hodges' Mets cruised past Glenn Beckert's Cubs to win the National League Pennant going away, Rico Petrocelli crushed a career-best 40 home runs, drove in 97 and batted .297, also a career best.

But Glenn Beckert had at least one more lesson in humility to learn his first afternoon in Waterloo, Iowa.

"Where do I find a locker?" Beckert asked his new manager.

"Just go see the clubhouse man. His name is Bill."

Following orders, Beckert hunted down Bill the Clubhouse Man.

"Bill, I'm Glenn Beckert."

"Ah, yes. I heard you were coming."

At last, Beckert was receiving the kind of respect due a rookie being paid $2,500 to play professional baseball.

"So, where's my locker?"

Bill the Clubhouse Man reached into a drawer and pulled out a hammer. Then he reached into another drawer and pulled out five nails. He handed them to the rookie and waved at a wall on the far end of the locker room.

"Make it anyplace on that wall that you want."

After he hammered those nails into the clubhouse walls, Glenn Beckert went to work honing the skills that would take him to the major leagues. Beckert's ego would have to endure one more bruise but it would be the one that expedited his journey to the majors. The Chicago Cubs acquired him from the Boston farm system.

As a Cub farm hand, Beckert remembers his playing days with Jesse White. He chuckles when he recalls several of the instances when they collided chasing flies in short centerfield.

"I did that to him a lot of times," Beckert laughs. "When I was in the minor leagues and there was a fly ball hit between the center fielder, the right fielder and myself, I lost track of what the other guys were saying. I got it! And I wanted to catch that ball every time. But that's what you do in the minor leagues because you always want to move up the ladder.

"I'll bet Jesse would remember that."

Jesse White does.

"He used to knock me down all the time," White agrees. "I got to the point where I didn't even want to come in on a fly ball because I was afraid he'd run into me and knock me down."

"We were all trying to make it to the major leagues," Beckert adds. "We never had any spats except when I ran him over a couple times." Beckert laughs. "He was a good guy to play with, a good teammate. I don't remember any problems on the team, any black or white or Latin differences on that team. There was nothing like that. We just came to play."

Beckert's big break to the major leagues came in the form of tragedy. On February 15, 1964, Cubs' promising second baseman Kenny Hubbs was killed in a private airplane crash at Utah Lake, Utah, less than fifty miles from where Beckert and White played their season together for the Salt Lake City Bees.

"The Cubs moved me from shortstop because I didn't have the arm to play there," Beckert says. "The reason I got to the major leagues was that Kenny Hubbs was killed. He was better than I was."

Whether Beckert is being hazy or just modest, a check of his and Hubbs' statistics gives ample reason to dispute any contention that Glenn Beckert was not as good as Kenny Hubbs. Beckert lived to overcome evaluation; Hubbs died filled with expectation.

Over an eleven-year career that spanned 1965-1975, Beckert hit .283 in 1,320 games. In 1971, he hit a sizzling .342, third behind Joe Torre of St. Louis at .363 and Atlanta's Ralph Garr at .343.

"I remember that year, '71. Everything I hit off the end of the bat would fall in. Every line drive would fall in."

In two full seasons with the Cubs before his tragic end, Hubbs hit .260 and .235.

Asked if the 1969 season was Beckert's biggest disappointment, he does not hesitate in answering.

"Yes, it was. We had an eight-game lead and ended up losing it by eight games." Time heals the pain and intensity of a pennant race and the grief the 1969 campaign inflicted on members of that Cubs team. In some cases resentment gives way to admiration, as Beckert notes:

"I just got back from a cruise with Ron Swoboda," who played right field for the Mets in 1969. "Here's a guy who came up in '65, too. And for three or four years he wore a helmet in right field and everyone wondered why. But I knew it was because he was going to eventually get hit in the head.

"Then in '69 he turns around and makes some great plays you just can't believe. I like to watch older films of games and I watch them in the World Series when they played Baltimore. He made one play that was simply outstanding.

"I hated those guys. I hated the whole team back then. But now as you get older, you run into them and they don't seem so bad.

"But they had a heck of a team back then. People wonder why the '69 Mets won. Because they had pitchers. Two of them (Tom Seaver and Nolan Ryan) are in the Hall of Fame. But they were young kids back then and the press hadn't picked up on them yet. I think the Man Upstairs was on their side that year."

Beckert understands the critics who blame Durocher's unbending desire to play the same lineup day in, day out. Durocher leaned on that core of all-stars and future Hall of Famers, but even the best athletes have limitations of stamina and skill.

"Leo loved me for some reason. I don't know why, he just did. He was a good man, but he liked to start the same lineup every day. But we had some talent on that bench that could have helped out, could have given us a rest for two days. But Leo didn't think that way. Leo was from the old school."

Beckert concedes that one hole in that 1969 Cubs team was in center field.

"Now that I look back, I wish we would have had Jesse as our center fielder," he offers. "I really do, I really do. I think Jesse could definitely have made a difference on that team because he was a very good center fielder.

"I wish he had been with us with the Cubs. I don't ever recall us having a great center fielder. We had some great infielders and we had Billy Williams in the outfield. But we never had a good center fielder.

"We had Don Young and he's a nice guy and all, but I didn't know what he was going to do when he was out there. The year before we had Adolfo Phillips. I wish I had Adolfo's ability. He could run. He could hit with power. But, no offense, Adolfo was a little scared. 'Me no feel good. I don't want to hit against Bob Gibson.' I didn't want to hit against him, either."

Ironically, Beckert's first major league hit came off of Hall of Famer Bob Gibson, whose incredible season of 1968 included twenty-two wins against nine losses; that summer he gave up an out-of-this-universe 1.12 earned runs per nine innings pitched. Following Gibson's '68 season the major leagues lowered the pitching mound from sixteen to ten inches in an effort to aid the overpowered hitters.

"I got my first hit in the major leagues off him. He struck me out, I think, my first time up and then I popped up. It was something like 33 degrees on opening day in Chicago. It was dark and gray and the wind was blowing; colder than heck. And my first hit was a swinging bunt down the third base line.

"I don't have the ball. I never thought of that. We never knew about that stuff at that time. I'm just an average player."

An "average" player of Beckert's caliber today would earn in the range of $6 to $8 million annually. But in his era money did not flow so freely.

"One time I worked for Ron Santo in his pizza business. That was my first year, 1965. My salary was $6,000 for the year. I think I spent $800 or $1,000 investing in the business and it didn't go too good – *look for us in your freezer case.*

"So that one died and I'd never known what a loan was at a bank. I still lived with my parents. I went back to John Holland, the (Cubs) general manager and said, 'John, how do I get back to Pittsburgh?'

"He said, 'Glenn, don't worry about it. We'll pay all your bills … and then take them off your next year's salary.'" Beckert chuckles at the recollection. "That's how things operated back then."

After retiring from baseball Beckert remained in Chicago where he worked at the Board of Trade. He now is retired in Florida, "and in October of this year I'll be on Medicare."

He thoroughly enjoys talking about his major league experience and the friendships he forged.

"What's great for me is that there were seven of us (Beckert, Santo, Williams, Kessinger, Hundley, Ferguson Jenkins and Ken Holtzman) who played together for nine years and we're still the greatest friends. Today, that will never happen. Players shuffle around too much, and when they're out of baseball, with their millions of dollars, they'll go their own way."

And his mind is still clear when he talks about the baseball talent of one friend who never quite made it to the major leagues.

"Jesse was totally penalized because he got a late start in organized ball. The owners back then didn't want a player that old to be in the major leagues. That's my opinion. Jesse was a danged good ballplayer.

"He ran fast. He was quick. He could move. I wish I could have run that fast. I believe it would have been easy for Jesse, if he had made the major leagues, to steal bases. He was that quick. He was like Lou Brock going down there."

Fellow Southwestern Conference Hall of Famer Brock, by the way, played for the St. Cloud Rox a year after Jesse White. In 1961, Brock hit a blistering .361 for the Rox, with fourteen home runs and eighty-two runs batted in. Brock's another one who could have helped the Cubs win that elusive 1969 National League Pennant, but Chicago traded him in 1964 to the St. Louis Cardinals for pitcher Ernie Broglio.

"If Jesse would have had a chance to prove himself, he might have compared with Brock and Curt Flood. I don't know. It's hard to look at what a guy does in the minor leagues and then compare them. But I think he could run as fast as Curt Flood. When you go from the minor leagues to the major leagues, it's a whole new, different situation. When you get to the major leagues, you see the ball better because the lighting is better and they treat you better. The pitchers in the major leagues are not as wild as they are in the minor leagues. They're close to the plate, so you have a better selection of pitches to hit.

"But Jesse had a good arm, too. He wasn't like a Roberto Clemente, but he was good. As I recall, he didn't strike out much but he still had some jerks on the ball. Yep. Jesse White could play."

Beckert pauses a moment and repeats his wish.

"I wish Jesse had been on that team. He would have been great in center field for that team because he could go and catch a ball." Beckert then returns to his devilish sense of humor. "Unless I was headed straight at him."

Let's play two today.

— Ernie Banks

Chapter Ten The man is an incorrigible tease.

"Jesse White, Jesse White. Do I know Jesse White?"

Yes, sir. You do. There's a picture of the two of you at a Cubs spring training dinner in honor of former Negro Leagues star Buck O'Neill.

"Jesse White, Jesse White. How do I know Jesse White?"

You played baseball for the same major league franchise.

"Jesse White. Did I play with him with the Yankees?"

No, sir. Had you played with him for the Yankees, you'd be Mr. Yankee. You're Mr. Cub.

"Jesse White. Did I play with him with the Chicago American Giants?"

No, sir. The Chicago American Giants was a Negro League team and the Negro League was disbanded by the time Jesse White made it to professional baseball.

"Jesse White. Did I play with him with the White Sox?"

No sir, had you played for the White Sox … let's not get into that.

"Tell me about Jesse White."

And that's how the most famous Chicago Cub of all time turns the tables on someone who's asking him questions about someone else.

Before there was Sammy Sosa, before there was Mark Prior, even before there was *Richard Pryor*, there was Ernie Banks. On September 17, 1953, the 22-year-old Ernie Banks of Dallas, Texas, became the first African American man to play for the Chicago National League Baseball Club known as the Cubs. Three days later, he hit his first major league home run off right-hander Gerry Staley of the St. Louis Browns and he didn't stop until he hit 511 more. His baseball exploits earned him election to the Hall of Fame. But his flirtatious charm has earned him a place in the hearts of all of Chicago, even the cold hearts of some White Sox fans. (Other cold-hearted White Sox fans will remind you that Staley, the man who gave up Banks's inaugural homer, made it to the World Series in 1959 as a member of the crosstown White Sox's bullpen staff. Banks, on the other hand, never played in a postseason game.)

Banks was blessed with titanium-strength hands and wrists and a disposition that could splash sunlight into an arctic December night.

"Jesse White," he recollects. "We never had a chance to play together because in spring training I was on the major league field and he was with the minor league players. But I knew of him. Jesse White was a *ballplayer.* He had some real ability. His reputation made itself known throughout the organization."

Told that former teammate Glenn Beckert believes that White could have made a difference in the Cubs' quest for the National League Pennant in 1969, Banks doesn't hesitate to respond.

"I believe that. Yes, I believe that. He had a lot of ability. This kid had a lot of talent. *I mean a lot of talent.* He put everything into it. He focused. He concentrated on being the best player he could be. He really focused on what he was doing."

Banks was half the reason Chicago basked in a golden era of shortstops in the 1950s and early '60s. In 1959, Banks won his second consecutive National League Most Valuable Player Award when he hit .304 with 45 homers and a league-leading 143 runs batted in. That same year, the White Sox were winning the American League Pennant with the Go-Go speed of shortstop Luis Aparicio, who led the league with fifty-six stolen bases. Aparicio wasn't able to win the AL MVP award that year because his keystone partner, Nellie Fox, was busy doing it. A golden era indeed. It marked the only year in more than a century of Chicago professional baseball that a player from both sides of town was voted most valuable player in his respective league.

Banks was as gifted a baseball player ever to wear a Chicago uniform, north side or south. Over a nineteen-year career in which he played only for the Cubs, Banks hit .274 with 512 home runs and 1,636 runs batted in. Twice he led the league in homers, an impressive statistic considering his contemporaries included Hank Aaron, Willie Mays, Frank Robinson and Orlando Cepeda, all of who earned their own elections to the Hall of Fame because of their gaudy power statistics.

Ernie Banks' baseball star shone as bright as any in America, which is why he caused more than a few eyebrows to arch in 1963 when he decided to run for alderman from the 8th Ward on Chicago's South Side. True, baseball had boosted his name identification substantially, although he arguably was better received on Wrigley Field's North Side. But why would a future Hall of Fame baseball player seek public office during the prime of his career?

"When I played baseball," Banks explains, "I had mentors. It started with my father. I always looked for a mentor at every juncture in my life. When I started playing in the Negro Leagues, I looked to Jackie Robinson as a mentor. And I took it right down the line. I looked at qualities in the men who I admired and I tried to emulate them.

"Jesse White was one of those men. He didn't know this, but he was always a great inspiration to me because of all that he did. Jesse White. You know what Jesse White is? He's a social entrepreneur. I kind of adapted his attitude to my life, this concept of being a social entrepreneur because of what I saw him do with those kids of his."

"Those kids," Banks refers to are, of course, the Jesse White Tumblers. Banks says White truly made an impression with him during the early 1960s.

"I decided to run for alderman in the 8th Ward because of his life. I watched what Jesse was doing with those young kids and I got the idea that I wanted to do something like that. I wanted to give something back to the community where I lived. I wanted to get to a place where I could help the people in my own ward."

Unfortunately, Ernie Banks didn't enjoy the same political success as his social entrepreneurial mentor, Jesse White. Here are the official results from the February 26, 1963, primary election for alderman from Chicago's 8th Ward, according to records with the Chicago Board of Election Commissioners:

James A. Condon	9,738
Gerald E. Gibbons	4,472
Ernest Banks	2,162
Coleman T. Holt	1,391

Since his retirement from baseball in 1971, Ernie Banks has moved to Marina del Rey, California. However, he is a frequent visitor to Chicago, especially during the summer when the ivy is in bloom at 1060 W. Addison Street.

"It's funny," Banks says, "but a lot of people in Chicago get Jesse and me mixed up. I would be going someplace and someone would call me Jesse. It's pretty funny. I'd go to a restaurant or a hotel or just for a walk in the park and people would mistake me for Jesse White.

"I've never shared this with him but one time I came to see him at his office and some people looked at me funny, thinking I was Jesse White." Or just maybe they knew he is Ernie Banks?

Anyway, Banks says he uses Jesse White as an example of what people can do for others.

"He's really inspired me and I've followed his career in politics pretty closely. He doesn't know that. But I read so much about him, about all the good things that he's doing, all the good deeds. I go to a Bulls game and see him and those kids of his and it inspires me. He's an incredible man and he's been a true inspiration to me. He doesn't know this. I've never shared it with him."

Sharing would have been nice in 1969, the kind of sharing that would have brought Ernie Banks the only thing he lacks from his Hall of Fame career with the Cubs: a World Series ring. It would have been nice if Ernie Banks and Jesse White could have shared the thrill of winning a World Series ring.

"Jesse White could have certainly made it to the major leagues, but I guess he got a late start after college and the military service. He really had a lot of ability and I thought he was going to stick, but he went in another direction. And even though he didn't make it to the major leagues, he was always an inspiration to me and he has been throughout his career.

"But all our lives take different turns. And Jesse White teaches lessons to kids that need to be taught. I've passed some of those lessons on to my children and to other people who have come into my life. Don't forget where you came from and be sure to give something back. And those are the qualities that I've learned from being around Jesse.

"Jesse White gets it done. He completes it. He finishes the job and he's proven that to be the case in everything he's done since he left baseball.

"He's a wonderful person."

Every year I said

I was going to quit . . .
and every year I'd

change my mind.

— Jesse White on the infancy of his tumbling team

Chapter Eleven Jesse White returned to Chicago in the fall of 1959 after his first season in organized baseball. He was the leadoff hitter and center fielder for the Carlsbad Potashers, who under Walt Dixon pounded out a 72-54 record and led the Class D Sophomore League in attendance. Carlsbad finished first in the North Division but lost two games to none to the Alpine Cowboys in the league championship series.

He hit .312 with two homers and 52 runs batted in for the Potashers, pretty good numbers for a rookie. But in 1959, when American League MVP Nellie Fox of the pennant-winning White Sox earned $40,000, baseball wasn't much more than a hobby for a low-level minor leaguer. At age 25, Jesse White had bills to pay and a backup career to pursue. Little did he know that what he was about to undertake would change his life and the lives of thousands of inner-city kids, most of whom weren't yet born.

"That off-season I started teaching school," White recalls. "I also went to work for the Chicago Park District and I was assigned to the Rockwell Gardens Fieldhouse near what is now the Rockwell Gardens housing project. I taught the kids how to tumble, how to wrestle, other physical education programs.

"Someone asked me if I would put on a gym show, basically a show for the parents of the kids I was coaching. So in October I started teaching the kids how to tumble. Two months later, we put on a gym show and there were about 400 people in the audience, mostly from the neighborhood.

"Remember now, these were all poor kids, all project kids right there from Rockwell Gardens."

Forty-six years ago, the birthplace of the Jesse White Tumbling Team was just another poor neighborhood. At one time, more than 1,100 units swelled the Rockwell Gardens housing project, crouching three miles northwest of the Loop. The U.S. Justice Department identifies the neighborhood as a drug-infested bunker for the Gangster Disciples. Nearly half a century ago, however, it was simply a place where kids needed direction and guidance.

"The kids did so well and afterwards the parents were so excited. They said they'd never seen those kids so well dressed, so well behaved and performing so well."

After the show, parents hugged their kids with one arm and threw the other around Jesse White's shoulders.

"That's great. We're done. This is it," he announced to the mothers and fathers.

"What do you mean? You spent all this time with our kids and now you're saying you're not going to take them any farther? You're not going to continue?"

"No, I just did this as part of my responsibility as a physical instructor."

"Hey, that's not right. That's like training a man to be a general and never giving him a command. You spent all this time with these kids and now you're going to just drop them? You gave them a bite from the apple and it tasted pretty good, but you're not going to give them any more?"

Dr. Frankenstein, your monster wants to know the meaning of life. And remember, George Bailey never did leave Bedford Falls.

"Every year I said I was going to quit, that this was going to be my last year. And then the kids would come to me with tears in their eyes and say, 'Mr. White, please don't give up the team.'

"And the parents would come by and tell me that if they didn't have this program, their kids would be on the streets and end up being prey for the gangs and all the other negative aspects of life.

"I said early on in life that I wanted to do something to make a difference in the lives of young people. I wanted to give back to the community. Some people will tell me that I've given back enough, and there were times when I thought that maybe they were right.

"And I'd do another year, but I'd swear that this one was going to be my last year. This is my last year. I'm not going to do it anymore. But every time I'd say that, I'd be inspired by the kids, be inspired by the parents to continue."

Forty-five "last years" later, the Jesse White Tumbling Team not only is still up and running, it is a world-famous troupe that has graduated, by White's own accounting, more than 10,000 kids. Not that it's been easy. For the first quarter century of the team's existence, Jesse White was not only its coach and creator, he also was virtually its sole benefactor.

"I paid for it from as many as three sources of revenue that I had during those times. I was a teacher and I worked for the park district and for a time I was a lawmaker," he explains. "So it was costing me about $19,000 a year from 1959 until about 1985."

Now, Jesse White may be a terrific teacher with a heart bigger than the Sears Tower, but he isn't much of a capitalist. What he shelled out for the team came after he paid taxes on the income because he had never bothered to organize his team as a not-for-profit organization. Not only did he never profit even a nickel from his tumbling team's performances, neither did he take advantage of allowable tax benefits for the first twenty-six years of his troupe's lifetime. It took a shout from outside his adopted family to provide some guidance and, ultimately, some financial assistance.

"Around 1985, Coca-Cola called and asked if we'd do a commercial for them," he remembers. "I talked with a fellow by the name of Chuck Morrison who was vice president of Coca-Cola. I told him that, since we did the commercial for them, we'd like to continue with the relationship.

"So he asked me if we were a 501(c)-3 and I told him we were not. All that money I was using and I couldn't write it off my income tax because we didn't have the not-for-profit classification. I didn't write off a dime from my income tax. So Coke came on board and the year after that, McDonald's stepped up and then we started to roll."

Today, the tumblers command on average between $1,500 and $2,000 for a performance. He maintains three troupes and together the teams perform more than 1,000 shows annually. All surplus revenues pour right back into the program. Each year, the Jesse White Tumbling Team performs at least once at twenty-nine of the thirty National Basketball Association arenas. They can be seen in dozens of minor league baseball parks and soccer stadiums when the dandelions explode in a sea of maize, and in scores of college and professional football stadiums when crimson leaves wave goodbye to the season of life. Parades? From Chicago's venerable St. Patrick's Day Parade down Columbus Drive in the bluster of March, to the scorching heat of the back-to-school Bud Billikin Parade, to the Sycamore Pumpkin Festival in the dying light of October, the best ones in Illinois feature the Jesse White Tumbling Team.

Today, the team's operating budget is well into seven figures.

Despite the explosive popularity of the team and the financial success that helped feed it, the man who runs the show is the standard-bearer of frugality. Until the past few years, he personally washed each tumbler's uniform in the laundry room of his apartment complex.

"I used to use up all the machines in the building," he explains, "sometimes five or six machines at a time, and there are only eight machines in the building. I used to use up all eight of the dryers. After all, I was with the kids prior to the show, picking them up and driving them to the event. When we'd come back, I would take the uniforms straight to the laundry room, clean them, dry them, fold them and get them ready for the next day's show.

"The people in the building weren't angry with me, they'd just say, 'Hey, Mr. White, why don't you have those kids clean their own uniforms?' After a while they didn't have to use a two-by-four to get their message across. So I decided to let the kids practice responsibility by cleaning their own uniforms."

The Little Tumbling Team That Could has exploded from a Rockwell Gardens mystery tour to a globe-trotting industry. With sponsorships and increased performance opportunities, White introduced etiquette lessons into his gymnastics regimen. As demand grew for his teams, so did the opportunity to teach the kids about something they were going to learn the right way or the gangster way. And he started to teach them about money, about its values and the responsibilities and dangers that come with it.

Money can be the root of evil or it can sow the seeds of success. Often it depends on who provides it.

Show me **the**

money!

– Rod Tidwell to Jerry Maguire

White

Chapter Twelve It's a long flight from Chicago to Tokyo.

But Jesse White's tumblers have become accustomed to long flights; it's a long flight from the embryonic stages of a park district gymnastics club to a world-famous, seven-figure group of performing artists. It's what they've become, you know. Gone are the days when the Jesse White Tumbling Team was a ragtag bunch of ghetto kids wearing taped shoes and uniforms washed each night by their coach. They have become bona fide performing artists. They are, by the very definition, professional tumblers.

As Jesse White speaks, you can almost feel Captain John Carpenter tugging at the reins of the American Airlines 767 Flagship Jet, hoisting its nose off O'Hare International Airport Runway 32L and banking west toward Tokyo and the Pacific Rim. This tumbling team, just like air travel, has come a long way since 1959. This was more an improbable dream than an impossible one because, after all, Jesse White harbored no aspirations beyond that first year in Rockwell Gardens.

Not long after he landed the Coca-Cola and McDonald's sponsorships, black ink began oozing from the pages of Jesse White's tumbling team ledgers. That's when he decided to begin paying his performers. In arriving at the decision, he envisioned as much value in the lesson as he did in the buying power of the currency he began dispensing to his kids.

"Today, the kids all get $185 per event," he explains. "It's a share and share alike proposition. I'm the only one on the team who doesn't get compensated. Eleven of us will perform, and when we're at an NBA game, we use the ball boys from the home team to help us with things like the mats and the trampolette.

"The home team will pay for our tickets, they will pay for our hotel and they give us per diem for food and for rental vehicles and six rooms."

The tumblers double up while their coach indulges himself of his only real perk as the team's patriarch – his own room.

In addition to rooms, meal money and a stipend for each performance, tumblers earn frequent flier mileage. All that, plus the opportunity to dazzle an arena filled with 18,000 professional basketball fans, serves as some of the incentive for tumbling team members to adhere to Jesse White's code of conduct. Team members are prohibited from using alcohol, vulgar language and tobacco products. They must maintain at least a C average in their studies. A tumbler who drops below the academic minimum must enroll in the team's tutoring program at the Chicago Latin School and regain academic standing before returning to the team. The death penalty comes into play if a team member uses illegal drugs or engages in gang activity.

White calls drug activity "street corner pharmacy – dispensing drugs without a license." There is no discussion, no negotiation, when it comes to illicit narcotics. A tumbler who becomes a drug dealer may just as well take poison. It has the same effect. Ingest poison or deal drugs and you will lose your ability to tumble for Jesse White.

In return for their good conduct, the tumblers, who range in age from 6 to 22, rub elbows with professional athletes, stay in fine hotels in big cities and receive a decent salary.

"They know my code of conduct," he says, matter-of-factly. "They know I will not tolerate them being part of a gang.

"I had a case a little while back, not a really bad incident, but one that required my attention. I got a call that there was a young man who was acting a little wild on the El while he was wearing his tumbling uniform. I knew who he was by the description they gave me and I confronted him. And I told him that he can never disrespect this program by making loud noises on the El or acting out of pocket.

"They'll get a warning. The next time they get a suspension and they don't want to get suspended. Suspension means they lose money; they're out of work. A one-week suspension could mean as many as twenty shows. It can also mean being denied a trip to an NBA game."

Throughout his personal and political lives, Jesse White has earned the reputation as a strict, but fair-minded, patriarch. No one gets out of this life alive, and even fewer get by without making mistakes. As tough as he has been known to be with the kids who violate his code of conduct, he is not a man without regard to redemption.

"When do I stick my neck out for them?" he repeats the question. "I stick my neck out for them a lot, but I pick and choose which kids I stick my neck our for. If they're right, I'll support them. If they're wrong, I won't. I'll give them a second chance but that's it – with some exceptions. If they're involved in illegal conduct, I won't give them a second chance. If they're involved in drugs, then I won't give them a second chance."

The threat of suspension hangs over the young entrepreneurs like an executioner's ax.

"Now, when we were in New York and New Jersey, each kid got $185 times two. And they got their frequent flier mileage, slept in hotels and met the players. Isiah Thomas came over and talked with them. They got autographs. If they get suspended, they miss all that. They lose their pay, they lose their contact with celebrities and they lose an opportunity to travel at someone else's expense. They don't want to get suspended, so they know they need to adhere to the code of conduct."

The salary, though, pales in comparison to what a kid can pick up off the street. In Rockwell Gardens, for example, a Gangster Disciple can make up to $10,000 a day dealing drugs, according to data released by the U.S. Justice Department.

So how *does* Jesse White compete with that kind of earning potential?

"For one, it's a lot safer to be on my tumbling team," he wagers. "And it's a lot more respectful. And the kids can walk around the neighborhood with their heads held high and they have bragging rights.

"They can talk about how they've been to Tokyo, Hong Kong, Bermuda, Canada and they get a chance to meet some very impressive people. They fly on airplanes, they get mileage-plus miles, they get free tickets to sporting events and they eat in wonderful restaurants. Just the other day we performed at Disney World. That's a pretty impressive statement to make when they go back to their community.

"So they have bragging rights. They can talk about the places they've seen, the people they've met, the experiences they've felt. And it doesn't cost them a dime. From time to time I talk with some of the old tumblers and that's what they remember – how they went to this place or that place and it didn't cost them a dime. They reminisce about the fun they had, the people they've met and the sights they saw. And they establish friendships that they take with them for a lifetime."

Jesse White does not tie strings to the money he pays his athletes. Essentially, the money is their own when they are paid. The coach does, however, offer them a blueprint for financial success.

"We ask them to put a third in the bank, take a third home to their family and they can keep a third for themselves. Each kid has a different set of circumstances, but that's one of the things we encourage."

Jesse White's blueprint gives his kids a guidepost for saving, sharing and understanding the value of earned income. But even the best blueprint is only as strong as the brick and mortar that frames the house.

"Let me tell you one story. One kid – his name was Terrence Lucas – he had gotten himself into trouble and he had just gotten out of jail.

"He comes up to me one day and says, 'Mr. White, I want to save some money.' I said, 'Okay, fine.'

"I want you to hold the bank book for me, Mr. White."

"Okay, I'll do that."

White took the young man to a neighborhood bank, helped him open an account, and made a deposit.

"Every pay period we'd put the money in the bank. One day, he says he had a conversation with his mother and she was complaining that he never had any money.

"He said, 'I've got some money.'

"She said, 'Where is it?'

"He said, 'It's in the bank.'

"She said, 'Where's the bank book?'

"He said, 'Mr. White's got it.'

"He calls me on the other line and asks if I'll call his mother and tell her that yes, in fact, he had been putting money in the bank. And I asked him if he was sure, was he sure that he wanted me to tell his mother that? And he said that, yes, that's what he wanted me to do."

So Jesse White called the woman and confirmed to her that her son had been saving money, that he had $3,400 in his savings account.

"That was on a Tuesday. On Friday he called me and he was hysterical. He's crying beyond control. When I asked him what was wrong, he said his mother had taken all his money out of the bank and used it up on drugs.

"And the reason he wanted me to handle the money is because that's what he was afraid of."

At first I thought, something's not right, **what is this dude,** some kind of **ghetto Nazarite?**

— from Be a Gentleman First

Chapter Thirteen It's a cold and dreary February day in Chicago. What sets it apart from most cold and dreary February days in Chicago is the absence of snow.

Jesse White and a campaign consultant need to pick up a few things from his campaign office on North Sedgwick Street, just down the block from the office of his celebrated tumbling team. As the two men step from a 1997 Mercury Cougar, a young black man ambles from the east side of the street. His hands are thrust in his coat pockets and he slouches against the wind. The young man is nondescript; nothing about him would lead you to suspect that he is anything but an ordinary citizen.

"Hello, Mr. White."

As the African American youth speaks, he nods toward his elder. Hell, he very nearly bows.

"How you doin' today?" responds the candidate.

"Take it easy, man."

"Keep yourself safe," replies White.

As White and his campaign aide part ways with this pedestrian, the candidate speaks up.

"You know who that is?" he asks his consultant, a middle-aged white man from central Illinois.

"How would I know who that is, Jesse?"

"He's a gangbanger. Leader of one of the biggest gangs in the city."

Jesse White's companion expresses surprise at the young man's pleasant attitude toward the politician.

"I know I'm naïve about this kind of stuff, but he called you *Mr. White.*"

"So?"

"Well, I guess I didn't know your neighborhood gang leaders were so friendly."

"Hey, the gangbangers don't mess with me around here. And they know better than to mess with any of my kids. They don't bother them. It's an unwritten law. Don't mess with Mr. White's kids."

"Or?"

"Or you'll have hell to pay. There have been times when we were out in other areas of the city where gangbangers wanted to exact a pound of flesh from my tumblers. I said that won't be. So I had to take care of some business."

You don't have to ask what he means by "taking care of business."

"I'm responsible for those kids when they're in my charge. I'm not going to let anyone harm them. If they violate the law, then I'm going to walk away from them. But as long as they follow the rules, I'll make sure that I stand between them and the harm that comes from gangbanging."

It just goes to show that, whether motivated by respect or by fear, they call heroes *mister.*

Well, he put some tacks
on teacher's
chair,

puts some gum in little girl's hair,
now, Junior,
behave yourself.

— Bad Boy, Beatles VI

Chapter Fourteen He remembers the trips through the fashionable neighborhoods in Chicago's north suburban Evanston. He remembers his surrogate father trying passionately to detour him away from playing high school football. He even remembers how this substitute parent taught him the proper ways to use tableware so that he and his friends wouldn't embarrass themselves in expensive restaurants and upscale hotels.

Mostly, though, Richard Blackmon remembers the day back in 1967 when he first met Jesse White. He laughs about it now, but the encounter terrified him back then, back when Richard Blackmon was just 6 years old.

"I was in first grade at Schiller School," Blackmon begins. "Mr. White was the gym teacher. And I had gotten myself in trouble. At that time, he was the disciplinarian, also. When you got in trouble, they sent you to see Mr. White."

Justice was swift for Richard Blackmon that day in 1967. Jesse White served as judge, jury and executioner. The disciplinarian spanked the 6-year-old boy for his mischievousness. In 1967, corporal punishment was as much a part of the curriculum as arithmetic, reading and civics. Not all schools had a disciplinarian like Jesse White, though. Not all disciplinarians followed through on the lessons they taught in the office.

"So he gives me a real spanking and he didn't spare anything. And then he took me home and asked my mom if I could join the Cub Scouts. I said, 'You gotta be kidding me! I don't want anywhere near this guy! He just whupped me. I don't want any part of this guy.'

"And then my mother says to me, 'Why is this man bringing you home? I don't even know him. You must have done something really bad.'

"And then my mother whupped me again."

Blackmon pauses for just a moment and chuckles again.

"That's how we met. That was my first encounter with him."

Little did the reluctant Cub Scout imagine that his painful introduction to the Schiller Elementary School gym teacher would blossom into a lifelong friendship of leadership, respect and — above all — love. After all, leadership, respect and love are in short supply in the Cabrini-Green neighborhood where both mentor and protégé spent their childhood. A little bit of it goes a long way. And when you get a lot of it, when the disciplinarian sees potential in the student, really good things can happen.

The Cabrini-Green housing settlement is a composite of four smaller developments built over a twenty-year period. The site originated in 1942 with the construction of the Frances Cabrini row houses. Known at the time as "Little Sicily," the development served as a stronghold for the city's Italian-American community. This was the community in which Jesse White earned his chops.

In 1962, the city added the William-Green Homes to the property, and Cabrini-Green became one of the largest public housing settlements in the city, populated almost entirely by African Americans. In the intervening years, two other wings were added to this community: Cabrini Extension North and Cabrini Extension South.

Blackmon is one of thousands of Cabrini-Green kids who enrolled in Jesse White's scouting program and graduated through Boy Scouts, the Jesse White Drum Corps and, ultimately, worked his way onto the Jesse White Tumbling Team. It was a natural progression for hundreds of kids from the Cabrini-Green public housing project. Just as millions of American kids graduate each year from first grade to second, Jesse White's kids naturally advanced from scouting to marching to tumbling. School prepares you for life and a job. The Jesse White programs kept you safe from the gangs. School teaches you how to make a living. Jesse White teaches kids like Richard Blackmon how to stay alive.

"Initially, I was one of those kids who just hung around the tumbling office. And if he doesn't really know who you are, you just keep hanging around until he decides to start making you do some stuff.

"I was one of those kids. I just wouldn't go away."

Gym rats hang out in gymnasiums. Rink rats hang out at ice rinks. Richard Blackmon was a Jesse White rat. He hung out wherever Jesse White was.

Blackmon's mother moved Richard and his five brothers and sisters to Cabrini-Green from Chicago's West Side.

"We had a fire and at the time Cabrini was emergency housing," he explains. "My mom raised six of us by herself. My stepfather was a drug user. He had been in Vietnam and he came back from the war and was all messed up."

This was a recipe for disaster, a recipe as easy to follow as boiling water. But oddly enough, Richard Blackmon's misbehavior as a 6-year-old actually caused his life's recipe to be rewritten by a master chef dedicated to the staff of life.

As a beneficiary of Jesse White's tutelage, Blackmon can say he is one of White's most successful projects. He never will, though. He's too modest for that. But his command of the English language, albeit still spiced with the ethnolect he inherited from his neighborhood, testifies to his commitment to learning.

His mother died in 1979, when he was 17 years old. As he talks about her, he's asked if his mother's death was the point in time when Jesse White became a surrogate father.

"No, that happened way before that. That happened way back in 1972, 1973.

"You've got to understand," he explains, "there were about seven or eight years of my life where I know that — 365 days each year — I was doing something with that man. I was with him either as a tumbler, or with the drum and bugle corps or just going fishing. You've got to understand: when I say I was with that man every day of my life during those years, I mean *I was with him every day of my life.*

"There were times when I worked in his office and just hung out, just in case he needed someone to run errands."

Birds teach their young how to fly. It's instinctive. It's nature's way that they are able to train fledglings to flap a pair of wings and they know when to nudge them from the nest. Richard Blackmon is clearly one of the young birds who was given a vision to soar. That vision came almost exclusively from Jesse White.

"Sometimes he'd just call me and say, 'Whaddya doin'?' And he'd take us up to Evanston – I'll never forget this – and he would just drive us up to the upscale neighborhoods in Evanston.

"When we'd get there, he'd say, 'You guys can live like this if you want to. But you gotta stay in school. You gotta stay away from the gangs and you've got to stay off drugs. You can't mess with drugs.'

"That stuff stays with you. You never forget stuff like that, especially when it's coming from someone like Mr. White. He doesn't just talk the talk. He lives the life he teaches."

Asked about Blackmon's recollection of the long rides up Lake Shore Drive and into another universe apart from the projects, Jesse White is almost dispassionate. Just another day at the office, he seems to say.

"It was all about exposure," White explains. "I wanted these young people to get out of their environment and see that there's a big, wide, wonderful world out there and I wanted them to feel it, touch it and be a part of it.

"I got that kind of opportunity when I was in high school playing basketball. That was my great exposure to areas outside my immediate environment. I just wanted to make sure that some of these kids got the same opportunity that I got when I was their age. Seeing what's out there, seeing what can be part of your life if you only give it a chance, sometimes that can make a difference in a young person's life."

Some of that exposure included such simple tasks as using forks, knives and spoons. Okay, so even a kid out of the projects knows the difference between a fork and a spoon. But Jesse White makes sure his kids know what utensils to use and when to use them.

Blackmon explains:

"The lessons he teaches you are so simple, so basic. He'd sit us down at a table in a gymnasium and show us which fork is a salad fork. And how to cut your meat, how to use a knife and a fork to cut your meat.

"He didn't want us to embarrass ourselves because after we performed, we'd go to places like the Conrad Hilton or the Pick Congress or the Palmer House and we're eating with bankers and lawyers and heads of state."

White affirms Blackmon's recollections. It seems so mundane until you remember who's doing the learning. Nearly all of Jesse White's kids come from incomplete families, from homes where a single parent is the norm and where basic survival is a triumph. Traversing neighborhoods is life-threatening when you live in gangland. The ghetto kids don't just hop in a car and go out with mom and dad for pizza on a Saturday night.

"I've taken them into communities they never would have had an opportunity to be exposed to. I've taken them into Polish communities, into the German community, into the Irish community, the Asian community and the list goes on. We've had the pleasure to perform before every imaginable ethnic group.

"And after the show we'll stay and eat with them. It's a sign of respect when you're able to use chopsticks at an Asian meal. So we try to teach the young people how to use chopsticks so they can demonstrate that we respect the customs and culture."

Leo Louchios, who has worked with Jesse White for a dozen years, says White approaches life the way the secretary general approaches the United Nations.

"He learns something special from each nationality," Louchios says, "and I'll give you an example. He knows how to dance a Philippine dance where they use bamboo sticks. He rolls up his pants, takes off his shoes and socks, and he starts doing the dance. Now, keep in mind that the people watching him understand that it's not so much that he knows how to do the dance, but they are impressed because he took the time to learn *how* to do the dance. When he says something about a culture, people know it comes from his heart because he takes the time to understand the culture.

"He's a peoples' guy because he's going to say something to you in your language or try your food, and he makes you feel comfortable.

When we go to restaurants, he will go back into the kitchen and talk to the dishwasher and take a picture with him. That shows that he understands the meaning of respect."

Sometimes that respect finds itself channeled into the form of corporal punishment. Jesse White likes to talk about his approach. Tough love, he calls it. Richard Blackmon met the man under those circumstances, when Mr. White distributed his patented brand of tough love in the form of a spanking. And Blackmon would never deny that he deserved the corporal punishment.

In Jesse White's world of discipline, you rarely spare the rod and spoil the child.

And you'd better never embarrass the program.

By the way, it took some effort to elicit a confession from Richard Blackmon about the providential transgression that brought him into Jesse White's life that day way back in 1967.

"I put a box of tacks on the teacher's chair," Blackmon laughs. "And all the kids told. So I got sent to him immediately for that and he spanked me. First grade. He whupped me. It wasn't a spankin', it was a whuppin'."

Most of the guys I went to high school with are either dead or in jail.

— former tumbler Marvin Edwards

Chapter Fifteen There is a death penalty in Jesse White's world.

Once again, it is Jesse White who serves as judge, jury and executioner.

His punishment is not arbitrary, but often it is swift. There are rules. When tumblers break those rules, they know the consequences. The tumbling team death penalty is banishment from the program.

"You might hear some stories about guys being disciplined," ventures former tumbler Richard Blackmon, "and you might think it's cruel. But he's told those guys a thousand times what he expects out of them. And if he did that to somebody, believe me, it wasn't the first time the guy got in trouble. It was just the time when Mr. White decided he had enough."

There's plenty of opportunity for the kids in Jesse White's neighborhood to find trouble. More often than not, trouble will find them. So if they decide that they would rather avoid the dark side, avoid living in the shadows of the Gangster Disciples, Vice Lords or the Stones, a viable option is the Jesse White Tumbling Team. And they can follow the rules or go back to gangland. The Jesse White Code of Conduct is the same whether you're a Cub Scout, a drummer in the corps or a tumbler. Break the code, suffer the consequence. It's your life. It's your choice.

Some lives have happy endings and other lives don't. Here's one of each from Jesse White's memory bank:

"One of my most embarrassing moments," White offers. "We were invited to a luncheon down at the Hilton, the largest not-for-profit fund-raising event in Chicago at that time. I had the largest Boy Scout troop in the country – Boy Scouts, Cub Scouts and Explorers.

"I'd spent some time teaching the young people how to use their knives, their forks and their spoons. Where to put the napkin, not to comb their hair at the table, not to wear their caps at the table. They placed one of my kids at every table. We schooled these kids on how to conduct themselves because they were being placed at a table with important members of the community. There was a table for Commonwealth Edison, one for Illinois Bell, the bankers association, the lawyers. The list goes on and on.

"We had well over 125 kids there. One of them – we'll call him Clifford – I put him with the bankers. First thing he did was he took out his hair pick and he started picking his hair, combing from back to front and right over his plate. Right in front of these bank presidents.

"I'm sitting a few tables away and I caught him in the downstroke. I grabbed the comb and said, 'Ladies and gentlemen, I'm sorry that Clifford was combing his hair at the table. That is not part of our training program.'

"I told Clifford to put his pick away and the gentlemen at the table told me not to worry about it, that they would take care of Clifford.

"I sat down again and the next thing I know, he's pointing at each of these bank presidents. I got up and moved a little closer and he's saying, 'Don't forget, you told me you were going to give me your potatoes, you were going to give me your peas, you were going to give me your dessert …'

"I went over again and apologized for Clifford being out of control."

Jesse White's normal carriage is tranquility. He is painfully soft-spoken to the extreme that he often is asked during media interviews to speak up because the microphone doesn't always capture what he has to say.

However, there are times – rare ones – when he sizzles. That day, Clifford boiled him over the top.

"We got back to the school, and I sat all these 125 kids on the floor of the gymnasium and I thanked them for their great performances by the drum corps, by the tumbling team, by the honor guard. But I indicated that I was really disappointed in one person, and I did something I normally don't do. I singled him out because I was really upset.

"I asked the kids, 'What's Rule Number 1?'

"Don't comb your hair at the table."

"Well, Clifford combed his hair at the table."

"Oh, no!"

"What's Rule Number 5?"

"Don't beg at the table."

"Well, Clifford was begging at his table."

"Oh, no!"

Whether he knew it or not, Clifford's world was about to collide with a hurtling asteroid, hell-bent with leather.

"I took Clifford to the washroom and I took off my belt and I gave him a couple whacks on the butt to remind him that he was completely out of order and that he was an embarrassment.

"The next day, I was working at the YMCA with another group of Troop 1151 and they asked me how things went downtown at the luncheon. I was right in the middle of telling them about the problem that we had when, next thing I know, here comes Clifford.

"I said, 'Clifford, come here.' And I took him to the washroom and I whipped his butt again.

"The next morning, I got to school and when I opened the door I looked to my left and there was Clifford. I said, 'Clifford, I had a dream about you last night. Come here, man.' I took him to the washroom and I whipped his butt again. Then I went to the office, called his mother and told her what happened.

"She said, 'When he gets home I'll get him, too.'"

Unfortunately, Clifford's backside never sent the message topside.

"He still didn't learn his lesson," White confesses. "In later years, he and one of his buddies stuck up a fellow and shot him in the neck and the man is partially paralyzed to this day. Clifford went to jail, came back out and got himself convicted of rape and went back to jail again."

On the other side of the coin is a kid we'll call Houston "Bad News" Black. Houston tumbled and was one of the team members sent to Morris, Illinois, for the annual Grundy County Corn Festival Parade, held each September as a summer's end celebration.

"It's such a warm town and people there always give us such a warm reception," Jesse White says. "I noticed when we arrived that two of my tumblers were late. I made note of it, and halfway through our show the two guys showed up.

"As we're pulling out of town, a couple of police officers wave me over and I notice that Houston and the other guy are standing there with the police."

"We have a little problem here, Mr. White. These gentlemen stole a radio out of this man's car."

The car's owner watched as the police officer explained the situation to White.

"Houston, did you break into this man's car?"

"No, I didn't, Mr. White."

The owner of the vehicle told White that he was walking out of a building nearby when he saw the two tumblers in his car, forcibly removing the stereo from the console. When the police arrived, the stereo was in Houston's lap.

"The officer said they were going to lock him up. I said, 'Officer, do what you have to do with him. He's in violation of the law and I cannot support that kind of conduct."

Somewhat surprised, the policeman asked if Jesse White was certain.

"You do what you have to do and I will do what I have to do. If you have to lock him up, so be it. Lock him up. Just know that I won't have any bond money for him."

"Mr. White, you gonna leave me out here?" Houston knew he was farther from home than a ride on the El. Morris is a largely rural community sixty miles southwest of Chicago. It would be a long walk home.

"You doggone right I'm gonna leave you out here. You can't come down from Chicago to Morris or go anyplace with me and embarrass me and this team like this."

As Jesse White was breaking the news to Houston Black, the owner of the vandalized automobile was telling officers that if Black would agree to pay for the damages, he would forgo charges.

"I said that if that was what he wanted to do, that was fine with me. But Houston still had a price to pay with me. So I gave the gentleman $100. I owed Houston for some shows he'd done, so I subtracted the $100. And then I dismissed him from the program.

"He became *persona non grata.* Gone."

Years later, Houston Black started a tumbling program of his own. And the man he approached for help was none other than his former coach.

"He has a little group of former tumblers from my program, some of the rejects. If I can help a person get his feet planted back on this earth and I have the ability to do it, then I'll help. I gave him mats and I gave him a trampolette. A couple times, he ran short of money to make his payroll so I gave him that. So we're fine.

"But he's not going to be part of my program. All is forgiven, but he's not going to be part of my program."

Although there's no written record, it's safe to assume that more kids tumbled for free than saw a paycheck from the Jesse White Tumbling Team. When they talk about the difference between today's tumbling team members and the way it was in their day, they sound like old men. But there most certainly is a difference between playing on a rock-strewn sandlot and stepping onto the emerald green carpet of Yankee Stadium. Not only is the surface greener in the Bronx, but so is the return.

"Money changes everything now," says Ronnie Baker, who joined the tumbling team in 1983. "Some of these kids think that because they're getting paid, they don't have to keep to the rules. But what they don't understand is that Jesse White doesn't need them, they need Jesse White. Tumblers are a dime a dozen.

"But he has ways of making them understand."

Tough love means sometimes having to walk home.

"There was an instance where one of the guys had a warrant and we were going out of town," Baker recalls. "And the guy knew Mr. White don't like to be involved in that kind of crazy stuff. We had to leave him at the airport. And he made him pay for his own ticket back home.

"He told him, 'You can't be a part of this team and represent us knowing that you have problems with the law like you do.'

"He stayed on top of that. He kicked the guy off the team and the guy apologized, paid his debts and worked his way back. He got himself together and he tumbled for a few years after that.

"He did let him back on the team. But it was under Mr. White's terms and that's something I don't think that guy will ever forget.

"And neither will I."

Give a man a **fish** and you feed him for a day.

Teach **a man to fish** and you feed him for a lifetime.

— Chinese proverb

Chapter Sixteen Sometimes life's best lessons are the result of planned spontaneity.

Sometimes you've just got to stop the car and drop a line in the water.

Sometimes a guy's just gotta fish.

"We'd be driving along and he'd get this gleam in his eye," chuckles Richard Blackmon. "We'd be headed somewhere and he'd pull the car over and say, 'This is a good spot to fish.' So we'd fish."

Blackmon, who has learned as much about life from Jesse White as he has from his nineteen years of formal education, remembers those lazy summer days when his tumbling team coach would pull over and let the world pass them by for just a little while.

"He would keep those rods and reels in the trunk of the car and he'd know all the good spots to fish. It's one of his favorite pastimes, you know."

White admits to a lifetime of weakness for angling. During a particularly long campaign drive one day in 1998, he was asked if he'd ever tried golf. After all, he'd succeeded as a baseball player where, as in golf, you need to strike a ball with a stick.

"Nah," he dismisses, "that's a rich man's game."

"Those guys who play at Jackson Park aren't rich."

"I'd rather fish."

And he confirms Blackmon's assertion that he's never without his equipment.

"Always in the trunk of the car," he admits. "As a matter of fact, in all the vehicles we have, we have fishing gear. It's my favorite hobby. It's a form of recreation that gets me away from the hustle and bustle of my job. It gives me a chance to have some quiet time to myself, whether I'm by myself or with others."

In fact, as a legislator, Jesse White rarely asked for a favor from a lobbyist. He made an exception, though, when he talked with Joe Spivey, a former executive vice president for the Illinois Coal Association. True Illinois fishing connoisseurs know the secrets of angling in the strip mines of Fulton County. Spivey, now retired as the state's chief coal association executive, prefers to call the spots "surface mining lakes," but laughs nonetheless when asked about Jesse White's affection for the some of the best spots in the state.

"The only thing he ever asked me for," says Spivey, "was to see if we could get him onto some of those surface mining lakes." And, of course, Spivey was only too happy to oblige.

White's election in 1998 as Illinois secretary of state has squeezed his schedule and limits his opportunities to indulge in his favorite leisure activity. But before he overstuffed his schedule with government commitments and lawmaking, Jesse White employed quiet time with a fishing pole to teach a few kids some of life's lessons. And he kept a barbecue grill in the trunk, right next to the rods and reels.

"When we'd go fishing, sometimes we'd cook the fish right there," he says. "And then there were times when we'd be driving past a park and I'd stop and pick up some bratwurst, hamburgers and cook right there.

"Sometimes the kids would have problems and I'd want to counsel them. What better way to do it than to take them to the park, place them on a bench and give them a hamburger and a hot dog and have a fruitful discussion as to how I can help them get their lives back on track."

Richard Blackmon was one of those kids whose life Jesse White switched back on the right track more often than he can count.

"It wasn't all work all the time," Blackmon explains. "The best thing about him is that it's not just discipline, it's the correct amount of discipline and love. Along with the discipline there's a certain amount of joking around that goes with him, too. He's a funny character; there's a certain amount of silliness that goes on. It's just kept to a minimum. I had good times with him because it wasn't just all work and no play.

"First time I ever went to a water park or a wave pool, Jesse White took me. I didn't know there was ever such a thing as a wave pool, places where they actually created waves. And when he kept those grills in the car and would throw some hot dogs or a chicken on there.

"Sometimes it was just man stuff. Sometimes it was about what it takes to be a man."

A year after his mother died in 1979, Blackmon became a father at age 18. Like it or not, he was a man.

"I was a kid with a kid," he recalls. "I was pretty much on my own after my mom died, but while she was living, she encouraged me to hang out with Mr. White as much as I could. But she also told me as I got older, 'You and Jesse White are different people. You don't necessarily have to follow in his footsteps. He should be a guide for you, but you still have to find your own way.'

"I can remember going to him and talking to him about my girlfriend being pregnant. At times, when I was at school in Carbondale and I couldn't get to my girlfriend and my daughter and they needed something, he'd take care of it for me. You don't forget that kind of stuff."

One of those days Richard Blackmon will forever remember was one on the football practice field at Southern Illinois University. He'd earned a football scholarship to the Carbondale campus after a star-studded career at Lane Technical High School in Chicago. Ironically, his decision to play football at Lane was one of the few times he rejected Jesse White's counsel. His tumbling coach did not want him to play football.

"I didn't want him to get hurt," White explains.

"He wasn't the only one," Blackmon chuckles. "He didn't want me to play football because he didn't want me to get hurt. But my mom made me quit during my freshman year in high school.

"She actually came up to the school and threw the equipment at the coach. I was so embarrassed, it took me years to live that one down."

But Blackmon had an idea that sports – in his case football – could provide a crack of daylight. Find that daylight, figure out a way to break through to it and maybe, just maybe, he could get out of Cabrini-Green alive.

Okay, so football wasn't exactly what Blackmon's mother and his mentor wanted him to pursue. But when Richard Blackmon was able to punch that ticket for a ride to Carbondale, it was clear that he was on a trip out of Hell's Kitchen.

"My thing was football and my other thing – the biggest thing – was just to get to college. I knew I had the ability to do the work if I could just get there. I just didn't have the money. And so I was willing to try anything to get myself enrolled in a university. I got a full scholarship to play football."

And on a stifling morning in Carbondale in 1983, Richard Blackmon was sweating out yet another tortuous football practice. Carbondale is nearly two full latitudinal degrees south of the Mason-Dixon Line. As Dan Rather might have said, Carbondale in August is hotter than a Times Square Rolex. Any reason to take a blow from the oppressive heat and choking humidity is welcome.

Almost any reason.

"They pulled me off the field," he remembers. "The coach said, 'Your brother is dead.' I said, 'Which one?' He looked at me funny. 'Which one?' 'Yeah, I got two of them up there, *living the life*.'

"So one of my brothers was killed in Cabrini in 1983. His name was William Dembry. His father was my stepfather. I was originally told that he was killed because he wanted to get out of the gang and join the marines.

"But my older brother told me the truth, that he was involved in something he shouldn't have been involved in. He said he was getting ready to turn his life around, but he and my other brother decided they'd pull one more big job before he did, and he got caught. And that's how he got killed, shot six times.

"So I had to come home from football camp in Carbondale and bury my brother, the gang leader."

William Dembry never went fishing with Jesse White. But his brother is alive today, probably because he did. Fish with Jesse White, be a tumbler, view the man as your mentor and father figure, and maybe you can have a chance. Maybe you can get out of Cabrini-Green, maybe get an education, maybe get a football scholarship and live to celebrate it all. In The Greens you don't have many other choices.

"There *was* no other choice," says Blackmon. "It's not like you've got alternatives. Either you were on the Jesse White Tumbling Team, you're going to church somewhere, or you're in a gang. Those were the three alternatives you had at that time."

After burying his gang leader brother, Richard Blackmon returned to SIU and earned his undergraduate degree in administrative justice with a specialty in juvenile justice. He could have stopped there and gone straight into law enforcement or corrections.

"I wanted to be a probation officer. At first, I thought that's what I wanted to do because of the work I had done with Mr. White. But, you know, strange things happen when you go and follow your own dreams. I was in that place because that's what I was supposed to be doing.

"But my mother had told me I had to find my own way, that I had to find my own niche. She told me not to get caught up in who he is and never to forget who I am. That was sound advice for me at the time."

So Blackmon followed a dream and won a full academic scholarship to the University of Notre Dame School of Law.

"He did that on his own," White explains. "We helped support him financially through high school and through Southern Illinois University. When he was at Notre Dame, he'd call from time to time and indicate that he had some financial problems and Mrs. Wicks – she's the librarian at Schiller – and I would pull our money together and send him a package."

Blackmon earned his law degree from Notre Dame and spent his first few years practicing family law.

"When I practiced law, the bulk of my work was in juvenile court," he says. "Abuse cases, neglect, DCFS (children and family services) kind of work. That was very important for me. It wasn't very lucrative, but it was important work for me.

"I've tried to stay close to kids. I've worked most of my life with young people and my relationship with Mr. White has aided me because he showed me so much about working with young people."

Now 43 and a resident of the Englewood Community on Chicago's

South Side, he is married and has five children, ages 14 to 25. The daughter born when he was "a kid with a kid" has graduated from the University of Illinois. He bursts with pride as he talks about his child's degree from a world-class university like Illinois. She clearly has enriched her father's life.

In turn, Richard Blackmon today is working to enrich the lives of others.

Seems like the acorn never falls far from the tree, even when the acorn's been adopted.

"I'm setting up a nonprofit organization. I've been working on this for about two and a half years. For the last four or five years I've had a chance to do some really good work. I work for a company called Options for People, one of the oldest welfare-to-work programs.

"One of the things I've been concerned about is welfare. One of the things I studied at Notre Dame was public housing, entitlement programs, that kind of stuff. I had some wonderful professors there. They encouraged me to look into those fields."

Those fields have enriched Richard Blackmon's life and he, in turn, is enriching so many other lives. The lesson learned from the master is a lesson learned by a wise and enlightened student. Kids can treat education the way a prisoner treats a sentence. They can serve the sentence by counting the days until their release. Or they can decide that, what the hell, I'm already here so I might as well make the best of it. I might as well make something of myself. I might as well take advantage of the opportunity and live a life better than that of my brother. I might as well live.

Of the thousands of kids whose lives Jesse White has touched, he is particularly proud of the life of Richard Blackmon.

"I would do whatever I could to help him out. I believed in the kid and I just wanted him to be a success in life."

Funny thing is, even though Jesse White has taught him more of life's lessons than he can count, Richard Blackmon doesn't hesitate when asked what the most important lessons have been.

"Be a gentleman first and we'll argue about the rest later," Blackmon responds. "I've heard that a thousand times. It's been his motto.

"The other thing he's said that's really stuck with me is that it's not what you do, it's how you do it. He has a standard of excellence that you can never get away from.

"You see, it's all about discipline. It's my way or the highway for him. And it works. I know it works. It's worked for me since 1967."

Right here in **Cabrini,**

just a few hours ago **a young man**
was killed

right behind my building.

A gang shooting.

Gangbanging, drug dealing.

— former tumbler Maurice Edwards

Chapter Seventeen Santa Claus must have a tough time working the projects.

At Cabrini-Green the white stuff flies all year long, not just when the cold air freezes the precipitation. And so do bullets. Bullets fly above and below the rooftops much more frequently than eight tiny reindeer.

So forgive Santa Claus if he decides that delivering even a lump of coal to the bad kids is too hazardous for his own health. Who could blame him if he takes a detour?

Maurice Edwards remembers a Christmas nearly a quarter century ago when it was a pretty safe bet that Santa Claus wouldn't be stopping at his home in The Greens. He and his twin, Marvin, knew that food was a luxury in 1982. Their single-parent mother had enough trouble feeding five kids without concerning herself with Christmas.

For the Edwards twins, hope that Santa Claus would visit them had faded years earlier. They were 14 and teenagers don't believe in Santa Claus. In The Greens, there's not much belief in anything for a teenager.

"It was back in about 1982," Maurice Edwards remembers, "and Christmas was really going to be a washout. My brother and I didn't even have any boots. We were sitting in the back room and my brother and I were saying to each other, 'It's Christmas and we don't have anything. We don't even have Christmas dinner.'

"Everybody needs something. Mother's trying to figure how she's going to get Angie a pair of shoes. How's she gonna get Marvin a shirt? How's she gonna get Maurice a pair of pants? How's she gonna get Melvin a coat? How's she gonna get Renee a dress?"

Most likely, it was cold and dreary on that Christmas eve in 1982. Chicago can be cold and dreary in June. The winters are exceptionally harsh and hopeless, especially when you have no money.

At about 7:30 p.m., there was a knock at the door of the Edwards's apartment in Cabrini-Green.

"Who is it?"

"Jesse White."

"Oh, man! Can you believe it? Mr. White."

Twenty-three years later Maurice Edwards's voice still radiates with excitement at the memory.

"Sure enough, Mr. White comes in and I don't even remember the other guy's name. All I know is he was a white guy. Our family was one of the families chosen and they presented my mother with $500 worth of gift certificates — $250 for Jewel and $250 for Sears.

"The next day, we had more than enough for Christmas and the next day and the next day. And my brother and I got a new pair of leather boots."

The excitement in Maurice Edwards's voice quickly yields to a deeper emotion and causes it to crack.

"To this day, I don't know why this guy chose our family. I just don't know."

That Christmas of 1982 wasn't the first time that Jesse White tossed a lifeline in the direction of the Edwards twins. Maurice and Marvin Edwards attended Schiller Elementary School, where Santa Claus worked part-time as a physical education instructor.

"We used to have tumbling and drum corps practice at Schiller School in the morning. This must have been around 1978. Marvin and I must have been about 10 at the time.

"One particular morning, Mr. White took his position outside on the playground area where the children were playing. It must have been about 15 degrees out there, and my brother and I were shielding ourselves from the wind by standing close to a wall. All me and my brother were wearing was a hoodie (hooded sweatshirts). Mr. White sees us and calls us over."

"Hey, Edwards. Hey, man, get over here."

The boys ran to him and White escorted them to his office, away from the elements and the other kids. He didn't want to embarrass them.

"Hey, man, where's you guys' coats?"

The Edwards twins looked at each other, then looked back at the teacher.

"We don't have coats."

"Hey, man, at 2:15 you guys get back down here to my office."

Maurice and Marvin did as instructed. Jesse White handed them a handwritten note.

"Here. Take this home to your mother and get right back to me."

Again, as instructed, the Edwards twins took the note and raced home to their mother.

"She read it," Maurice says. "She wrote something back and we ran the note back over to Mr. White. So then he gives us an envelope and says, 'Take this home to your mother.'

"We never looked in that envelope. We gave it to our mother, she got dressed and said, 'Come on. We're going to the store.' Turns out there was a check in that envelope and my mother took us out and bought me and my brother coats."

Not the end of the story. In fact, this story doesn't appear to have an ending.

"A few weeks later, he signed us up for Santa Claus Anonymous and he took us to get another coat.

"Now, here's the rest of the story. Every year, to this current day – and my brother and I have good career jobs – we've received a coat from Mr. White. Every year from that time, he has never let us go without a coat.

"Any time I tell that story I can't help but get very emotional."

Santa Claus can perform some pretty miraculous feats. How he fits down the chimney would be one. How he manages to navigate the circumference of the planet in twenty-four hours would be another. How he does it remains his secret. How Jesse White is able to pour goodness into a needy community is rooted in part to some of his own angels.

Bob Lozins is one of those angels. Introduced to White by a mutual friend a quarter century ago, Lozins has quietly poured goodness into Jesse

White's programs in the form of toys for kids, gifts for senior citizens and untold financial support.

"He's from heaven," says White.

"That's what Jesse tells me," Lozins says humbly, "but I tell him that he's the one from heaven. The rest of us are just here to help him out."

One way Lozins helps out is by underwriting much of the cost of White's Christmas turkey distribution program. Another is by generously contributing to the tumbling team's scholars program. Hundreds of "angels" contribute to the myriad of charitable efforts in the world of Jesse White. Lozins is one of them, and he asks for nothing in return.

"I was in the car one day," Lozins recalls, "and I heard him on WBBM Newsradio, and he was talking about how he was getting ready to take the tumblers to Hong Kong, but that he needed about $10,000 to cover expenses. So when I got home I called him up and said, 'You got it.'

"And it didn't come up again until a couple years ago, long after they made the trip. We were talking about it and I told him, 'You know, I was pissed off that you didn't call me for the money, that I had to hear it on the radio.'"

"That's the way Bob Lozins is," White says. "He takes care of people because he has a deep regard for people in need."

The Edwards twins were two of those people in need, a pair of Cabrini-Green miracles performed by Jesse White. Maurice has worked since 1997 as a security officer for the Cook County Recorder of Deeds. Marvin is a deputy for the Cook County Sheriff's Department.

Ask either of them where they would be without the guiding light of Jesse White and you'll get the same answer, something you might expect from twins.

"We'd probably be well on our way through the penitentiary or the graveyard," ventures Marvin Edwards.

"You know," agrees Maurice, "coming from an urban ghetto like Cabrini-Green, you're considered to be blessed if you make it to age 21. Watching a guy like Mr. White, I want to grow to be 70. When he makes it to 71 in June, I want to make it to 71. Right now I'm 37, so I'm a long way from 71. But my brother and I pattern ourselves after Mr. White.

We want to live our lives the way he's lived his.

"We've seen so many people who we went to school with, who are from our community, who end up on the wrong side of the law. Or they end up having a funeral before age 21, or in most cases before age 35, let alone 70 years old."

In fact, just three hours earlier, a young man was gunned down within 100 yards of the Edwards apartment in Cabrini-Green. It begs the question why these two men, both gainfully employed and with heads screwed on straight and tight, would continue to live in the community where they were raised. After being attached to so many memories of poverty, misery and a scramble for mere survival, why not escape?

"Until Mr. White came around, if someone said that there was going to be a group of fifteen kids from Cabrini-Green coming around, the first thing you'd do is hide your purses," says Maurice. "But it wasn't like that when we showed up with Mr. White. When my brother and I were on the tumbling team and we went to an event outside the neighborhood, people actually expected something positive and it's because of all the work he's done to build that reputation.

"Mr. White has made people understand that there are some good things that can come out of the projects, too.

"It's funny, but any time that the Jesse White Tumbling Team van rolls up on the street in this community, people hide their wine bottles, take their hats off and shake the man's hand. They know he's been here for their community, almost since it's existed."

The Edwards brothers say they believe in Jesse White's commitment to the community to the level that they want to be a part of the renaissance.

"My brother and I have taken his leadership to heart. Currently, I'm the local advisory council vice president of Cabrini-Green and my brother has had the opportunity to run and manage seven of the Cabrini-Green high-rise buildings under the resident management program."

Cabrini-Green is valuable territory for would-be developers, and in the 1990s there was a move to raze most of the units within the seventy-acre complex. Eight buildings that once housed 1,300 families started coming down in 1996. But the redevelopment plans snagged when residents sued the Chicago Housing Authority and the City of Chicago. The suit alleged families would be displaced and their ability to find other affordable housing would be drastically inhibited. A 2000 consent decree required the CHA to rebuild 700 units.

Marvin, the sheriff's deputy, said his law enforcement status helps him survive in the community and conveys a sense of decency and propriety to his neighbors.

"My brother and I took on the responsibility of being community activists, dealing with youth," says Marvin. "A time came when the gangs were getting stronger and they started to threaten us for being too active in this community.

"So our only true backup, the only way we can really protect ourselves, is to get into law enforcement, since we've decided not to move out of the development.

"We wouldn't want to move away. All of our roots are here. We don't want to leave this place because Mr. White was here and we want to remain here for the youth of today. What he taught us sank in, tailor-made. Everything about Mr. White, his discipline, his commitment – all of it rubbed off on us. We try to lead by example from what we learned from Mr. White."

The Edwards brothers, just as thousands of kids before and after them, have lived the tumbling team experience outside the urban ghetto. Rather than flee to a world outside Cabrini, they've remained committed to the people who do not yet have the option of moving away.

"Whenever we performed outside the neighborhood when we were kids, from the time we left the neighborhood until the time we got back, things seemed strange," marvels Maurice. "It was almost as if we were someone else, like it wasn't happening to us. 'Man, did you see those lights downtown? Can you believe we're staying in this big hotel?'

"Then people would applaud and cheer, and it made us feel like we were wanted in society. It made us feel like we weren't isolated anymore."

Like so many other kids who've gravitated to Jesse White, the Edwards brothers were steered to his program by their mother.

Maurice Edwards remembers:

"As a young man growing up, growing up here in Cabrini-Green without a father – I never had an opportunity to meet my father – there was a serious need. My mother found surviving very difficult without a male presence. At the time, Mr. White was the only guy around who could offer the help she needed while she was trying to raise young males without a father.

"When she ran into Mr. White and that strong disciplinary character, that's what caught her eye. Our mother wanted us to get involved with him because she saw the things he was doing for other kids. He stood out like a sore thumb because he was taking time with children and it was something that he didn't have to do."

Perhaps because of an inferiority complex, the Edwards twins believed early on that Jesse White favored the kids who came from better homes outside the projects.

"We had some other kids in scouts with us who weren't from Cabrini-Green and they came from two-parent homes," Maurice recalls. "And we were starting to believe that he treated those kids a little better than he treated the kids from the projects who only had a mother at home.

"One day, we're sitting at a table and there was a young man who came from a two-parent home, and he made the mistake of calling Mr. White by his first name. When he did it, we figured this guy had to be out of his mind. He has no idea what's about to happen."

Maurice Edwards chuckles at the memory. Misery may love company, but if it's the other guy who's miserable, then you're better off alone.

"Sure enough, Mr. White looked up rather strangely from his salad at the guy. The rest of us looked at each other and thought, 'Oooohhh boy, wow. Something's about to happen.'

"Mr. White took the guy behind a curtain – we were at a big hotel downtown – and he administered tough love to the young man.

"At that point all bets were off. We knew that it wasn't just the guys from the projects who could suffer the wrath of his discipline. It's everybody that's under the age of 21. All doubts were removed after that episode."

Maurice then refers to one of Jesse White's favorite lessons.

"He has a saying. If you walk up and make the mistake of calling Mr. White by his first name and you're under the age of 21, he'll say, 'I'm Mister to you and Jesse to your mother.' And right away you know never to make that mistake again."

As her young man dies,

on a cold and gray Chicago

mornin',

another little baby

child is born in the ghetto. And his mama

cries.

— Elvis Presley, In the Ghetto

Chapter Eighteen There used to be desolate, empty lots in Cabrini-Green, tiny parcels of land chock-full of broken glass, rusty cans and spent rocks. Today, it's called real estate.

The poor people are being pushed out by the rich ones. It's the American way. The Indians were pushed out by the white men, and today the rich men are pushing the poor men out of their ghettos. For the most part it's white men again, this time pushing black men out of their neighborhoods. It's the American way.

Those empty lots of Cabrini-Green's yesterday didn't exactly remind you of the great Midwestern prairies of the early nineteenth Century. Where purple foxglove, butterfly milkweed and prairie phlox once flourished, shards of broken glass, beer cans and cigarette butts blossom. Twentieth century concrete crumbs have replaced the loam tilled by pioneers.

Spirit, however, somehow survived the migration of the species west. So it must have been a burning spirit and a dearth of toys that inspired dozens of Cabrini-Green kids to drag old mattresses onto those empty lots and into those alleys so they could do what the big kids were doing on red mats and springy trampolettes.

The tumbleweed is a prairie flower, too. And it thrives in Cabrini-Green.

"I went to Franklin School, and we didn't have a tumbling program there," explains David Johnson. "So we used to flip around on old mattresses.

"On my way home from school I'd see some of the Jesse White tumblers practicing on old mattresses. That's the way we used to do it – on old mattresses and in sandboxes. Old mattresses were all over the vacant lots.

"So that's kind of where I got the first idea that I'd like to do that. That's where I got the idea I wanted to be one of Jesse White's tumblers."

Now 40, Johnson and his family live in the Austin neighborhood on Chicago's West Side. He carries his carpenter's union card and is a building inspector for the City of Chicago.

"We called them Mattress Men," Jesse White says of the kids who risked skin and limbs bouncing on the old beds. "They'd get out there on those old, smelly mattresses and they'd try to impress me after the tryout period had passed by doing routines on those old mattresses.

"Sometimes it would even work. Those guys were like walk-ons on a sports team. They came on board without scholarships."

As a child, David Johnson's family lived in a Cabrini-Green row house at 950 N. Cleveland Avenue. Johnson was one of the fortunate tumblers because he came from a home with two parents. It was his father who took him to see Jesse White after David told him he wanted to be more than a Mattress Man.

Ronnie Baker grew up in Austin, where Johnson now lives. He tried out for the tumbling team after seeing them on television.

"I was lucky because I was pretty good," says Baker, now 42 and employed as an electrician for the Chicago Park District. He was also lucky because he made it to adulthood without much of a home life.

"I went into the Marine Corps after high school so I was never really in any trouble with the law," Baker says. "But most of the kids grow up without a father. The hard part of growing up in those neighborhoods is that there is so much negativity. There's always two or three members of your family who turn out bad.

"I had two brothers who died from drugs – one from heroin, one from cocaine. I have other brothers who have been in prison for drug-related crimes."

Virtually every person who grows up in the Jesse White system lives in the shadows of gang violence, intimidation and death. But here's the deal: if you abide by his rules, if you don't drink or smoke, if you stay away from drugs and gangbangers, and if you refuse to engage in racist activity, you become one with the safety zone. The gangbangers will leave you alone.

"I've seen him go to blows with guys about his kids," says Richard Blackmon, the attorney and former tumbler. "If somebody's trying to sell his kids drugs or if somebody's trying to recruit his kids into a gang, I'm talking physical fights. I've seen him get physical with people about that kind of stuff."

Physical encounters aren't the only threats to a child's well-being. In The Greens there are intense psychological pressures on kids to become one with a group and grow up with a feeling of being wanted or accepted. Baker said the pressure to join a gang was omnipresent.

"There were a lot of pressures to join a gang. I grew up with six brothers. There were always opportunities to get into violence and the other stuff that goes with being a gangbanger. Tumbling was really the only thing that kept me away from that."

Although there are no absolutes in behavior, it appears that those who make it to Jesse White's safety zone live a life free from gang violence. The hands-off orders from the gang leaders emanate from two sources: first, they understand that retribution from the Man Himself will be swift and without mercy.

They know not to mess with my kids.

"That's what it is, it's the fear of the unknown," White offers. "When the gangbangers see me they say, 'How you doing, Mr. White?' These guys are in the toughest gangs around, but they know not to cross the line.

"But along with the fear of the unknown, they also have a respect for me and for what we do because we're doing something that no one else has ever done. And don't forget, I had a lot of these guys in school and I know their families. They remember that we've done some good things for their mothers, their brothers and sisters."

But there's another theory among those who have lived life in the safety lane.

"Actually," Ronnie Baker theorizes, "no matter how bad they are, no matter what you see or hear about them, if there's a child in the neighborhood who's trying to be something, it's known by the gang members not to be involved with that child.

"If a gangbanger messes with a regular gangbanger, they may get some jail time. They're just gonna get whatever they get. But if they kill a person who's about something, who's trying to be something, they look at it like they'll get triple life in prison.

"So if a kid has a goal or an ambition – like they know the tumblers have – then they stay away from them. The tumblers don't mess with them. The tumblers aren't doing drugs, so they don't need to mess with the tumblers."

Baker isn't blowing smoke. He grew up around the Vice Lords and many of his friends took the alternate route. So he knows what he's talking about.

"Oh, yeah. I look back now and go through my old neighborhood and half the guys I knew are dead. Half of them were dead ten years ago. The ones who are still around will see me and say, 'Oh wow, man, you made it.'"

Sheriff's Deputy Marvin Edwards agrees that the gang leaders view Jesse White and his followers with equal parts fear and respect.

"They fear Mr. White," Edwards explains. "They respect Mr. White. So there's a combination of fear and respect. A lot of these guys are former students of Mr. White's and they know he means business. And he's done a lot for almost everyone who lives in Cabrini.

"He's given their families food, clothes. He helps crime victims from around here get relocated into a more peaceful environment."

Johnson says he'd have been among the dead or imprisoned.

"You know what? If it hadn't been for the tumblers, I'd probably be in jail. If not gang-related, then probably something else." Johnson pauses. "I would have done something stupid. I just would have. I would have been just like everyone else. I would have been influenced by the neighborhood, by friends.

"But I made a choice when I decided to follow Mr. White. He taught me how to work hard, how to help other people and that's something I take with me every day of my life. He taught me how to get my life ready for the future. My father didn't teach me that.

"A lot of my friends are dead, strung out on drugs. I look at my life and I feel like I've been one of his success stories. I don't brag about it. I don't boast about it. But I know that I've been able to do something good with what I've been given. And if you think about it, that's the example he's set for all of us."

David Johnson credits Jesse White with not only helping build a foundation for his life, he knows that the walls around him were raised by his coach and mentor.

"He knew what I wanted to do. I wanted to learn how to be a carpenter. So I got myself into a school, got myself to where I was able to learn the trade and then he was able to put me in a position to make it happen. He put me in touch with the right person and all he had to do was say, 'This is one of my tumblers.'

"He put me in touch with Burton Lipman (a Chicago building contractor) and I haven't stopped working since."

Jesse White's playful side surfaces when he's asked about David Johnson. And Johnson knows the punch line before you even ask him the joke.

"He remembers everything," Johnson laughs. "I can call him right now and he'll say, 'Well, if it isn't Won't Pay. How you doin', Won't Pay?'

"He gave me that name a long time ago because I wanted to buy a car from him. And I thought I paid him for it, but he said I didn't. So he calls me Won't Pay. But that's him. That's Mr. White."

"He didn't tell you the whole story," Jesse White teases. "I told him, 'I'm going to give you an Indian name. I'm going to call you Won't Pay.'

"So he says, 'How about if I give you some of the money?' And I said, 'If you do that, then I'll call you Partial Pay. But what you really want to do is pay me all of the money so that I'll be able to call you Full Pay.'"

Funny stories and nicknames aside, an austere Marvin Edwards, the sheriff's deputy, puts his life and the lives of fellow tumblers into common perspective.

"The kids I grew up with? Those who are still alive, I can count them on one hand if they're doing something productive in life. Most of the guys I went to high school with are either dead or in jail themselves.

"The most important value that Mr. White taught me and my brother is to be a gentleman first. The rest is debatable. And get up off your butt and contribute, give back to the community you came from.

"Have self-respect. Get up and work for what you want. Don't try to take any easy routes out of tough situations.

"We need another fifty more of Mr. White. You notice I call him Mr. White because that's the respect we have for him. We never call him by his first name. Thank God for him. He's a great part of who we are now."

The quality of mercy is not strain'd, it droppeth as the gentle rain from heaven upon the place beneath. It is twice blest: It blesseth him that gives and him that takes.

—William Shakespeare, The Merchant of Venice

Chapter Nineteen Carl Davis screwed up and now he was scared.

As he sat in his jail cell his mind raced.

What the hell was I thinking?

What indeed. The night that Carl Davis and two of his buddies decided to knock over a north suburban diner may well have provided him with the epiphany that his parents and Jesse White could perhaps preach but not demonstrate. Redemption doesn't happen to the pure of heart; you've got to make a mistake before you can correct one. Until the night he and his friends tried to rob the restaurant, Carl Davis was nothing but a good kid from the projects at Cabrini-Green.

Fortunately for Davis and his misguided colleagues, no weapon was involved. But the absence of a firearm and a blade did not spare Carl Davis a trip to jail and the opportunity to reflect.

"We were suspicious black youths and we weren't from that neighborhood," Davis explains. "This was the kind of pressure that could have landed me in jail for a long time. I was with a couple gentlemen, and we were accused of trying to rob a restaurant in Evanston.

"There was no weapon involved and I was more or less trying to talk them out of it, but we were picked up by the police, taken into custody and questioned. The first person I called was Mr. White."

Carl Davis has known Jesse White since Davis was a third-grader at Schiller Elementary School. One of six kids growing up in Cabrini-Green, Davis was a neighborhood rarity. He had a mother and a father who worked as a truck driver. Coming from a two-parent family has its advantages to be sure. But coming from a whole family unit does not inoculate a child from the evil that runs rampant in gang life and the urban ghetto.

"I was afraid of the gangs, of being recruited or being harassed, but the things I was doing with Mr. White gave me the opportunity to avoid gangs. As a tumbler, I felt like I was a celebrity. The other kids used to tease me that I was Mr. White's Number One Boy, and the opportunity to be involved in Scouts, in track and with the tumblers gave me a way out."

They say a horse freed from his stall will turn around and return to a barn engulfed in flames. Maybe Carl Davis understands such misguided instinct.

"Mr. White took special care with all of us. He kept me out of trouble so I was around him all the time. He became more than my gym teacher and track coach. He became more like a father."

After police booked him into the Evanston lockup, Carl Davis called Jesse White.

"First of all, he told me he was very disappointed in me and he told me that he'd have to inform my parents. I can't describe to you how bad I felt that night. I felt that I had not only disappointed my family, but that I had disappointed Mr. White.

"Two weeks later, because no weapon had been involved, the charges were dropped and we were released to the custody of our parents. From that point I realized that was not where I wanted to be in this life. From that point on, I felt like I was disappointing Mr. White if I wasn't giving my best at anything I did. If I didn't live up to the standards that he set for us, I felt like I was letting him down.

"When I look back, I almost feel as if that experience was something that was supposed to be. I could have wound up in a gang. I could have wound up in drugs. I could have wound up in jail for a long time.

"But all those track meets we went to, all those tumbling events we did, they exposed me to different situations and different people. I got to see more than just my own neighborhood. Cabrini-Green was predominantly black, but because of the programs I was in with Mr. White, I got to interact with white people, different ethnic people. And it allowed me to see a world outside of the projects.

"Because of what I saw, I wanted more. I didn't want to just end up in the projects. I wanted to live outside those boundaries."

Davis used his experience to reevaluate his life. That's what an epiphany is, a manifestation of a miracle. If his turnaround was not exactly miraculous, the Evanston jail experience did provide a guiding light.

"After I got out of that trouble with the law, I went to thank him for what he did. I was looking for work and he gave me a card. He told me they were hiring over at Oscar Mayer. He set me up with an interview, and I went over there and got hired. I worked there for eight and a half years before I went into the service."

Today, at age 47, Carl Davis is a Navy aviation support mechanic at a base in Ft. Worth, Texas. His work assures Navy pilots that their airplanes don't fall from the sky. It's the kind of responsibility that not only requires commitment but teamwork as well, just the sort of lessons he learned as a Jesse White tumbler. With nearly nineteen years service and at the rank of E-6, he plans to retire after two decades in the Navy. He also is enrolled at Columbia College and is taking courses at the naval base.

"My wife's been telling me that, because I like being involved so much with kids, that I should look into teaching," Davis says. "It's something I've been contemplating. I need to light a fire under my butt so I can get the credits I need to get a teaching degree."

If the day comes when he stands at the front of the classroom, he knows precisely whose lesson plan he'll follow.

"Last year, I made it a point to get to Chicago and try to see Mr. White. I wanted to let him know how much I appreciated what he's done for my life and to congratulate him on what he's done for everyone in the neighborhood as well as for his personal accomplishments.

"I had a hard time getting in to see him, but God gave me a stubborn head. I walked away from his office because his secretary told me he was busy. I went downstairs and I bought a card, signed it and went back upstairs and gave it to the receptionist. Then I walked four, maybe five blocks away from downtown, on my way back to the North Side. Then I said, 'Wait a minute. I've come too far to quit.'

"I turned around and walked right back, went up the elevator in his building and just as I was getting off the elevator, he came walking toward me. He looked at me and I could tell that he recognized me. He said, 'Carlos!' which is the nickname he gave me.

"It was great. I told him that I just wanted to thank him for all the things he had done for me. I know how many people he helps, how many people he helps get jobs. But I wonder how many people stop just to say, 'Thank you. Thank you for helping my life be a better life for me.'

"He doesn't truly realize how many peoples' lives he has touched. He's heaven-sent, a true blessing to me. I just love him. He is my father."

It's good that Carl Davis decided to turn around.

On election night I

called the mayor and said,

'Mr. Mayor, I've got good news for you.

We beat Dexter Watson.'

– Jesse White, after Walter Burnett was elected alderman

Chapter Twenty To this day, Walter Burnett is excruciatingly pained when he talks about his life's biggest mistake. Yet the mistake is the defining moment of his life.

Most kids meet Jesse White before they get into trouble. Walter Burnett lives on the flip side. He didn't get to know his future mentor until after he had spent thirty months in Illinois penitentiaries.

Asked about the wrong turn that landed him in stir, he sighs and hesitates before the words escape his windpipe.

"I don't like talking about it, to be honest," Burnett says apprehensively. "I made a mistake. I was 17 and I was intoxicated."

Walter Burnett's mistake was in getting behind the wheel of a car. No, his transgression wasn't impaired driving, unless your definition of impairment includes bank robbery.

It's been nearly a quarter century since Walter Burnett and two accomplices, both older than he, were stopped in their getaway car as they sped from a bank robbery in rural Momence, fifty-five miles due south of Chicago's Loop. Burnett was behind the wheel.

"One of my mistakes was being under the influence and hanging around with older guys. I was trying to act older than the 17 years that I was."

Acting older included driving the getaway car, but Burnett and his partners didn't get far.

"Oh, yeah, I was scared," he remembers. "Scared, but most of all I was disappointed with myself. See, our situation was a little different. I wasn't a bad kid. I had a job already. I had just graduated from (Wells) high school and I had my own apartment, a car – I had everything.

"And at that point I lost everything."

For his role, Burnett was sentenced to six years in prison and found himself sitting in a cell at the Graham Correctional Center near Hillsboro, Illinois, 250 miles from Chicago and a million miles from home. His partners were sentenced to twenty years each.

The only similarities between Hillsboro and Cabrini-Green are the planet where they are located and that both are arguably prisons. The penitentiary is located on 117 acres surrounded by rich, bountiful Illinois farmland and the slow pace of rural life. Cabrini-Green is surrounded by concrete and crime, narcotics trade and terror.

"I felt as though I had let my parents down because I wasn't raised like that. I let my parents down. I let my boss down. Everybody had believed in me. Peer pressure, trying to impress other people, can lead you down the wrong path."

Behind the chain link fences topped with razor wire and barbs, Burnett found himself locked up with more than a few men from his neighborhood. These weren't fraternity brothers, guys with whom he played in the youth soccer leagues. These were gang leaders; these guys were Disciples, Vice Lords. Ironically, the tough guys who knew him from Cabrini-Green were as much his buffers on the inside as they were his nemeses on the outside.

"A lot of the guys I grew up with were in there. I come from Cabrini-Green," he laughs now. "You go to any penal institution in Illinois and there's guys from Cabrini-Green, unfortunately. I call 'em my homeys. All my homeys are there.

"But that was to my benefit because they were some of the gang people and I didn't have to join a gang in prison to stay safe because my homeys wouldn't bother me because I was from the 'hood. So I never had to indulge in that kind of activity because I grew up around guys who were involved with it. They protected me as what they called a 'neutron.'"

Even at progressive correctional facilities inmates have plenty of time on their hands, time to think and time to reflect. At Graham, prisoners are offered educational and vocational programs to reduce recidivism.

They didn't have to ask Walter Burnett twice if he wanted to take advantage.

"One of the things was that I didn't have any goals," he remembers. "My only goal when I was 17 was to graduate from high school because my parents wanted me to stay in school. I didn't have any goals to go to college. I was working as a janitor for a maintenance company and I was satisfied with my situation – work, go to school and get buzzed with my partners.

"After I was incarcerated, I made up my mind to set some goals. One of those goals was that I wasn't going to try to impress anyone anymore. I was going to go to school and get a college degree. During incarceration I got an associate's degree. I knew that after I got out I was going to have to sell myself."

Hillsboro's Graham Correctional Center is to Stateville Prison in Joliet what purgatory is to hell. Neither can be confused for paradise, but in hell there is no hope. Burnett wasn't country-clubbing his way through the penal system, to be sure, but he clung to the hope that one day he'd put more than just flashing red lights in his rear view mirror.

"Everything that was going on in the streets was going on in the institution," he says. "There were drugs, there were gangs and there was homosexuality. You name it, it was there. But I stayed to myself. I humbled myself. I surrounded myself with motivational books and motivational tapes. I read the Bible and tried to communicate to people on the outside that I was trying to do something positive while I was on the inside."

On the inside, Walter Burnett discovered that well-heeled white guys make mistakes just like the destitute black guys do.

"There were a lot of guys who were incarcerated who were big businessmen out in the street. They just messed up somewhere down the line. So I learned about real estate and stocks. I learned about how you should have an accountant if you go into business, that you should have a lawyer when you go into business. And so I tried to hang around with guys like that and try to learn a little bit of that stuff on my own."

After his release from prison, Walter Burnett returned to the only home he knew on the outside. The Greens may have been a figurative prison to those trying to get out, but to Walter Burnett The Greens were still his only home.

It was in Cabrini-Green that the rest of the Burnett family had come to know Jesse White.

"As a child I knew about Mr. White, but I wasn't involved with him. I wasn't on the tumbling team. When I found myself in trouble at the age of 17, I left behind me my kid brother, who is a lot younger than me. My little brother got on the tumbling team and he tumbled with them since he was a little bitty kid."

The little bitty kid who learned from his big brother's mistake is Eugene Jerome Burnett.

"They call him Jerome," says his big brother. "When you're a tumbler on the Jesse White team, you're more than just a tumbler. Mr. White is just like your father and he would help our family out.

"As a tumbler, my brother would get a lot of clothes donated to him. He'd get coats, bikes and things like that because people would be charitable to the tumbling team. When Momma wasn't able to buy a new coat, every year Jerome would get a new coat through the tumbling team.

"They'd get gym shoes, Christmas trees, toys. All of those things really helped my family out a lot. And everyone knew that when they donated something to Mr. White, it was going to be put to good use. Anytime people would think about donating to The Greens, they knew that once they gave it, he'd give it to the people who needed it the most."

Burnett also acknowledges the tumbling team's contributions to keeping Jerome safe from gangs.

"Just so you know," Burnett explains, "the tumbling team is actually stationed in the Vice Lords and Stones area. The Vice Lords and Stones can go into each other's territory, but the Disciples can't go into the Stones and Vice Lords territory.

"Like my little brother. We grew up in a Disciples area. We grew up in the row houses, but because Jerome was a tumbler, he could go everywhere. He could go to the Vice Lords, the Stones, everywhere.

"The gangs know that Mr. White will not let his kids be gangbangers. And also, they have a great deal of respect for Mr. White because Mr. White raised most of these kids. He was a schoolteacher and he helped them out, gave them things out of his office, gave things to their families to help them survive. So they know that if they're hard on one of his kids, Mr. White will connect with them. They know he means business."

Jesse White vividly remembers Jerome and the lady who came to be known throughout the tumblers' ranks as Momma B.

"Walter's brother lived in a gang-infested neighborhood and he was on the verge of becoming a gangbanger when he came to the tumbling team," White relates. "His mother – we call her Momma B – she was like the den mother of a scout pack. Whenever we'd go on trips, she'd go with us. When we were on the road, she'd walk the halls at night to make sure everyone was okay. Just a wonderful lady."

When Burnett returned to White's legislative district in 1984, he volunteered to help his state representative and work precincts in the 42nd Ward.

"At first, I volunteered as an assistant precinct captain. And every Thanksgiving and Christmas, Mr. White would donate turkeys and hams to the precincts and I would help pass them out to the seniors and the needy families throughout the entire district. He'd feed between 6,000 and 8,000 families with those hams and turkeys."

By the time Jesse White decided to run for Cook County recorder of deeds in 1992, Walter Burnett had risen to the rank of sergeant-at-arms for George Dunne's powerful 42nd Ward Regular Democratic Organization.

"So I asked Mr. Dunne if I could work on Mr. White's campaign for recorder of deeds, and I became his deputy campaign manager. I drove him everywhere, all over the county."

At 92, George Dunne still is sharp and lucid. He recalls the ambitious Walter Burnett as "a nice kid who had earned a chance to turn his life around. I told him that working for Jesse White's campaign was a smart and honorable thing for him to do. I encouraged him to do it and he did a magnificent job."

"This was an unbelievable opportunity for me," Burnett volunteers. "Whenever you saw Mr. White, you saw Walter. I will tell you this: I may be thirty years younger, but I was never able to outwork him because he went all out, day and night.

"I would work my night job as an engineer with the county, get a couple hours sleep and then I'd be out on the campaign with Mr. White during the day."

The critical concern of that first campaign for recorder of deeds was White's repudiation of campaign advisers' warnings that his time with the tumblers was potentially fatal to his political effort. He refused to abandon the tumbling team that he founded on a string, and he wasn't about to trade his kids for a political office.

He made a conscious decision that if he had to choose, politics would be his second choice. Burnett explains:

"His campaign manager would become extremely upset because he would miss political events to be with the tumblers. Mr. White did everything for the tumblers during their events. He made sure they had shoes. He made sure their hair was combed and their uniforms looked sharp.

"His manager said to him one day, 'What are you doing? You're going to lose. Walter, you'd better make him understand that he has to go to these political events or he's going to lose.'"

So Burnett did the best a sculptor can do when he's given a jar of grape jelly instead of a palette of clay.

"I would try to get him to the political events, and I had to help him with the tumblers to make sure that he would get the shows done in time to do the political events. He loved the campaigning because he loved people, but he had to take care of his kids first.

"We'd be in the car, heading to a political event, and instead of reading the briefing about the event, he'd be on the phone with his assistants, talking about the number of shoes they needed, uniforms and making hotel reservations."

The more he exposed himself to the work ethic of his candidate, the more Walter Burnett understood that hard work is not only a requirement for success, it's a reward in itself.

"Man, he actually inspired me to work hard because I could never feel like I was working hard when I was with him. His energy was unlimited. He's driven and he loves those kids, but he's very disciplined.

"If a kid wanted to act tough with him, he'd put the kid in check and let him know that he is not a chump. If a kid tried to act tough, he'd let them know he'd put them off the team and that they'd better not disrespect anyone. If he had to, he would jack them up. Mr. White's policies were all military."

After Jesse White won election as recorder of deeds, he hired Burnett as an administrative assistant. Less than three years later, it was Burnett's turn to place his name on a ballot for alderman from the city's 27th Ward.

"A couple years after I was elected recorder of deeds, Walter came to me and said he'd like to run for alderman," explains White. "I told him I thought that was a wonderful idea. Then he tells me that he's a convicted felon. I said, 'What?'"

"That's when he told me the story."

White conferred with his press secretary, Bob Yadgir, who called the late *Sun-Times* political columnist Steve Neal to preempt the opposition with a story about Burnett's redemption.

"And Steve Neal wrote a column about it. It was negative in that he wrote about the bank robbery, but he put a positive spin on it in that here was a man who was able to get up off his back and onto his feet, so to speak.

"So I went to the mayor (Richard M. Daley) and I told him about Walter Burnett. I told him that he was a dear friend of mine and that he wanted to run for alderman against Dexter Watson. Now, Dexter Watson was a thorn in the mayor's throat. The mayor wanted to know if Walter could win, and I said that I thought he could, in spite of the fact that he had a criminal background.

"I told him that Walter had become an integral part of his community and that he had turned his life around. As it turned out, of course, Walter won. On election night I called the mayor:

"Mayor, I've got good news for you. We beat Dexter Watson."

"You what? Is there any possibility of a recount?" "No, we beat him something like 70 percent to 30 percent."

Indeed, Walter Burnett thrashed Daley nemesis Dexter Watson, 3,621 to 1,525.

"Some of the people who were with the mayor that night said they had to peel him off the ceiling. He was so excited that we'd gotten rid of the thorn in his throat."

With Burnett's victory, Jesse White took his seat at a table reserved for the prominent Chicago political players. Not only had White demonstrated his own prowess as a vote getter, he had begun to produce a string of candidates who would carve yet another legacy for the erstwhile minor league baseball player. Jesse White was a winning candidate who was beginning to groom new generations of winning candidates.

But election night euphoria invariably melts by morning. Then it's time to get to work, to the business of doing what elected officials have to do so they can get themselves elected again.

Walter Burnett attacked his new job and won praise from the Chicago media. There are fifty wards in the City of Chicago, and not many of them command the attention of the mainstream media outside their neighborhood press. But Burnett's ward encompasses one of the nation's most notorious housing projects, so the 27th Ward alderman automatically assumes a seat under the microscope.

Burnett was generally acknowledged to be a conscientious and energetic public official. In a column published July 14, 2004, the *Chicago Tribune's* Mary Schmich wrote:

The day Mayor Richard Daley summoned Walter Burnett to ask whether he would support tearing down Cabrini-Green to make way for a mixed-income development, the new alderman knew exactly what he had to do: He had to talk to his mother.

Burnett's mother lived in Cabrini then and he had grown up there, a credential that had not, however, brought him Cabrini's trust.

In 1995, when he ran for alderman in the ward that included his old housing project, the gangs spread word that he was conspiring to kick Cabrini people off their land. Even the older Cabrini women whom Burnett considered his surrogate mothers eyed him as a kid gone wrong.

Daley's puppet, he was called. Uncle Tom ...

Housing authorities ... assure Burnett that displaced Cabrini residents won't wind up homeless. But where are all those squatters going to go? And when he looks at the lists of where people are moving, Burnett winces. They're going to his ward's worst neighborhoods. Gang members are settling next to members of rival gangs, a toxic mix.

As the late Speaker Thomas P. "Tip" O'Neill was fond of saying, all politics is local. In the 19th Ward on the city's far southwest side, police and fire contracts are a major concern among the locals. In a ward like the 33rd, garbage pickup is a local concern. In the 27th Ward, Walter Burnett should be so fortunate.

"We deal with the gangbangers the same way they deal with us," Burnett explains. "They're constituents. Our doors are open to everyone. So if they come to us or their mothers come to us or their wives come to us for help, for something the government can do for them, then of course we will do it.

"They might be involved in negative activity, but they are still citizens of the City of Chicago and so we have to serve them the same as we have to serve anyone else. But I try my best not to acknowledge the gang stuff.

"If there's a gang war going on in Cabrini – and there has been since I've been alderman – then I'm sure I know somebody who knows somebody who's involved in the war. And so I can talk with them to try to get them to stop the killing, to keep innocent people from getting hurt."

Most recently, the gang wars have been between the Disciples and the Vice Lords. But civil war breaks out occasionally.

"Every once in a while, it's the Disciples against the Disciples, the white (colored buildings) projects against the red projects. We just do what we can do to keep innocent people from getting hurt."

By all accounts Walter Burnett was doing a good job as alderman. But when his term was up and it was time for a re-election effort in 1999, his criminal record reared its head. In a story headlined, "When Politicians Seek Pardon for Past Crimes," reporter Laura Gatland wrote in the *Christian Science Monitor:*

Half a lifetime ago, when he was a teenager living in Chicago's notorious Cabrini-Green housing project, Walter Burnett Jr. was convicted of an armed bank robbery and sent to prison.

Today, Mr. Burnett is an elected official, a city alderman whose short political career is now in jeopardy because of that criminal record. Like most states, Illinois bars ex-felons from holding political office unless the candidate-to-be gets a pardon from the state.

When Burnett ran for and won an alderman's seat in 1995, his opponents declined to challenge him under the state law.

Anticipating that challenge in 1999 by a prospective opponent, Burnett began feverishly to seek a pardon from then-Governor Jim Edgar. What a contrast: Here steps convicted African American felon from one of the nastiest urban neighborhoods in the nation. He's active in a true-blue, never-say-die Democratic organization from the inner city of Chicago. The man from whom he must seek clemency is a white, button-down conservative from deep downstate Illinois. He is a Republican first, last and always, a GOP stalwart who owed his very statewide career to an appointment from a Republican governor and who never hesitated to parade his party banner before the public.

The *Tribune* said Burnett was an "excellent, responsible" alderman and that he was the "perfect example" of why officials should overturn laws that bar felons from serving in their government.

In a business where loyalties are often no longer than a wink and no tougher than the tensile strength of a butterfly's wings, Jesse White put his friendship where his friend needed it.

"Here was a man who was an elected public official who had kept his nose clean, had become a deacon within his church, an assistant coach for the Jesse White Tumbling Team and had paid his debt," argues White. "First of all, here is a man who helped me get to where I was – to where I am – and who we helped become alderman.

"There he served with honor and distinction, so I didn't have any reservations at all about whether I should stick my neck out for him. I didn't have any reservations at all."

In an era where most politicians consult their pollsters before covering their nose to sneeze, Jesse White never hesitated. Besides, he got where he is in the first place without polls. Damn the risk. This was a friend and his friend was in need. Moreover, a needy friend who has earned your trust and faith is someone who also earns your every effort.

"Sure it's risky," White concedes. "But Walter proved himself to be a stand-up individual, a reliable, honest, dedicated and committed person. Some people thought I overextended myself, but I did the right thing and I'd do it all over again if I had to."

White spearheaded a letter writing and telephone campaign to urge Governor Edgar to pardon Burnett for his felony conviction before the lame duck chief executive left office in January 1999. This was time-sensitive stuff. Burnett was required to file his nominating petitions in December of 1998, just a month after Jesse White was elected to his first term as secretary of state. So before he was even sworn into office, Jesse White stepped forward and stared controversy right in the eye.

The secretary-elect called on a host of elected officials. And the stand-up guys, the ones Jesse White knew would step forth to be counted, went on record to support Burnett.

U.S. Senator Richard J. Durbin, who knew Edgar when both men were legislative staffers in the 1970s, remembers getting a call from White, who was asking for a favor on behalf of Burnett. Would Durbin send a request to Governor Edgar asking for the state's chief executive to grant a pardon for Burnett?

"It was easy to sign up for that because I really believe in Walter," Durbin explains. "I know how close he is to Jesse. He probably owes his political career to Jesse and George Dunne, particularly to Jesse."

Durbin, who was elected in December 2004 as the Senate Democratic whip and who serves as his party's second-ranking official in the Senate food chain, has worked his way up through the Illinois Democratic Party ranks. A native of East St. Louis and a longtime resident of Springfield, Durbin has had to prove his worth to the powers in the party's Chicago base and has done so through uncommon intelligence and hard work. He understands the hurdles that faced Burnett and says he believes in the divine ability to forgive and grant second chances.

"Here is a man who deserved a second chance, and Jesse has spent his entire life standing in the corner of people who deserve a second chance," Durbin offers. "I think that's why Jesse is almost mythical in terms of his reputation for helping people get back on their feet."

White recalls:

"I called Jim Edgar and gave him a blow-by-blow account about how Walter arrived at where he was, about how he got into trouble and about where he is today. The governor promised me he would look at the paperwork and get back to me."

Today, former Governor Edgar serves on corporate boards of directors and has taught at the University of Illinois at Champaign. He clearly remembers the Burnett pardon issue.

"I remember Jesse was concerned about the issue and he, along with others, expressed support for the alderman," Edgar says.

"When we reviewed the petition, it was clear that Alderman Burnett served his time and paid the price for the mistake he made in his youth. But I always wanted to see what individuals had done since then. Alderman Burnett had lived an exemplary life afterwards.

"The voters knew about the issue and still made the decision to elect him to public office. So we took a look at the facts and felt a pardon was warranted. I felt very comfortable with our decision."

Senator Durbin has rightfully earned a reputation for his liberal philosophies and fierce party allegiance, and he also has gained status as one of the sharpest political minds in Illinois. Durbin readily admits there was an element of political risk in going to bat for a man convicted of taking part in a bank robbery. Nonetheless, Durbin says Burnett demonstrated he was worthy of any risk.

"There was risk to it, but I've said this many times: I believe in redemption, both personally and politically. I've told my colleagues around here in Washington that I've made some mistakes and I'll make some more. But I believe in redemption, and Walter Burnett proved that he was worth any political risk that might have come from this request."

Jesse White says Burnett is testimony to that same kind of sense of redemption, a forgiving spirit that abounds within the African American community.

"They have a giving and caring spirit in the community," White explains. "Like Bill Clinton. Very few people in the African American community walked away from Bill Clinton, even though they realized that he made a mistake. They believe – like I believe – that everyone is entitled, with a few exceptions, to a second chance."

Armed with that second chance and with the support of a cadre of true believers, Walter Burnett never looked back. In the 1999 election for alderman of Chicago's 27th Ward, Burnett crushed challenger Rickey Hendon with a landslide for the ages. Burnett whipped Hendon 8,137 — 2,443, a percentage breakout of 77-23.

In a story filed by Northwestern University's Medill News Service, reporters Janet King and Andrea Woo wrote:

Partying under a chandelier made of vodka bottles, Alderman Walter Burnett, Jr. easily won re-election in the 27th Ward Tuesday night over challenger Rickey Hendon …

Burnett gave his victory speech at 9 p.m., thanking campaign workers who waved white victory pennants bearing his name as the song "Celebrate" by Kool and the Gang blared on loudspeakers … Burnett ran for re-election after former Governor Jim Edgar granted Burnett executive clemency for an armed bank robbery Burnett committed at age 17 …

Burnett's party was a lively one at Drink, a trendy downtown Chicago nightclub. It featured R&B music, a glimmering disco ball and three bars. Party-goers feasted on fresh fruit, vegetables, quesadillas, chicken wings and pizza …

Among the festive supporters that night was the Illinois secretary of state. With second chances come new responsibilities. For those who thought Jesse White was sticking his neck out a little too far for a convicted bank robber, this was as much about loyalties as it was responsibility.

Blind loyalty — allegiance without reason — is a dangerous approach to life. But in the rough and tumble world of government, politics and community, Walter Burnett had proven his commitment to his people and to his mentor. There was no doubt in the mind of Jesse White that his protégé was ready to prove that the reward would be well worth the political risk.

"No one ever used my support of Walter Burnett against me in a political way," White says. "I think it's because they know what kind of a guy

Walter is, the kind of guy who got himself into trouble, but who demonstrated that he is not only a dedicated public official, but an all-around good guy.

"But it never mattered. My politics, the way that this issue might have played out against me, it never mattered because this was all about what was right and what the man was all about. People who know me know that I wouldn't wrap my arms around him if he wasn't a person of character."

Think not, Percy, to share with me in glory any more. Two stars keep not their motion in one sphere.

— Prince Hal, Henry IV

Chapter Twenty-One When she was 5, Glenna White moved to California, 2,000 miles from her father and his rapidly growing extended family. When Jesse White tells you're part of *la familia,* he is dead serious. The human race is a pretty big family, but it's not much bigger than Jesse White's.

Glenna White, who returned to Illinois at age 14 and now is 40-something, is wistful when she speaks of the time with her father that was spent somewhere else, with someone else. But she, as well as Jesse's other daughter, Lorraine, also seems to understand that one child's loss is another's bounty.

"I have felt that I've had to share him with a lot of people," Glenna states matter-of-factly. "I believe he loves me, but I also feel that tumbling is his first love."

Now married with two children (her 10-year-old son is Jesse White III) Glenna White Jones is a certified public accountant with a bachelor's degree from Illinois State University in Normal. Her captive smile is a gift from her father, and it adds to her beauty. Glenna White Jones also inherited her father's engaging personality and affability.

"I guess our relationship has kind of evolved from some degree my being a little resentful of it to an understanding that this is the way it is and it's the way it's going to be. From when I was a teenager and right up through my adult years, I have felt like I missed some valuable time with him. He was trying to get established.

"When I got back to Illinois there was the tumbling team. And it still takes some getting used to today. Everything in his life is on a schedule.

There are times when I've had to say to him, 'Hey, I'm not a constituent. I'm your daughter and we shouldn't have to schedule time together.' But everything now revolves around a schedule. I guess that's the way it is when you occupy a position of responsibility like that."

Glenna White Jones is selfish when it comes to sharing her father, as is the apt inclination of loving daughters. But she also understands that her father's commitment to sons and daughters without fathers is a high calling.

"My dad is a very genuine person who wants to help people," she says. "A lot of it you can see, but there's still a lot of it that you don't. He gets an awful lot of satisfaction from helping others. His reward is what happens after he helps those people when they go on to college, when they go on to become successful people. That's his reward.

"It's not a numbers game, but I'm one success story among many, many successes in his life. I went off to college, got my degree and became a CPA, and I'm sure he's proud of that. But there are other successes, other accomplishments, and he views them in the same way, with the same kind of satisfaction. That's his reward."

These days, Glenna's father sets aside time in his schedule to take in his grandson's piano recitals.

"Someday he'll play with Yanni," he beams. If so, it would be a union of his progeny and his favorite musician.

"He has very high standards," Glenna recognizes. "He can get on you hard about some things. But there are times when I have to pull him aside and say, 'Hey, it's time for you to relax. Take off your shoes, put your feet up and watch the basketball game. Just enjoy some time together with your family.'"

A ministering
angel
shall my sister
be.

— Hamlet

Chapter Twenty-Two George White had it all going for him as he was hitting the backside of 40.

A pharmacist at the Lakeside Veterans Administration Hospital in Chicago, Jesse White's baby brother, six years younger, had been married just a month when he began experiencing severe headaches. Julia White, their mother, pestered George's older brother to get George to a doctor.

"I told my mother that he was a pharmacist and that he was perfectly capable of taking care of himself," Jesse White remembers. "He was a grown man and he didn't need me getting involved in his personal affairs."

Eventually, Jesse capitulated.

"He was not feeling well. And my mother kept after me, kept asking me to make George go to a doctor. He kept having these headaches.

"So we finally got him to a doctor, and the doctor examined him and told us he was suffering from an aneurysm. It was deep-seeded and we had to take him to the hospital right away. So we took him to Loretto Hospital on the West Side, where he lived. But after they examined him, they rushed him to the hospital at the University of Chicago. It was that bad."

The aneurysm was situated too deep within George White's brain to allow surgeons to repair it. His condition was critical by the time he got to the University of Chicago.

"That night at the hospital," Jesse recalls, "we were asked that if George passed away, could they use his organs for transplantation purposes? I told them no. I told them I didn't want him to be bothered and I didn't want the rest of the family bothered. We were worried about my brother's condition, and I didn't think it was appropriate for the organ donor program representatives to be asking those questions at that time."

Jesse White left the hospital late on the night of July 30, 1981. Within minutes after he arrived at his home on the near north side, the phone rang.

"I got a call saying that he had a bleeding episode. His brain had drowned in blood."

The next day George White was dead at the age of 41.

"That was pretty hard to take," George's older brother says today. "He'd just been married the month before. Here he was, a young guy, strong as an ox. He was a drummer. He was a basketball player. He was a pharmacist. He had a kid and he'd just gotten married the month before. It was tough on all of us."

Jesse White didn't give another thought to the conversation he had with medical personnel regarding his brother's vital organs until nearly a decade later. By that time his sister, Doris Ivy, was suffering from kidney failure. She was forced to undergo painful dialysis to cleanse the toxins from her blood.

Doris Ivy was a candidate for a kidney transplant. And no one in the family had a kidney that matched her type.

Jesse White's older sister is blessed with remarkable candor. Asked what advice she has given her little brother over the years, she unabashedly replies:

"I have tried to get my brother not to do two things. I have asked him not to kiss people in the mouth, and I've advised him not to leave his drink and then come back to it."

"I didn't think anymore about the conversation I had with the gentleman about donating my brother's organs until my sister needed a kidney a few years later," Jesse White explains. "At that point I began to understand the value of life that we have right inside of us, the ability we have to share our own life with other people, even strangers. I wish I would have been better informed about the program when my brother passed away. If I had been better informed back then, if I would have known more about the organ donor program, I would have said, *yes, yes, yes.*"

Doris Ivy was fortunate. On June 14, 1991, nearly ten years after her brother George died and after four years of dialysis treatments, she received life's gift of a new kidney.

Because the Illinois secretary of state administers the issuance of drivers' licenses and monitors motor vehicle safety, the state's organ donor programs have gravitated naturally to the office. Starting with Republican Jim Edgar, secretaries of state have promoted organ donation as a means of giving new life after another life comes to an end. So it is no small irony that Jesse White today spends hundreds of hours every year coaxing motorists to sign the back of their drivers' licenses to certify them as organ donors. His redemption as an organ donation advocate has thrust Illinois into the forefront for organ transplantation.

The gift of life has enabled Doris Ivy to brag about her baby brother in the bluntest of terms. Her candor is refreshing when you ask her if she's his favorite relative.

"Basically, I think I give him less trouble than the rest of our relatives. Everybody else wants a piece of him because of who he is and they know how much he does for other people," Doris says. "But he and I click because I think that what's his is his. What he has, he has earned and that does not mean that he has to give it to me or anybody else.

"He's not like a lot of these politicians who get into office and think they are above the people. Jesse is always down to earth, and anybody can talk to him because he is able to relate to people and their problems.

"If you really need something and ask him for it, he will give it. Many people ask my brother for help and even if he does not know them, he will help. He does not think of himself first, and if you ask him if he's tired, he will say no. If you ask him if he is hurting, he will not tell you because he thinks he's immortal.

"My brother is not the type of person to hold grudges and he forgives anybody. The old motto is, *'Do unto others.'* I don't think that way. My motto is, *'Do it first.'* I used to get so upset when I would hear people talking negatively about my brother and they didn't know who I was. I would talk with him about it and he would always tell me that I didn't have to defend him. I have seen people who did not like Jesse come to love him dearly."

The apostle Thomas didn't believe that Christ had risen from the dead until he placed his hand in Jesus's wounds. There's irony in the Doris Ivy story, not so much because her brother didn't believe in organ transplantation until his sister needed one. Rather, Doris Ivy's second chance at life is pretty much what Jesse White is all about. Throughout his adult life he's given second – and more — chances to deserving kids who needed a break to escape from the mean streets of Chicago. He leads by example as much as by words.

That time, he just needed someone else to set the example.

He has a saying, 'If you can think of 100 ways of hating someone, let the color of their skin be the last one.'

— Thomas N. Benigno,
chief of staff,
Office of Secretary of State

Chapter Twenty-Three In one town they threw you off a bus because your skin is the color of Hershey's syrup. Then there's the town where the boss threw your career off the tracks because you shared a table with a white woman. Your own neighborhood was a refuge, but an island in a sea of ugliness, senselessness and abject disparity. The home state your mother didn't want you to leave when you went off to college wasn't exactly a model for racial harmony; Illinois was 160 years old before a man of your race could win statewide office.

Your natural reaction should be to arch your back and retaliate with every ounce of energy you can muster. It would be your right, your duty to your people, to practice a little in-your-face vengeance, to rub some white noses in some black dirt. Go ahead. It's not like many of your people wouldn't encourage it.

Besides, if you take the easy way out and work within the white man's system, you're an Uncle Tom and then no one respects you. You're welcome nowhere and by no one. You abandon your people and the others won't accept you, just tolerate and control you.

And, besides, don't smart African Americans know that to succeed within the system is to manipulate it and milk it to your every advantage?

"My parents always taught me to love my fellow men and women."

In speeches before school kids, Jesse White never fails to remind them that racial bigotry is the ugliest form of hatred.

"My parents never talked about racial hatred. Sure, they might talk sometimes about how they were discriminated against in the South, but they never encouraged us to behave that way.

"I could tell by their voices, I could tell by their mannerisms, that they were still deeply hurt by what they experienced. That's why I always tell people that once you've been discriminated against, once you know how deeply it cuts, you know how badly it feels. You don't ever want to do that to another human being."

In fact, the Jesse White Tumblers have avoided some Chicago neighborhoods in the past because their coach and founder detected racial animosity toward his team. Rather than bait those who might bait them, he chose to follow the advice of his former minister, the Reverend Dr. Martin Luther King, and avoid the confrontation altogether.

"I won't let them go into some sectors of the city," he admits. "The bulk of the people are the finest people in the world, but you will always find those one or two who will try to knock some kid's eye out because the kid is black. That's the dumbest thing I've ever heard of in my life.

"You're going to beat up a kid when he had nothing to do with how he came into this world? You're going to do harm to him just because he's different? That's ugly."

Yet sometimes conflict is unavoidable. Sometimes it finds you in the most peculiar fashion and venue.

"I had tickets for about 125 kids to go to a game at the old Comiskey Park," remembers White. "And I made sure we had enough money to give to each kid so they'd be able to get something to eat at the park. I had some friends who came along, and they said they'd be able to feed two kids apiece."

During the fourth inning, an usher came to White and explained there was trouble brewing.

"Mr. White, you're needed downstairs. One of your scouts is downstairs and he's in trouble."

Then a state representative, White was escorted to the underbelly of the ballpark, where he was met by a south suburban police chief who happened to be white.

"Chief, what's the problem?"

"Representative White, I know who you are and I want to tell you that I think you do a terrific job with your tumblers and for your community.

But this young man beat up my son."

Not exactly the kind of news an elected official wants to hear from a law enforcement officer. Jesse White remembers the details, and he's careful to point out that the boy was a tag-along, a kid who wasn't one of his scouts.

"Apparently one of the kids – we'll call him Michael – went up to the police chief's son and asked the boy for some money. When the boy wouldn't give him any, he punched him in the jaw.

"I guess that Michael had seen some of the guys from the South Side walk up to some of the white boys and intimidate them, telling them that if they didn't give them a dollar they'd beat them up.

"So the kid who got punched ran up and got his dad, and his dad held Michael until the park police arrived."

"Gentlemen, do what you have to do with him," he told security officers. "I have to be very honest with you. I brought him here and I'm responsible for his actions. But he's not really part of my unit and I hope that you would not let his actions reflect poorly on my kids. Still, I assume full responsibility for him.

"And I assure you this: Whatever you do to him, what I'm going to do will be worse."

The police chief and his son accepted Michael's apology and all involved agreed to release the boy to Jesse White's care. That wasn't exactly a good thing for Michael.

"I thanked them all, apologized again for Michael and excused us. It was time for me to take care of some serious business. So I took him down to an area that I thought was hidden from everyone.

"I took off my belt and I whipped his butt, right there in Comiskey Park. And while I was spanking him, a black lady came over to me and asked me what was going on."

"Why are you spanking that boy?" the woman demanded.

"Ma'am, he beat up a kid who refused to give him money."

"Was he a white kid or a black kid?"

That's exactly the wrong kind of question to ask a color-blind man who is in the midst of teaching a polychromatic lesson to a child.

"Ma'am, it doesn't matter if he's black or white. I'm trying to raise these kids the right way. No matter what color that other kid was, this young man is out of order and I'm going to take care of business with him. And you have a good day."

Nearly twenty years after the incident, Jesse White bristles at the audacity of the woman's question, to the point where he uncharacteristically utters an off-colored phrase to emphasize his displeasure.

"It really pissed me off that she would be concerned whether the kid he hit was black or white."

The story reminds Jesse White of a long-ago day when a proud father took his son into a local tavern for a cold, wet beer at the end of a hot, stifling Chicago day.

"One day, I came home from the service and I met my father in Logan Square, where he did most of his janitorial work. We walked into a tavern and there was a fellow sitting at the end of the bar.

"When we walked into the bar, my dad said hello to the gentleman and the fellow responded in a very negative way. He used the n-word. My father still sat down beside the guy."

Jesse White remembers the ensuing conversation to have gone something like this:

"Do you want to have a drink?"

"No, I don't want to have a drink with you."

"You shouldn't have that kind of bitterness in your heart. There's enough room in this world for all of us. I'm Jesse White and this is my son, Jesse White Jr. He has a contract to play ball for the Chicago Cubs. He's just back from the military. He's a paratrooper for the 101st Airborne Division, and one day you're going to be able to see him play at Wrigley Field."

The white man was taken aback.

"I like your style."

It's the kind of style Jesse White inherited from his father that impresses attorney and former tumbler Richard Blackmon.

"Let me say this about him: I've never once heard him say, 'I'm a proud black man.' He's never had to say it because he's too busy doing it. Some people walk around wearing their nationality – their race – on their sleeve. But here's a man who's living it. He never has to tell you who he is because he shows you who he is.

"To me," Blackmon continues, "that's the greatest testament to who he is. That's the example I follow.

"When I tell people I'm a lawyer they say, 'You don't act like a lawyer.' Well, how exactly does a lawyer act? But they mean it as a compliment because I don't wear that phase of who I am like a badge of honor. That's something I learned from him.

"You don't have to tell people who you are. It's more important, when the time comes, that you step up to the plate and get the stuff done as opposed to just talking about it."

The Jesse White code of racial conduct treats favoritism and discrimination with equal contempt.

"The one thing he's always stressed," says former tumbler and current Cabrini-Green resident Maurice Edwards, "is that you never play the color or the race game. I don't know what he would do if he ever thought that we would get away with playing that game."

Much of avoiding racial gamesmanship is rooted in the foundation of respect for others as well as respect for self.

"When I think of him, I think of respect," says former tumbler David Johnson. "Massive, mega, ultimate respect. I would never do anything that I think would upset Mr. White. The race card to him is the ultimate in disrespect. So he's not only taught us that racism is wrong, he teaches us that to use it is disrespectful to others as well as yourself."

And that's why Jesse White says he keeps his race in his back pocket.

"Never. I have never used my race as a club and I've never used it as an excuse."

When he says this, Jesse White's chocolate brown eyes are concomitantly ablaze with pride and wilting with sadness.

"I always thought that people can look at you and see that you're an African American. I always wanted people to look at my young people and understand that they are not a stereotype of what people might think African Americans are. These kids have their heads screwed on right. They conduct themselves like ladies and gentlemen.

"I want always to dispel the myth that African Americans don't know how to act, don't know how to conduct themselves, or have anything positive going for themselves. I always wanted to show that there's another side that people might not know about."

His old legislative running mate, Dawn Clark Netsch, is recognized as one of the most successful liberal politicians in Illinois history. Despite her leftward leanings in a decidedly moderate state, she managed to shatter the statewide glass ceiling for women in 1990 when she won the race for state comptroller. She can spot an opportunist when she sees one and she can feel the depths of a person's soul. Jesse White, Dawn Clark Netsch believes, is incapable of playing the race card, especially as a role model for disadvantaged kids.

"He's worked with kids who have clearly needed a male to look up to," Netsch says. "I have known him for so long that I find it natural for him not to play that card. I think it's a reflection of who Jesse is, unless I'm being totally naïve.

"In a sense, he didn't come out of the projects, even though he lived there. Maybe that makes some difference. He had lived for a long time in a world that was probably not as polarized as many others.

"But there is something basically gentle about him that it's always been about doing what you have to do and do it your way, as comfortably as you can."

I represented the most cosmopolitan district in the state of Illinois. My district stretched from the Gold Coast to the Soul Coast.

— Jesse White

Chapter Twenty-Four

George Dunne's office at 400 N. State Street is startlingly simple for a guy who over four decades was one of the most powerful men in Illinois.

The photographs in his office speak of the respect he has for those depicted: Mayor Richard M. Daley, Cook County Board President John Stroger and Secretary of State Jesse White. On a shelf below those three images is an aging picture of a man far less renowned than the others. His name was Robert Thompson and he's the answer to this question: Who preceded Jesse White in the Illinois House of Representatives?

Throughout his career, Jesse White has been the picture of the atypical politician. Unlike so many of those men and women he has defeated at the ballot box, Jesse White never plotted a course in politics. Never did he sit down and put pencil to paper and draw a time line complete with goals, aspirations and projections. He has been first and foremost the reluctant candidate.

In 1973, the Democrats began to seek a replacement for veteran state Representative Robert L. Thompson of the 13th District. In those days, Illinois had in place a unique system of legislative representation.

The Senate consisted of fifty-nine members elected from single-member districts. Each legislative district was also represented by three members in the House of Representatives. The system, sometimes referred to as the cumulative voting system, provided for minority party representation for each of the state's fifty-nine districts. That meant that in even in Chicago, a bastion of Democratic machine politics of old, there were Republican members of the House of Representatives.

A retired fire fighter, Thompson had been president of the 42nd Ward Democratic Organization prior to George Dunne's ascension. As he prepared to step down from his house seat, he was the only African American legislator from the 13th District, which consisted of independent Democratic Senator Dawn Clark Netsch, Democratic Representative James M. Houlihan and Republican Representative Paul J. Randolph.

When Thompson sent out word that he would not seek another term, an idea started percolating in the mind of Warren Chapman, one of the mentors in Jesse White's youth.

"When we were looking for someone to run for state representative to replace Bob Thompson," Chapman recalls, "I recommended Jesse. I was more than just a playground director in those days. I was deeply involved in the community. Bob came to me and asked if I could recommend someone to take his place and I recommended Jesse. I happened to know George Dunne and I went to George Dunne and I told him that I thought Jesse White would make an outstanding candidate for the legislature."

George Dunne, the 42nd Ward powerhouse who also was president of the Cook County Board at the time, liked the idea.

"I thought that Jesse White would make an excellent legislator," Dunne says. "There was never any doubt in my mind. He was well respected in his community and had been a role model for young people throughout the area. As a teacher and the coach of the Jesse White Tumbling Team, he was respected by everyone who knew him or knew of him."

Maybe there was never a doubt in the mind of a political veteran like George Dunne, but there certainly was some doubt in the mind of the man who would be the candidate.

"When they first approached me, I turned them down flat," remembers White. "I didn't want any part of it. I was happy working as a schoolteacher and serving as coach of the Jesse White Tumbling Team. I had all that I wanted and I didn't really want anything more."

But the likes of George Dunne, Warren Chapman and others didn't let go. They tried to persuade the tumbling team coach that he'd have room in his life for a little more public service.

One of the friends who urged Jesse White was the late Ned Benigno, a precinct captain who was one of White's closest friends from the 42nd Ward. Today, Ned Benigno's son, Thomas, is one of Jesse White's closest confidants and advisers.

The friendship between Ned Benigno and Jesse White embodies the kind of relationships that were fostered in the racially and ethnically diverse neighborhood of Chicago's Lincoln Park.

"I'll bring up an interesting story about (White) because he doesn't like to talk about himself that much," Thomas Benigno begins. "But during the 1960s, when Dr. King was assassinated, there were an awful lot of black families that were afraid to come out of the house to buy groceries for their kids. The riots, you'll recall, were really frightening.

"During that time, Secretary White and my dad got together and got all of the workers that they knew – we had a lot of African American workers – and we filled their trucks up with bags. We'd tell them, 'This one goes here; give it to Mrs. Smith. That one goes there, give it to Mrs. Jones.' We'd fill bags with groceries and take them to the people who were afraid to leave their homes.

"So back during the worst and most terrible times, here were two guys working together to accomplish the same thing. It didn't matter what race those people were. That never entered their minds."

Within the ward organization, Jesse White had plenty of support and the confidence of a legion of friends. There was just one more person who needed to be convinced that Jesse White was up to the job: Jesse White.

"Finally, I went on a ski trip to Michigan," White says. "And after I got to the top of this tall mountain I thought to myself that if I'm strong enough to ski down this mountain, then I can accomplish anything that I set out to do."

For the first time in his forty years on the planet, Jesse White stepped out of the bleachers and onto the field of politics. He made it down the mountain, ski-side down. He figured if he could do that, politics would be a cinch.

Jesse White won that first election for state representative in 1974 but suffered a setback two years later when he was defeated in a three-way

Democratic primary for two slots on the November ballot. But by 1978, he was back on track and recaptured the legislative seat he would hold for fourteen more years. He would never again lose a campaign for public office.

Throughout all but the last two years of Jesse White's sixteen-year term in the Illinois House of Representatives, Dawn Clark Netsch served as his counterpart in the senate. Fiercely independent, Netsch is a portrait in contrasts with her former legislative colleague.

Jesse White is proud of his political heritage and will tell anyone who listens that George Dunne is his "godfather," and he regularly dines with the former Cook County Democratic Party chairman. Netsch, on the other hand, represented the liberal wing of her party and was a member of the "Crazy 8," a maverick group of Democratic state senators that, in 1977, fought for and won concessions before agreeing to help elect a Senate president from the regular organization.

Jesse White and Dawn Clark Netsch are studies in contrasting political styles, yet are eminently compatible as public servants. Their differences begin on the surface and penetrate deeply into their personalities. Their similarities can be unearthed with just light excavation.

Jesse White not only has never used tobacco, he strictly prohibits his tumblers from engaging in the habit. For years, Dawn Clark Netsch sneaked off the senate floor to her capitol office to steal a drag off a Camel, which she stuffed into a cigarette holder a la FDR.

He's a former Chicago Cubs farm hand. She's a longtime season ticket holder for the Second City's baseball stepchild, the Chicago White Sox.

He's an African American son of a public aid household. She's a wealthy, white lakefront liberal.

She's a law professor at Northwestern University, known throughout legal circles as a brilliant legal mind with incredible recall of the Illinois Constitution she helped draft. He's the guy who was unable to attend Northwestern as a young man because his math sequence was deficient.

She's been unabashed in her lecturing against the evils of Chicago machine politics. He's been some of the grease that lubricates the engine.

Like fire and ice, peanut butter and mustard, these two were made for each other.

Despite their obvious differences in basic political philosophies, they share a true compassion for people in need. As a high school student growing up in Cincinnati, Dawn Clark and a group of her friends got together to help disadvantaged kids find something to do with their time aside from simply hanging out.

"When I was in high school, a friend of mine and I organized a youth canteen," she explains. "We had a very mixed high school. It ranged from fairly poor to what was in those days very well-to-do. We got the school board to give us an old, abandoned elementary school and we got it all fixed up.

"Then we got the local businessmen to contribute money and various things, and we bought second-hand pool tables and second-hand ping pong tables and jukeboxes."

En route to winning a hotly contested Democratic primary race for governor in 1994, Netsch gained fame for a television commercial that portrayed her as a "straight shooter." In the thirty-second spot she demonstrated the pool-shooting skills she learned as a high school coed in Cincinnati. No stunt doubles were used in filming the commercial. The lady can shoot some serious stick, even in her 70s.

"When the youth canteen opened, someone had to stay there and be in charge, and that was my job. So I was there every Friday and Saturday night, and what else did I have to do? I learned how to shoot pool."

Netsch was elected as a delegate to the 1970 Illinois Constitutional Convention before she ran successfully against the regular organization and captured the 13th District senate seat in 1972. Early in her legislative career, Dawn Clark Netsch focused on battles with Mayor Richard J. Daley's political organization. More often than not, the regulars considered her to be a nuisance.

Because of his ties to the organization, Jesse White was not a natural ally for an independent liberal like Dawn Clark Netsch. Moreover, her approach to government was the new-style liberalism born in the 1960s while White was satisfied to focus on constituent services and the needs of his party leaders.

Journalists have always marveled at Netsch's candor and her uncanny and innate ability to generate good copy. She never has been at a loss for a quotable quote, nor has she ever been accused of duplicity. Dawn Clark Netsch – take her or leave her – is either refreshingly honest or a lovable pain in the ass, depending on the point of view of her audience.

"My sense when he first got to Springfield," she confides, "was that Jesse was not a man of enormous substance. From time to time he might ask for some input about an issue that pertained to our district, but my sense was that the first issue of substance that he took on was the one (in the 1980s) that addressed AIDS (acquired immunity deficiency syndrome) confidentiality.

"He was well liked and popular and very well regarded for what he has done with the boys in the project. That was well known. But he was not a major player in the legislative process." She then chuckles at the memory of the days when she and her senate colleagues were too often frustrated in their bid to defeat the house team in the annual legislative softball game.

"I'll tell you where he *was* a major player was at the annual house-senate softball game."

One bill dear to Representative Jesse White's heart was legislation he introduced to allow food pantries and organizations that feed the poor to receive portions left over from events such as fund-raisers and institutional dinners. Until White's Good Samaritan bill became law, the food was pronounced to be waste and discarded.

"That's a very important law," Netsch admits. "That's a very good piece of legislation. I still go absolutely bananas when I see food being wasted when there are so many people who have nothing to eat. He should be very proud of that. That's a very good piece of legislation."

Netsch's assessment of White's legislative record is subject to debate, particularly as it pertains to two left-leaning issues, labor and human rights. Jesse White's pro-labor voting record as a state representative was 98 percent, a fact that was not lost on unions when he first ran statewide in 1998. Voting in the interests of blue collar men and women is a tradition among Chicago Democrats. And fighting for the civil rights of citizens is a badge of honor for Democrats, too, although it takes guts sometimes to assume the lead.

One such issue that captured the lawmaking passions of both Dawn Clark Netsch and Jesse White was the civil rights of traditional minorities. Some legislative observers may be more inclined to remember Netsch's public – albeit unsuccessful — fight for ratification in 1979 of the Equal Rights Amendment to the United States Constitution. However, it was Jesse White who quietly went about fighting for equal rights for another minority.

Before it was trendy among politicians, White sponsored legislation to grant equal rights to gays and lesbians in Illinois. In fact, the Illinois Human Rights Amendment, signed into law by Governor Rod Blagojevich in 2005, contains the language sponsored by Jesse White three decades earlier. Characteristically, it's not a crusade he wears on his sleeve. He simply approaches human rights with the same sagacity he showed when he rode the city bus as a college student in Montgomery, Alabama.

"Once you have felt the sting of discrimination," White says, "you never forget it. Discrimination is ugly, whether it is based on ethnicity, race or sexual orientation. I sponsored human rights legislation because I believe in eliminating discrimination and all of the ugliness associated with it."

As a result of his pursuit of human rights for the gay community, Jesse White was inducted in 1999 to the Chicago Gay and Lesbian Hall of Fame, as a "friend of the community." Ellen A. Meyers, a longtime human rights activist from Chicago's lesbian community, first met White in 1998. She says that even before she'd met him, she was fully aware of his commitment to human rights, regardless of political cost.

"Jesse White was an original sponsor of the human rights legislation in 1975," Meyers says, "and he's the only original sponsor still in elective office today."

Meyers, who now serves as the secretary of state's deputy director of intergovernmental affairs, says White has never wavered on the issue of human rights.

"In the time that I have worked with him, he has really taken a public lead on this issue," she explains. "It says of his character that he does the right thing, regardless of what it may mean to him politically. He doesn't think of personal costs. He does the right thing because he believes in it."

It's an interesting chemistry that binds a regular Democrat like Jesse White and a feisty reformer like Netsch, who still marvels at the incredible diversity that existed within the 13th District.

"What's most fascinating, in a sense, is the way that Jesse came out of the regular organization and he's paid a price for it, although obviously not too enormous of one. There are good government, independent types up there who still think of him as a machine Democrat. That's also true among some of those who come from the black political world.

"But you've got the lakefront with its strong, independent, antimachine streak, plus a good hunk of the district that was very regular Democratic. I suppose it would not have been possible to elect us both at the same time if it had not been a district that had been so different.

"When I ran the first time and didn't think I would win the primary, I got clobbered in some of the areas like Cabrini-Green and the projects. It has always been one of the most fascinating districts in the state because it has been the most diverse – wildly diverse – from the Gold Coast to Cabrini-Green."

Or as Jesse White is fond of saying, *from the Gold Coast to the Soul Coast.*

"So I guess," Netsch continues, "it was possible to spawn two sort-of-separate movements. And Jesse was so nice and so well liked personally that even among the usually antimachine, independent Democrats, he was accepted. He was accepted certainly more than the traditional regular Democrats from the area."

A longtime observer of the careers of both Dawn Clark Netsch and Jesse White is Charles N. Wheeler III. Today, Wheeler is an associate professor and director of the Public Affairs Reporting Program at the University of Illinois at Springfield. As a university professor, Wheeler helps select graduate students to serve a yearlong internship in the capitol press corps in Springfield. This elite group of student-reporters is privileged to learn at the knee of a professional with the breadth of experience compiled by Wheeler.

Before moving into the world of academia, Wheeler toiled for two dozen years as a reporter and Springfield bureau chief for the *Chicago Sun-Times.* In fact, one of Wheeler's first assignments covering Illinois state government was the organizational meeting in 1969 of the Constitutional Convention, where Netsch served as a delegate.

Wheeler concurs with Netsch's assessment that Jesse White's legislative career was not typically heroic. However, he is quick to emphasize that White exhibited unmistakable humanistic qualities.

"He was chairman of the House Human Services Committee," Wheeler recalls, "and some committee chairmen tend to be very imperious. They tend to be disrespectful to witnesses, disrespectful to the minority party. Really, they let it go to their heads. They take on the attitude that I'm the committee chairman, kiss my ring. Jesse was never that way.

"He was always very courteous. He was kind and gentle to witnesses who, in some cases, were just rank-and-file people. As you know, many of the people who testify in committee hearings tend to be lobbyists. If a committee chairman treats them brusquely, well, they're used to it. Whereas, for an individual citizen who shows up to testify on an issue, never having been to a committee hearing before and this may be their only experience with state government and the legislative process, I think it's really important that they be treated with respect. It's important that they be allowed to speak their piece.

"I thought that was one of the hallmarks of Jesse as a chairman. He was very considerate, very respectful of the average citizen. On the other hand, that's the way he is as a person."

Now in his fourth decade as an impartial, yet eminently insightful, observer of Springfield and Illinois state government, Wheeler has earned the respect of journalist colleagues and lawmakers alike. As a reporter, he was renowned for his fairness and accuracy and expertise in state budget matters. As director of the Public Affairs Reporting Program at UIS, he imparts to graduate journalism students the importance of depth, accuracy and fairness. Twenty-first century journalism needs more teachers like Charlie Wheeler to turn out more reporters like Charlie Wheeler.

Wheeler's experience gives him the ability to understand the diversity, yet similarities, between Netsch and White as legislators.

"There are some similarities. Neither of them sees government as an avenue for self-aggrandizement, as an avenue to power or prestige for themselves. In my judgment they were both legislators who looked at government as a device to help improve peoples' lives."

Wheeler also understands the significance of Jesse White's electoral success in a district where his race was in a clear and distinct minority.

"During his career in the legislature Jesse was the only black lawmaker who was elected from a district where the majority of voters were not black." Wheeler's observation is key to the overwhelming electoral success White has enjoyed since entering politics more than three decades ago. "All the others were elected from black majority districts. He was a regular Democrat. He was part of the 42nd Ward organization, so that, of course, helped. George Dunne was his patron.

"But it says to me something about the individual that Jesse White was – somebody whose qualities transcended racial considerations, somebody who is very much people oriented. All his life he's lived the life of an Eagle Scout."

Told the circumstances surrounding White's indecision in running first for the General Assembly and later for higher offices, Charlie Wheeler says he's not surprised.

"See, I think that's in keeping with the approach of a guy who's not in it for self-aggrandizement, who's not on a power trip. I suspect that in all the offices that he's held, that deep down inside, the thing that he's proudest of, the thing where his affections truly lie, is with the tumblers.

"All this other stuff," Wheeler continues, "is fine, but the real focus of his life is those young people that he works with in those projects. A couple years ago, he brought our public affairs reporting class into his office.

"He talked about the secretary of state's office, some of the security stuff that had been implemented in the wake of 9-11; and before they left he said, 'I want to show you a video.' And he showed them a video of the tumblers.

"That, to me, sums up Jesse White's priorities. He's been a committed public servant in the jobs he's held, but I think his first love is those tumblers, working with those kids."

Wheeler admits that during the sixteen years he covered Jesse White as a legislator, he did not envision him as a candidate for higher office.

"I probably didn't. He was not really an aggressive type of guy, not someone who sought these offices out. They always came to him. Other people would see something in him that told them that this guy could handle a certain office. He was not one of the guys who you would see as rising up the political food chain. Usually the guys you'd see doing that were the guys who were very aggressive at it, who would set themselves up."

Ironically, the way Jesse White has lived his life has been the inadvertent trigger mechanism in his political weaponry. Objective observers like Wheeler have witnessed his successful passivity, as have a handful of perceptive former protégés.

Margaret Houlihan, now director of state and local government affairs for United Airlines, worked as White's campaign manager for his first run at the recorder of deeds office. Afterward she served as his chief of staff.

Houlihan is a seasoned political veteran who has worked in the administrations of such Democratic powerhouses as U.S. Senator Richard J. Durbin and Illinois Governor Rod Blagojevich. She saw yet another side of Jesse White, the side that gives potential the opportunity to succeed. When White appointed her as his chief of staff in 1993, Houlihan was just 28 and became the youngest female executive in Cook County. Without the proving ground provided by Jesse White, Houlihan may never have had an opportunity to serve a senator and a governor.

"He took a chance on me even though I was only 28 at the time," Houlihan remembers. One of the lessons Jesse White learned from his political godfather and mentor, George Dunne, is the lesson of loyalty to those who share responsibility for success. Houlihan explains:

"Jesse White is the most unique and selfless person I have ever met. He is a man of his word. I recall him saying on countless occasions that you, 'should never forget those who brought you to the dance.' He always believed that former Cook County Board President George Dunne brought him to the dance and he never forgot that."

Houlihan underscores Charlie Wheeler's observation that Jesse White's political pursuits were role reversals: politics pursued Jesse White, not the other way around.

"Jesse White never entered politics with an expectation that there was something in it for himself," she ventures. "His skills and personality would have made him a wealthy man in any other career field, but he chose public service."

Some of the obstacles that stood between Jesse White and recognition of his potential as a candidate for higher office is an unflattering general perception that most Chicago legislators are organization shadow puppets.

"There are some who come to Springfield with absolutely no agenda," says Wheeler. "People sometimes refer to those who come from regular organizations in Chicago as being *hacks.* Now I don't think that's uniformly true. Yeah, there are some guys who are just there to fill a chair and push the red button or the green button as the leaders indicate. They're interchangeable. When they're gone, they leave no footprints.

"And then there are people who begin in the organization and in the beginning are hacks until they prove themselves differently. Some of them pretty quickly rise to the top and show that they're anything but hacks. They're not afraid of hard work. They have a willingness to expand their boundaries beyond their own ward. (House Speaker Michael J.) Madigan is a perfect example."

There is a third category of legislator from Chicago who can fall into either of the aforementioned groups: the black caucus. Wheeler has watched dozens of African American legislators come and go, from Chicago to Springfield and home again. And he is careful in his choice of words to describe the talents and potential of this select group of lawmakers.

"Much of the time that I covered the legislature, blacks could be divided into sort of two groups," he explains. "This may sound pejorative. One group might be referred to as *plantation blacks.* They were the folks whose skin was darker pigmented than the Poles or the Italians or the Irish, but other than that pigmentation, they voted the same as the white ethnics.

"Then there were the *movement blacks* who had their roots in the civil rights activism, as opposed to having them in the regular Democratic organization. Harold Washington is a good example."

Harold Washington served in both the Illinois house and senate before his election to congress and prior to exploding into the history books as Chicago's first African American mayor. Wheeler said Washington's behavior in the legislature typified black legislators who set out to turn over some tables in Springfield.

"Harold Washington was a protégé of Ralph Metcalfe. On issues where it was Republicans versus Democrats, he'd always be with the Democrats. When it was Chicago versus the suburbs, Chicago versus downstate, he'd be with Chicago. But when it was the white ethnic power structure against the black community on issues like police spying, police brutality – things like that – he'd be with the community. Harold Washington would be a perfect example of a legislator who was a movement-oriented person."

Into which pigeonhole does Jesse White fit?

"He didn't fit either way. Jesse was like a noncombatant. He wasn't from a district with a minority population that was suffering from these kinds of economic and social problems that were caused by racism in the City of Chicago. His area was pretty well integrated. His area has always been a cosmopolitan area."

Some political stars burst across the horizon flashing fleeting brilliance in the inky night sky. Others simply twinkle modestly in that same black majesty, traveling westward each night, often without the notice of all but a few dedicated stargazers. Sometimes beauty is in the understatement.

"I've always respected Jesse White as being a good guy, a hardworking legislator," Wheeler confides. "He's always been someone who didn't let his committee chairmanship go to his head.

"He's tried to be a conciliator, someone who has tried to reconcile opinions and advance a progressive agenda. He's always been someone who would use government programs to help people who needed help or who couldn't always help themselves. He's just a serious, committed guy."

As Professor Wheeler and others have attested, Jesse White is unique among politicians of his era. His ambition is eclipsed by his commitment to values he discovered outside politics, but that have helped guide him through public service. The values of service and commitment to others have served as his life compass.

"Basically, once you spend time with him you realize that he's really for real," says longtime friend and 47th Ward ally Ed Kelly. "For one, I think he's a very contented person. Jesse is not a political animal. Most people in politics will ask how he can survive in politics by being so nice. To me Jesse is not a politician. He's not a mean person, but I tell people that you'd better not underestimate him.

"He's underestimated by some people, absolutely. But he reads people better than most people I know. He'll sit and talk with you and he comes across as the nicest person in the world, but he does read people. I'm a little surprised that a guy like Jesse White can survive in today's political world. He's got that athletic ability, that competitive instinct to fight you. You try to push him, but he's not going to be pushed. There's people who think he's soft, but I know him. You push him too far and you're going to end up being in a war. He's not going to be pushed. "

To be sure, don't ever mistake Jesse White's gentility for timidity. His initial reluctance as a candidate should never be confused as a deficiency in passion for victory. Once in a race, this runner sprints all out until he hits the tape. Once he laces up the track shoes and coils into the starting blocks, his focus is singular and myopic.

It's best to stay out of his way. He doesn't run to lose.

I find that the **harder**
I work, the more luck I
seem to have.

— Thomas Jefferson

Chapter Twenty-Five

Thousands of men have spent their American lives working toward the unattainable goal of being elected president of the United States. Someday the same will be said of thousands of American women. So many embrace the ambition of working to one day become the elected leader of the free planet. So few succeed.

Success can be defined in many ways. By raising the bar so high that it is realistically unreachable, humans set themselves up for failure. If your reach exceeds your grasp, it may be what a heaven's for, but you may spend more of your days miserable than happy.

There's another life philosophy that may be the one of true happiness. By putting yourself in a position to win, opportunity becomes a realistic means of attaining self-fulfillment; happiness is comfort in your own skin, not necessarily what happiness seems en route to the final destination.

Jesse White dreamed of being a ballplayer when he was a little kid. And a ballplayer he was. He was good enough to reach the penultimate rung on the ladder to baseball's ultimate goal, which is the major leagues. Beyond that, hard work and the satisfaction it returns appear to be his only goal in life.

He never plotted a route to the Illinois General Assembly; he answered the call when it felt right. During his sixteen-year career in the Illinois House of Representatives, Jesse White grew comfortable as a lawmaker because the job allowed him to do what he does best. As a legislator he was able to serve his community, his city and his state. Simultaneously, the part-time nature of the job enabled him to continue his life's work as a schoolteacher, a role model and a community leader.

Never driven by the lure of money, never tempted by an ego that required high praise or a higher office, Jesse White took aim at happiness and contentment and did his best to spread around as much as he took in.

Bobby Knight says a basketball team can't win until it puts itself in a position to win. Jesse White played his fair share of basketball and helped put his high school and collegiate teams in the position to win more often than not.

But Jesse White also loves to fish, and there's a distinction between fishing and hunting. True, a fisherman has to bait the hook and put the line in the water. In doing so, he puts himself in a position to catch a fish.

Ultimately, however, it's the fish's decision to get caught. The fisherman doesn't jab the hook into the fish; the fish rises to the bait. It's the experienced angler who knows *where* the fish are in a position to bite.

Similarly, there are two kinds of politicians. There are politicians who plot an exact course for success and never deviate. Most likely, they are the majority. They're most likely the ones who, like Bill Clinton, decide at a young age they want to be president and a negligible number of them reach their destination.

The other kind is the accidental victor, the politician who sets no course aside from a desire to achieve some measure of service. They're the ones like Harry S Truman who, by virtue of hard work more than anything else, find themselves in unlikely positions to win and succeed.

Every ten years across the nation, a new crop of politicians get their maiden opportunities to launch careers toward the White House and other, more likely destinations. It's called reapportionment.

Every year after the decennial United States Census, the Illinois General Assembly assumes responsibility for reconfiguring its legislative districts to reflect population shifts and changes in its racial and ethnic makeup. The reapportionment process is a furtive one, a cloak-and-dagger method in which the two major political parties set the course for power and incumbency for the subsequent decade. The party that controls the legislative redistricting process can determine public policy for a full ten years, and it's naïve to believe what you may have learned in your grade school civics books.

During the reapportionment process, legislative staff members crunch population statistics and fuse them with voting patterns. Like political meteorologists, they build hundreds of separate and distinct models that produce majorities and minorities that ultimately sway power and influence to the party of their hire. At the behest of the respective party leaderships, staff members twist and cajole their computer software programs to configure district maps that sometimes exceed the imagination of the most creative of graphic artists.

Bound by a constitutional mandate that districts be "compact and contiguous," the mapmakers push the envelope to the deepest reaches of political outer space. Legislative districts that may have assumed the shape of squares during their previous ten-year life cycle will sometimes transform into political subdivisions resembling a mealworm in heat. The goal of the reapportionment mapmaker is the production of a map that will survive a judicial test and that will ultimately swing legislative power to the political party that puts food on his table.

Following the 1990 federal census, the Illinois political power base was poised for a standoff. The governor's office was manned by Jim Edgar, a Republican. The senate and the house of representatives were controlled by the Democrats. During spring session of the Illinois General Assembly, neither party was able to enact legislation to create a legislative map for the next decade.

This is where the process becomes extremely technical. This is where the constitutional mothers and fathers came up with an ingenious method to break ties, to ensure that a political map will reflect the racial, ethnic, economic and political makeup of all 12 million Illinois citizens. In the last decade of the twentieth century, a full twenty-two years after the first humans set foot on the moon, in an era when technology enables automakers to build cars that tell the drivers where on the planet they are at any given moment in time, this was when the genius of government showed its true potential:

They flipped a coin.

Well, it could have been a coin flip. Instead, it came down to whose name would be drawn from a crystal bowl provided by then Secretary of

State George H. Ryan. A decade earlier, the question came down to the same method of resolution and the Democrats emerged as the victors.

This time, in 1991, it was the Republicans' turn.

When the Illinois GOP won the lottery to determine who would sculpt the state's legislative district map, the Republicans essentially eased themselves into the driver's seat for the 1990s. The GOP would use its voter data, its political experience and its election expertise to craft a map to virtually guarantee a shift in legislative power until the turn of the century.

That same year, in the fall of 1991, another legislative body was setting a political course of providence in Illinois. At the nation's capitol, 700 miles to the east and seven years in advance of the 1998 race for Illinois secretary of state, there would be a vote that would change the course of Jesse White's life. When U.S. Senator Alan J. Dixon voted to confirm Clarence Thomas as President George H.W. Bush's next Supreme Court justice, the wheels were set in motion to change forever the political life of the little boy who just wanted to be a ballplayer.

But first there was that matter of the legislative map.

In its effort to reconfigure house districts to favor a GOP majority, the Illinois Republican Party set out to draw districts in which incumbent Democrats could not win. Part of the process in changing the majorities in the two legislative chambers is to beat incumbents before they even file for reelection. In some cases, the mapmakers will dump two or more incumbents from the opposing party into the same district, thus guaranteeing attrition. In other instances, the legislative cartographers will draw an incumbent to the outermost reaches of his old district so as to make his reelection nearly impossible.

Such was the case with the reelection prospects of Jesse White. After representing the near north side of Chicago – from the Gold Coast to the Soul Coast – for sixteen years, Jesse White found himself nearly drawn off his own political map. The map drawn by Republicans eliminated his major power bases from what would be Jesse White's new house district. The map erased the public housing projects of Cabrini-Green and much of his mentor George Dunne's 42nd Ward. Displacing those Democratic strongholds were upscale, high-rise residences occupied by young and Republican-leaning professionals who had no allegiance to the Democratic Party and no inclination to embrace its social philosophies.

White had three choices. He could take his chances and run in the new district against a Republican opponent who most assuredly would be well financed and attractive to the new voter base. He could move across the district boundary and into his old power base. Or he could hire legal counsel to challenge the district boundaries.

He chose the third option. He hired the lawyer.

Jesse White called on an old friend and tumbling team benefactor, Loop attorney Lawrence J. Suffredin of Evanston. Suffredin, a longtime lobbyist and Democratic loyalist, had earned the reputation as an expert in state government legal affairs. He also came to White as a trusted political adviser. Suffredin not only chaired the Illinois Democratic Party's Delegate Selection Committee, he had been elected as Evanston Township Democratic Committeeman and, in that capacity, carried considerable sway within the Cook County organization as a loyalist able to reach out to independent-minded Democrats.

Because White is African American, Suffredin began to craft a strategy that would challenge the district's makeup based on requirements contained in the federal Voting Rights Act of 1965. Plain and simple, it is illegal to displace a minority legislator from a minority-dominated district with a white candidate. But the strategy was not without its risks. True, White spent his legislative career representing African Americans living in public housing projects – the Soul Coast, as he likes to call it. But he likewise was a state representative for all those white voters who populated the wealthiest neighborhood in the city of Chicago – the near north lakefront known as the Gold Coast.

Since then, Suffredin has himself been elected to public office and serves as a Cook County Board commissioner. Today, he vividly remembers the days leading up to the decision that would change Jesse White's political career.

"The Republicans had determined that there were potentially enough Republican votes to maybe pull off an upset and pick up a seat if they had a moderate, Yuppie kind of a candidate," Suffredin recalls. "To be able to pick up a seat in the heart of the city would have been a bonus to their chances of maintaining a majority in the House.

"They were contending that Jesse's district didn't have to meet the criteria of the Voting Rights Act because it never was, quote, unquote, a minority district. They contended that it was a place where a minority had gotten elected, but who had gotten elected in a district that was not populated by minorities.

"So all they were doing was shifting it to pick up what they thought were the new people who had moved into the condos and other residences. What they had basically done was turn his district into a Yuppie Gold Coast district. While he'd always represented part of that community, he always had it balanced out with Cabrini-Green and other parts of the 42nd Ward.

"They were targeting the Yuppies who were working in the banks and the law firms and who were Republican by inclination."

Republican by inclination, Republican by birth. It didn't matter. If there more people were inclined to vote for a Republican instead of Jesse White, the political risk to the tumbling team's founder and coach was potentially fatal.

Suffredin is unabashed in his partisanship when speaking of his former client.

"The Republican proposal was rather Draconian in that they were trying to marginalize Jesse's strengths. And when I was representing him, I was offended at three levels.

"First, I was offended that they would do this to Jesse because there was no member of the General Assembly who was as well liked as Jesse was. So why would they pick on Jesse?

"Second, they really were trying to push the envelope on the Voting Rights Act to go after a minority member and to me that just didn't make any sense.

"And, three, this concept that they were going to be able to elect a Republican in that area, to me it was just crazy."

In Suffredin's law offices at 333 S. Wacker Drive, the attorney and his client were brainstorming a strategy for challenging the proposed map when the phone rang one October afternoon.

"Jesse was in my office, and we were piecing together some ideas to go after the validity of the map," Suffredin remembers. "The phone rang while he was sitting in the office with me, and it was Carol Moseley Braun. And she proceeded to tell me that she had made up her mind and that she was going to challenge Alan Dixon and run for the U.S. Senate."

Indeed, the entire nation was about to witness a sea change in American politics during the campaign of 1992. In what is arguably the worst vote of his long and illustrious political career, Alan J. Dixon sided with a 52-48 majority to confirm President Bush's Supreme Court nominee, Clarence Thomas. But the vote did not come until after a contentious series of nationally televised confirmation hearings with a star witness by the name of Anita Hill.

Hill testified during the hearings that Thomas sexually harassed her during a period when the two of them worked together. The Museum of Broadcast Communications describes the resulting firestorm that marshaled female voters across the country:

During the three days of televised hearings, the senators and the viewing public heard testimony from both Hill and Thomas, as well as their supporters. Hill referred to specific incidents of Thomas's behavior, including repeated requests for dates and references to pornographic material.

Thomas vehemently denied Hill's allegations and responded with outrage, at one point, by calling the hearings "a national disgrace … a high-tech lynching for uppity blacks who in any way deign to think for themselves, to do for themselves."

Ironically, Thomas and Braun both are African Americans.

Suffredin remembers telling Braun that she could count on his support in the upcoming primary against Dixon. He returned the phone to its cradle and then turned his attention to his client.

"Jesse, I think we just won our case."

"What do you mean?"

"That was Carol Braun. She's not running for reelection as the recorder of deeds. Jesse, you ought to run for recorder of deeds. Then you won't even have to worry about the map."

White later admitted he'd not given even a moment's thought to the prospect of becoming the Cook County recorder of deeds. Suffredin continues:

"When I hung up the phone, I told Jesse that if we continued to challenge the Republican district map, it was going to cost us a lot of time and effort. It's not like we were going to pick up an extra Democratic seat. It's not like we were going to be able to subdivide a district and end up with an extra Democrat in the house. The best we could have done was redefine the boundaries.

"So when Carol told me that she, for sure, was going to run for the United States Senate, I suggested to Jesse that he start making phone calls immediately and see what kind of support he could get for running for recorder of deeds."

From Suffredin's offices on Wacker Drive, White headed directly to the 42nd Ward offices of his political mentor, legendary Democratic powerbroker George Dunne, who was just a year removed from a twenty-two-year reign as Cook County Board president.

"I have supported Jesse White for every office he has aspired to," says Dunne. "When he asked me if I thought he should run for recorder, I told him that whatever he wanted to do, he would do it with my full blessing and utmost support."

"That night," Suffredin adds, "they began lining up support and by the next morning Jesse White was the recorder of deeds candidate."

Indeed, with former county party chairman Dunne's backing and a satchel full of high-powered political friends and outstanding favors, White became the odds-on favorite to win election as the next recorder of deeds. Still, there were the formalities of the nominating process and a general election.

In the March primary, White bested county board Commissioner Bobbie Steele and Mary Ellen Considine, who added her maiden name O'Hara to her ballot moniker because the primary was to be held on St. Patrick's Day.

On November 3, White defeated former house colleague Susan Catania, a liberal-leaning Republican who managed 46 percent of the vote to White's 54 percent.

In reflecting on his role as a rocket booster for Jesse White's launch into political outer space, Suffredin chuckles.

"This is where you know there is such a thing as divine providence," Suffredin ventures. "For Jesse to be sitting in my office when Carol called? I interrupted our meeting to take her call because I knew she was thinking about running for the senate.

"Jesse and I had just spent a good hour trying to analyze what our options were. And as it happened, the best of all options came to us in the form of a telephone call from someone who wasn't even involved in the remap process.

"Now, had the Republicans drawn a different map, Jesse would still be in the legislature. The whole thing was just fortuitous. I look back and I talk with Jesse periodically about it, and it just goes to show that there is such a thing as divine providence. The answer was Jesse White. I just didn't know it until the phone rang that the question was, 'Who's the next recorder of deeds.'

"And I contend that being the recorder of deeds is what put him in position to run for secretary of state."

You'll get no argument from Jesse White.

"Larry Suffredin is right about that," White concurs.

You can also make the argument that the more people got to know Jesse White, the more they began to trust him as an administrator. In his first campaign for recorder of deeds, he lost suburban Cook County 60 to 40 percent. Four years later, he won the suburbs with 60 percent of the vote.

And Suffredin was right about one more thing. It was crazy for the Republican mapmakers to believe they would elect a Republican from the new district, with or without Jesse White running from within. In the 1992 election for what became the Eleventh Representative District, Democrat Judy Erwin trounced Republican Jeff Perlee with 61 percent of the vote — 32,618 to 20,883. The Republicans temporarily won the war by seating a majority in the new House of Representatives, but they lost the battle for Jesse White's old seat.

Erwin held the seat until the twenty-first century.

For the second time in his political career, Jesse White ran for an office that never was on his radar screen. He was perfectly content to serve as a legislator from the *Gold Coast to the Soul Coast.* But just as tomorrow is guaranteed to no one, neither is a political futures almanac. An irony in this is that an opportunist may never get the opportunity to run for the office he believed himself destined to hold.

Sometimes Forrest Gump throws away his leg braces and wins the race.

Charles N. Wheeler III, former *Sun-Times* reporter, assesses it this way:

"As a reporter who deals with politicians or public officials, you kind of categorize them as who's for real, who's sincere, who's a phony. I think most reporters have more respect for politicians who are more sincere. You have respect for someone who's not a phony, someone who is genuine.

"Maybe part of it is that sometimes you can be so hungry and so obvious in your lusting after higher office that it turns voters off. Whereas someone who is more reserved, more reluctant about it, has more appeal to voters. Sometimes the voters prefer someone who they recognize as a genuinely good guy."

I consider myself a **hero.**

I take it so personal

because it's my **life's** work.

— Jesse White, in announcing his candidacy for secretary of state, October 21, 1997

Chapter Twenty-Six The 1998 Democratic primary for Illinois secretary of state was shaping up to be a classic donnybrook, a political dogfight for the ages.

In one corner stood Tim McCarthy, the burly police chief from Chicago's south suburban Orland Park. A former Secret Service agent, McCarthy had gained international acclaim when he stepped in front of an assassin's bullet intended for President Ronald Reagan. McCarthy, Reagan, presidential press secretary James Brady and Washington, D.C., police officer Thomas Delehanty all were wounded by gunfire from a .38 caliber revolver wielded by John W. Hinckley Jr. The television cameras had captured the rapid-fire shootings that morning as Reagan walked from the Washington Hilton to his bullet-proof limousine. The videotape had been viewed by seemingly everyone on the planet in the succeeding sixteen years. For the rest of his life, Tim McCarthy would be defined by an event of March 30, 1981.

In another corner stood Jesse C. White, the Cook County recorder of deeds. His political dossier was considerably thicker than McCarthy's, but the March 17 primary looked early on like it would be decided based on who the candidates were instead of what they were. White, too, had been often featured on national television, albeit not nearly as spectacularly. Getting shot with the president of the United States is considerably more macabre than directing a group of gymnasts on the *Tonight Show*.

In a third corner paced the diminutive Penny Severns. A state senator from Decatur in downstate Macon County, Severns was the only one of the three candidates who had tasted blood from a previous statewide political campaign. At 46, Severns was the youngest of the three but had already posted a 1-1 record as a statewide candidate. Four years earlier, she won her party's nomination for lieutenant governor following a nasty primary campaign in which she blasted the woman who would ultimately be her running mate.

In the fourth corner of the ring lingered Fate, Providence and Guile. The eventual winner of this political prizefight would be the candidate able to cajole these three opponents to cross the ring into his or her corner. Fate, Providence and Guile were the early line favorites in this brawl. They always are.

McCarthy saved the life of a U.S. president. Hands down and without debate, he was a hero.

White arguably saved the lives of hundreds, if not thousands, of young men who otherwise may well have died from the sort of gunfire that nearly cost McCarthy his life. To those kids, their parents and knowing residents of Chicago's inner city, Jesse White was a hero.

And Severns, the petite, yet fiery, lawmaker who cut her political teeth watching the Kennedy-Nixon debates three and a half decades earlier, well, Penny Severns was a hero, too. Less than three months after she prevailed in a bitter battle for the Democratic primary for lieutenant governor in 1994, she found herself in a battle for her very life. As two sisters before her, Penny Severns was diagnosed in the summer of 1994 as having breast cancer. With running mate Dawn Clark Netsch at her side, Severns campaigned relentlessly through the 1994 political season, literally munching meals while chemical drips pumped cancer-fighting drugs into her veins. To thousands of young women – and men for that matter – Penny Severns's courage earned her the title of hero.

Three heroes.

One office.

One winner.

Two losers.

Winner advances to the championship round.

Losers go home.

It's a hard thing for a hero to lose.

What Jesse White has done with the tumblers is wonderful. He has done a lot of wonderful things with children's lives. But that doesn't necessarily qualify him to be secretary of state.

— Kitty Kurth, media consultant to secretary of state candidate Tim McCarthy

White

Chapter Twenty-Seven The Illinois political season is more grueling than a marathon race.

The average marathon runner trains three months to conquer a 26.2-mile racecourse. In Illinois, the average political candidate must train five times as long and traverse a course that snakes 450 miles north to south and as much as 250 miles east to west.

Within minutes after the polls close and Americans have elected a president, elbows get thrown and combatants unsheathe the long knives as potential candidates for Illinois's six constitutional offices begin a ritual mating dance with their voters. Every four years, Illinois voters select a governor, lieutenant governor, attorney general, secretary of state, comptroller and treasurer. In two out of every three statewide races, throw in a United States senator for good measure.

Grueling? The Illinois political season is too long.

By the time the Illinois State Fair ends its ten-day run two Augusts before election day, the political landscape has already taken form. Before Illinois farmers have had the chance to harvest their corn and soybeans, candidates begin to sow seeds of their campaigns a full fifteen months before election day.

There are speed bumps on the road to elective office and glory. After the state fair speeches echo into the blue skies over Springfield, candidates turn loose their political operatives to gather thousands of signatures on nominating petitions. To qualify for the March primary election, a candidate for statewide office must gather no fewer than 5,000 legally certified signatures from 5,000 legally registered voters. Think it's easy? Think just because there are 12 million people living in the Land of Lincoln that 5,000 authentic, registered voter signatures are easy to come by? Give it a try. At least once in the twentieth century, a statewide candidate from a major political party thought it was easy enough, only to get tossed from the ballot five weeks before the primary.

In Illinois, politics ain't beanbag.

On October 20, 1997, a year and two weeks before the 1998 general election, former Secret Service agent Tim McCarthy staged a news conference to proclaim he would be a candidate for the office of Illinois secretary of state. A day later, Cook County Recorder of Deeds Jesse White did the same.

By the time candidate petitions were filed in December 1997, state Senator Penny Severns had announced that she, too, would seek the office of secretary of state.

Each candidate read from a carefully crafted text. Each text extolled the virtues and qualifications of the candidate. Each announcement attracted a pack of print and electronic journalists, movable pieces on the news conference game board, each piece flashing microphones, recording machines, pens and pencils.

McCarthy, who didn't dodge a bullet, but who prevailed over one, was primed to hit the campaign field like the former University of Illinois football player he was. Big and strong, Tim McCarthy cut an imposing figure. He cast a wide shadow. But he'd never sought public office before.

Still, Tim McCarthy was a hero. Some even believed his resume beckoned to a new flank of voters who sought a fresh and clean approach to an office scarred by scandal and swelling in unseemliness by the hour. Tim McCarthy was a formidable candidate.

The day after McCarthy's announcement of candidacy, former legislator Jesse White stepped up to the podium at the Palmer House, a venerable Chicago hotel dripping with political lore. To no one's surprise, White confirmed what *Chicago Sun-Times* political columnist Steve Neal had predicted six weeks earlier. At 63, White would be the oldest of the three candidates for secretary of state. But a genetically engineered athlete's body and a lifetime of physical discipline belied his age. He was fit and he was spoiling for a fight.

Privately, White pulled no punches: he knew he was the hero. To Jesse White's way of thinking, Tim McCarthy was shorting the ante for this poker hand. White believed his time had come, his dues had been paid and that his reward should be his party's nomination for the second largest political office in the state. Jesse White had a chip on his shoulder, and he was daring the former Secret Service agent to knock it off.

Meanwhile, the physically slightest of the three was flexing her considerable political muscle. Penny Severns had spent a quarter century preparing for this race. In fact, Penny Severns spent every waking minute of every single day of her adult life preparing to hoist herself up to the ladder's next rung.

While a student at Southern Illinois University at Carbondale, Severns in 1972 broke her political maidenhead when she won election as a delegate to the Democratic National Convention. At age 20, she was the youngest person ever elected to serve as a delegate to a major party's national convention. It was the first election in which 18-year-olds exercised their right to vote.

After earning her degree from SIU in 1974, Severns took a position at the State Department in Washington, D.C. As an analyst and auditor, she traveled to Thailand, India and Nepal, evaluating the United States' missions in those developing third world countries.

After Severns resigned her position at the State Department, she returned to her hometown of Decatur, where she began to move the pieces around the board and train for her next political bout. In 1983, she was elected to a seat on the Decatur City Council. She had sketched her political blueprint and had launched her political star.

Penny Severns was on the rise.

In 1986, after just three years as a councilwoman, Severns's keen political eye spotted her next campaign opportunity. The time was right, she figured, to challenge incumbent Republican Jim Rupp, a likeable gent who was serving in his tenth year as Macon County's state senator. In the decade before he ascended to the Illinois Senate, Rupp ran Decatur from the mayor's office and was generally viewed as a popular political figure. Even as a Republican, Rupp was a comfortable fit for the blue-collar, Democratic-leaning voters in the rustbelt town of Decatur. His portly physique, bushy eyebrows and warm smile exuded his image as everyone's grandfather. In a town that leaned Democratic, Rupp was able to draw votes away from his previous Democratic opponents. Rupp's paternal image, though, was about to be shredded by a cool and calculating opponent.

Severns sensed his vulnerability the way a shark smells the blood of a wounded sailor. By the time she was finished with him, Rupp was launched to the watery graveyard of Illinois politics. Severns swept 53 percent of the vote and was sworn in as state senator from the 51st District in January of 1987.

Political observers had learned quickly that Penny Severns was nothing, if not a political animal. Sharks must swim relentlessly and feed incessantly to survive in the deepest end of the ocean. Penny Severns was a political shark.

And she swam with the big fish. Senate President Philip J. Rock, the powerful leader of the Senate Democratic Caucus, immediately recognized Severns's potential and appointed her to key committee posts. She earned a reputation as a no-nonsense lawmaker whose job was to be a legislator, whose secular religion was to be a legislator, and whose recreation was to be a legislator.

By 1997, with ten years of service in the General Assembly and a statewide campaign already under her belt, Severns's uncanny ability to sense opportunity rang her bell one more time. The office of secretary of state, which for eight years was occupied by Republican George Ryan, would be open. Ryan, who was doggedly fighting allegations of scandal within the secretary of state's office, had announced in the summer of 1997 that he would seek his party's nomination for governor. Unlike 1986, there would be no incumbent for Penny Severns to unseat. Unlike 1994, there would be no sitting officeholder to battle, no insurmountable Republican war chest to match. Her keen sense of political radar told Penny Severns that the time had come for her to ascend to the next rung of the political ladder. That rung – the office of secretary of state – was just one small step beneath the platform she had aspired to long before she was a legislator, long before her days as a Decatur city council member. After she was elected secretary of state – this is what Penny Severns knew – she would be just one election away from becoming the first woman in Illinois history to win the office of governor.

But unlike Tim McCarthy, Penny Severns was not a strapping, towering physical specimen. And unlike Jesse White, Penny Severns had not spent her life sculpting her physique in gymnasiums and on baseball diamonds. In her mind she was ready for a knock-down-drag-out fight. But Penny Severns was at a distinct disadvantage in comparison to her two male adversaries. She could match their political resumes. Given the chance, she might even give them a run in raising political funds. Some people may even have argued she was the most intelligent of the three Democratic candidates for Illinois secretary of state in 1998.

Christi Parsons has covered state government and politics from her perch in the *Chicago Tribune's* state capital bureau since 1994. Parsons saw in Severns a toughness that set her apart from her legislative colleagues.

"Penny was a senator with chops," Parsons remembers. "She could be hard-assed and hard-edged, but still come off as the girl next door."

Chops aside, former running mate Dawn Clark Netsch was not comfortable with Severns's decision to seek the office of secretary of state. As she is in almost all matters, Netsch is brutally candid in offering her opinion.

"I just did not think it was the right thing for her to do," Netsch says. "I always thought that she should have run for treasurer. That would have been a good place for her to be, a good steppingstone. It just made an awful lot of sense."

Netsch, viewed by many political observers as a mentor to a young Senator Severns when the Decatur woman was cutting her teeth in the General Assembly, was in a box. As a state senator, she had served the same legislative district as Jesse White when he was a state representative. But her fiery feminism and desire to boost the careers of women – both politically and economically – tugged at her loyalty to Severns.

In the end, though, she believed White was the better candidate between the two for secretary of state.

"That was another factor," she says of Severns's candidacy. "Why go into a race where, number one, you have a personally popular person like Jesse White? Why take that on?

"I can understand that Penny may have viewed secretary of state as a pretty good launching pad. But I don't think it's the only launching pad. I just don't think it was right for her for a lot of reasons and one of those reasons was getting into a primary race with Jesse. Even if she would have won the primary – and I wasn't at all sure she would win the primary – she'd have left sort of a bad taste in the mouths of some people. It just wasn't the place to be.

"The impression was – and God knows that the powers-that-be in the party never confided in me – it was pretty clear that she had a pretty good shot at treasurer. Having a successful statewide race for an office where you can do almost nothing wrong short of someone stealing the state's money, it just would have been a good place for her to be. Much better than a messy secretary of state's primary."

In retrospect, Netsch was prescient in her doubts about a Severns candidacy in a three-way primary for secretary of state. She may well have been at a disadvantage in a fight against a man who saved a president's life and a man who saved thousands of ghetto souls.

But there was one disadvantage that even Penny Severns did not expect. The legs of her political ladder were about to be sawed off from under her.

The first hint of trouble arrived around Thanksgiving 1997.

Penny Severns was dying.

For a man of courage, **Mr. McCarthy**

is committing a cowardly act.

He is running

scared from a real primary battle.

— State Senator Penny Severns,

December 23, 1997

Chapter Twenty-Eight There is a time stamp on the document. Likely, hundreds of thousands of Illinois voters were focused on shopping, wrapping and baking when a clerk punched the stamp that marked the moment. To those hundreds of thousands of citizens, *3:27 p.m., 12-22-97,* meant there were just two shopping days before Christmas; just a couple of days before the kids could rip the shiny paper and ribbons off the boxes and stuff them into the garbage. At 3:27 p.m. on any December 22, the aroma of a pumpkin pie can tug at nostrils and awaken taste buds.

But on this December 22, at this 3:27 p.m. in this, the year 1997, a time stamp at the Illinois State Board of Elections proclaimed that someone had something other than holiday cheer in the oven. On Monday, December 22, 1997, at 3:27 in the afternoon, the signatures of Patricia M. O'Sullivan and Imogene Bosak etched themselves forever into a footnote of Illinois's rich political history.

In an objection signed and witnessed by O'Sullivan and Bosak, Tim McCarthy and his campaign for secretary of state officially challenged the legality of state Senator Penny Severns's nominating petitions. If the flurry of candidate announcements in the fall served as this civil war's Ft. Sumter, Gettysburg happened on December 22, 1997, at 3:27 p.m. This was to be a lawyers' battle, waged in conference rooms and before appointed election officials, but the blood would spill onto the pages of newspapers all over Illinois and across television screens throughout the state. It was the battle that would mark the beginning of Penny Severns's political end.

Illinois law requires that candidates for statewide office file petitions containing the names of no fewer than 5,000 registered voters. The nominating petitions can include as many as 10,000 signatures, but at least 5,000 must be genuine and valid. You can't sign for your neighbor and you shouldn't sign for your spouse. If you print your name, you're a suspect. If you never bothered to register as a voter, you are technically in violation of state statute. And if you hang your hopes of winning an election on the signatures of people who forge, or who don't live where they say they do, or who sign more than once, or who do not comply with a plethora of other bureaucratic rules and statutory regulations, you'd better come in with more than the minimum number of signatures. And if the folks who circulate your petitions flout election law, you'd better find a good attorney.

Penny Severns called the attorney, the best attorney she could find.

"I first met Penny sometime in the mid- to late-1970s." John R. Keith is sitting behind a desk in an office cluttered by a row of packing boxes filled with thousands of pages of legal documents. The boxes stretch five feet across the floor and stack three feet high. "Back then, we had an inheritance tax in Illinois that was supervised by the state treasurer. The director of the inheritance tax division resigned on short notice and (then Treasurer) Alan Dixon named me as acting director."

Back then, Keith was a bright, young and talented attorney just a couple of years out of Baylor University Law School. "I'd go in at 6 o'clock in the morning and work until 9 o'clock in the morning before I went to my job at the Giffin Winning law firm. I stayed there and trained the new person for the job. That new person was Penny Severns."

Over the years Keith, and Severns tacked a friendship to their professional relationship. As an attorney, Keith had earned a reputation as a tough and no-nonsense counselor with a sharp analytical mind. Penny Severns and her lawyer had a lot in common.

Around the time Keith met Severns, he was teamed with Springfield attorney Herman Bodewes in a state government case they argued before the Illinois State Supreme Court. They won the case. In 1981, he and Bodewes represented Senator Phil Rock after a Republican minority attempted to wrest from Rock the senate presidency in a shrewd parliamentary move engineered, in part, by then-Governor James R.

Thompson. As cocounsel in *Rock v. Thompson,* Keith again found himself arguing before the state's highest court. He won that one, too.

By the time Severns approached her longtime friend to represent her before the State Board of Elections, John R. Keith had earned the reputation of being one of the most tenacious and relentless election attorneys in the Midwest. If Keith couldn't keep Penny on the ballot, no one could.

During the two weeks between the deadline to file nominating papers and the last day to challenge them, the Severns petitions were subject to intense scrutiny. First, the Jesse White campaign combed the petitions. White's campaign officials decided they would not raise questions about the validity of signatures.

"We pulled her petitions and looked them over," explains Thomas N. Benigno, a longtime White aide and director of White's 1998 campaign. Rather, the White campaign people were more interested in who circulated the petitions than in how many people signed them. It's always good to know who's supporting your political opponent because, after all, the friend of my enemy is my enemy, too.

"We knew she might have had some problems with signatures, but we were more interested in knowing where her support was," says Benigno. "And besides, Jesse told us that she was his friend and that he had no intention of challenging her petitions. But we did want to know who was supporting her and a good way to find that out was to see who circulated the petitions."

Keith, whose legal expertise folds into a vast well of political experience, said the White campaign's interest in Severns's petitions was political common sense.

"At this stage of a campaign you'd want to see not only who's supporting a candidate, but also the areas of support," explains Keith. "In a statewide race such as this, oftentimes you'll see that petitions were filed from only six (of the state's 102) counties. If I'm involved from the other side or if I'm a candidate, I'm going to want to know what union might be involved over here or what group might be involved over there, and a good way to figure that out is by the petitions.

"In this case, even though I may not challenge the petitions, I'm going to want to know that she had a lot of petitions from the 33rd Ward. And then we make a decision. Do we write that one off or do we beef it up?"

The McCarthy campaign had in mind a different strategy, one that went beyond the need to know who was backing Severns.

A McCarthy campaign inspection of the Severns petitions would indicate she did not file the maximum number of signatures. Seasoned political operatives know that the nominating petition is the underpinning of the political campaign. Just as a fractured foundation will collapse a house, sloppy candidate petitions can cause a political campaign to cave in.

Fred Lebed of Western Springs, Illinois, is a veteran political organizer of more than a dozen statewide campaigns. He and others like him insist on perfection – or as near to perfection as humanly possible – when gathering and submitting petitions and signatures.

"You can never underestimate the importance of the candidate's petitions," explains Lebed, who directed the campaigns of such luminaries as former Attorney General Roland W. Burris, the first African American elected statewide in Illinois. Lebed also worked as a key consultant to the White campaign in 1998.

"You keep double books so that you have backups. You line up two means of transportation so you're guaranteed to get the petitions from Chicago to Springfield for filing. The people in charge need to personally supervise the bindings so that every *T* is crossed and every *I* is dotted. You can't get a hit in the big game if they don't let you step up to home plate. Without good petitions you don't even have a bat in your hands. You strike out without ever leaving the dugout."

Severns's biggest mistake was filing fewer signatures than the maximum allowed under Illinois law. State Board of Elections records show her campaign filed 7,914 signatures, 2,086 under the limit. The fragility in the number of signatures filed caused a red flag to flutter in the breeze.

In that fluttering the McCarthy camp saw an opportunity to cut the opposition in half, to narrow the field from three to two, to create a mano a mano battle between their candidate and Jesse White. As they inspected the Severns filings, they also began to see potentially fatal technical errors in her petitions.

And so they challenged the legality of Penny Severns' candidacy in the March 17 primary.

In reconstructing the case one cold and rainy Sunday morning, attorney Keith explains that the basis of the McCarthy challenge was rooted in patterns of suspicion that they used to create doubt over the validity of the signatures.

"Part of their complaint was that if you can find enough of a pattern of false filings, then an entire batch of petitions can be stricken," Keith says as he rolls his chair to the stacks of packing boxes containing copies of the Severns petitions. "So if I have twenty circulators and you challenge me and can show that seven of those circulators were using fraudulent tactics to get signatures, not only do those get thrown out, but if you teed it up right, you can have all of them thrown out. That's because the fraud is permeated in the process that none of the signatures should be counted."

In legalspeak, what Keith was saying is that some circulators may have had good signatures mixed with the bad, but that because the bad ones were rooted in a pattern of badness, the good ones became bad, too. Easy stuff, this law.

The Severns campaign found itself in a bad situation. Without a 5,000-signature cushion as would have been allowed by state law, they needed to cut their signature losses to 2,914. Severns's confidante and campaign press secretary, Terry Mutchler, began cranking up the campaign response machinery.

On Thursday, Christmas Day 1997, *Springfield State Journal-Register* political columnist Bernard Schoenburg fired off the first of Severns's defense salvos. In part, Schoenburg's column read:

Severns Slams McCarthy in Letter to Democrats

State Sen. Penny Severns, D-Decatur, has what could be a big fight looming in her attempt to stay on the ballot for the Democratic nomination for secretary of state.

While the legal battle over an objection filed to her nominating petitions is key to her candidacy, she's also taking time to pick a fight with the opponent she blames for the challenge – Orland Park Police Chief Tim McCarthy.

In a letter sent to Democratic officials following the challenge Monday by Patricia O'Sullivan and Imogene Bosak, Severns likens the challenge to her petitions to the "spirit of Scrooge."

McCarthy, she said, "is attempting to kick me off the primary ballot and has a Republican hired gun – Senate President Pate Philip's election lawyer to help him."

Severns calls the objection to her petitions a "frivolous filing designed to eliminate the only downstate candidate for such a critical office.

"For a man of courage, Mr. McCarthy is committing a cowardly act. He is running scared from a real primary battle. It should be troubling to all Democrats that Mr. McCarthy has decided to employ a politically and ethically underhanded tactic and that he is using the legal counsel of the most powerful Republican in the state to accomplish this goal."

The attorney to whom Severns's letter referred was Burt Odelson, a Chicago lawyer who has been retained in election code cases by Democrats as well as Republicans.

Oddly, the McCarthy campaign never strenuously denied Severns's assertion that the former Secret Service agent and "man of courage" was the force behind the challenge. Schoenburg's Christmas morning column carried what may have been the campaign's only nondenial denial:

Kevin Lampe, a consultant to McCarthy, said the McCarthy campaign is not paying for the challenge. He does say that "people who support our campaign have worked on this," and a computerized voter file kept by forces of House Speaker Michael Madigan, D-Chicago, was also used.

Typically, challengers veil their challenges behind "people who support our campaign." Atypically, the McCarthy camp did little to veil the challenge.

Kitty Kurth, Kevin Lampe's wife and business partner, served as McCarthy's chief campaign voice. She and Lampe are veterans of numerous political campaigns, including the presidential efforts of former Massachusetts Governor Michael Dukakis and the late Senator Paul Tsongas.

"To be clear," Kurth remembers, "the decision to challenge her petitions was not a unanimous decision within the campaign. There were people who thought it was a good idea and there were people who thought it was a bad idea. Politics is a little bit of math, a little bit of science and a little bit of art.

"There were people who believed that the math would be better in a one-on-one race" pitting McCarthy against Jesse White. "Also, there's a certain amount of fairness at stake. Once we took a look at the petitions and saw how crappy they were, our people who had spent so much time gathering petitions and organizing field operations were maybe a little miffed. They were upset that somebody was trying to get around the process and not follow the rules."

Kurth, who subscribes to the same petition philosophy embraced by political veterans like Lebed and Benigno, believes Severns's campaign got sloppy.

"The rules are not that complicated. They're not that difficult. They are there to level the playing field for all candidates. (Severns's petitions) were the worst and the lightest in number of any statewide petitions I've ever looked at."

Another McCarthy veteran campaign aide was Timothy S. McAnarney of Springfield. McAnarney, whose campaign experience dates to the early 1970s and whose client list includes the names of such prominent Democrats as former U.S. Senator Alan J. Dixon, former Attorney General Neil F. Hartigan, Congressman Jerry Costello and Aurelia Pucinski (who later switched party allegiance), said there was never a doubt that Severns's signatures should have been challenged. He remembers the postprimary debacle of 1986, when Democrats found themselves saddled with two statewide candidates who embraced the teachings of fringe politico Lyndon LaRouche.

In that primary, Mark Fairchild upended state Senator George Sangmeister, the slated candidate for lieutenant governor, and Janice Hart upset Pucinski, who'd been tabbed as the party's candidate for secretary of state. The result instantaneously erased Democrat Adlai Stevenson's chances to win his rematch against Republican incumbent Governor James R. Thompson.

"Democrats realized after the LaRouchie debacle that a challenge of petitions is not an underhanded, dirty thing," explains McAnarney. "It's standard operating procedure. I think that Democrats realize that if you're going to be a stand-up statewide candidate, you've got to have good petitions. We worked very hard to get good petitions. We worked our rear ends off to get good petitions. It's tough getting good petitions, but it's part of the process and it's a legitimate part of the process to challenge them."

Terry Mutchler, who was closer to Penny Severns than any other campaign or legislative aide, recalls Severns's anger at the McCarthy challenge.

"First, I think she was hurt," Mutchler says. "For someone who had given her entire life to politics in Illinois, for that challenge to occur, I think that hurt her feelings. I guess it was hurt and disbelief initially. I also think it angered her.

"She felt that Illinois voters should have the opportunity to make a decision like that. She felt the voters were smart enough to decide whether or not she should have been on the ballot.

"I remember Penny saying many times, 'McCarthy was not afraid to take the bullet, so why should he be afraid of the ballot?' She used that quote time and again."

In his Christmas day column, political writer Schoenburg concluded:

For his part, McCarthy issued a statement saying he supports the rights of voters to object to a candidate's petitions.

"It is the responsibility of all candidates to submit petitions which are right and proper," McCarthy said.

With all this back and forth, it's almost hard to remember that Severns has also showed great courage fighting cancer and McCarthy was the Secret Service agent who was shot by one of the bullets intended for then-President Ronald Reagan in a 1981 assassination attempt.

Jesse White, a former state lawmaker who has made his mark in part by years of leading a tumbling team of inner-city youth, is probably not doing somersaults about all of this. Conventional wisdom would say that White's chances in the primary are better if two challengers steal votes from each other instead of him.

Indeed, for the White campaign, the Christmas of 1997 was a silent night.

If **you want**

a friend,

get a dog.

— Carl Icahn

Chapter Twenty-Nine Politics is a game of addition, not subtraction or division. You can forge working relationships and alliances, but alliances change with the seasons. Politics played by survivors is a game played for survival. Sometimes you'll take a swing for an ally, but often the blow is intended to help your own cause as well as that of your ally. Jesse White played to the college level in basketball and to the Triple A level in professional baseball. In politics he plays in the major leagues, where you survive with friends and without, but mostly you survive.

Penny Severns was a friend. Penny Severns, in this particular instance, was an opponent. But Penny Severns and Jesse White were never adversaries.

"Penny and I went back to when she was first elected to the senate," White remembers. "There was a time when both of us were having problems with our knees and I had told her that she needed to have that knee 'scoped or it would just get worse. Neither of us wanted to run against the other one. In fact, the last time we talked, which was while she was still on the ballot, she said, 'Jesse, if it can't be me, then I hope it's you.' And I told her the same thing: 'Penny, if I don't win, I hope it's you who wins.'"

Linda Hawker, a friend and adviser to Severns and who has served as secretary of the Illinois Senate, says Severns often said the same about White. "She used to say that if it wasn't her, she hoped that Jesse would win," Hawker says.

Severns confidante Terry Mutchler confirms White's assertion that the two were friendly ballot opponents.

"I know this for certain," Mutchler recalls, "Penny's feeling was that if she didn't win, she wanted Jesse to win."

At the same time, White was not so chivalrous that he would throw down his cape for Severns to bridge the mud puddle. He was astute enough that he knew he'd incur the wrath of a significant slice of the Democratic electorate if he dared challenge Severns's nominating petitions. Furthermore, Jesse White knew Penny Severns well enough to understand that she faced a daunting battle against a relentless disease.

The White camp maintained public silence a full seventeen days after McCarthy filed his objection with the State Board of Elections. There was really no urgency to assist either opponent. McCarthy filed his objection just three days before Christmas and the holidays do not provide optimum opportunity to political candidates. The Christmas-to-New Year holiday offers a final respite before an all-out ten-week sprint to primary election day.

But by January 9, 1998, Jesse White was ready to enter the petition challenge mix. For two and a half weeks the media covered the petition story and, invariably, the newspaper coverage and television footage focused on just two of the three candidates in the race for secretary of state. If Jesse White wasn't being left at the station, he didn't yet seem to be aboard the train, either.

In a news release dated January 9, 1998, Jesse White took sides:

Jesse White: Severns Should Stay on the Ballot

Jesse White, Democratic candidate for Illinois secretary of state, said today he supports efforts to certify fellow Democrat Penny Severns's candidacy for secretary of state.

White said Severns, of Decatur, has a "constitutional right" to seek statewide office and should be allowed to have her candidacy considered by voters in the March 17 Democratic primary.

"From all indications, Penny Severns has fulfilled the spirit of the law in filing the requisite number of signatures to have her name placed on the Democratic primary ballot," White said.

"I believe in giving the voters the ultimate decision of who should be considered for office in Illinois."

White said he has offered his own campaign resources to Severns to sup-

port her efforts to be certified by the State Board of Elections.

The news release caught the attention of Dennis Conrad, Springfield bureau chief for the Associated Press. In Conrad's story, McCarthy spokeswoman Kitty Kurth said White's motives were based in a belief that Severns's presence on the March 17 primary ballot would improve White's chances. Kurth's assertion was that a three-way campaign between two white candidates and one African American tipped the balance in White's favor.

In part, Conrad's story read:

White denied any ulterior motive in defending Severns.

"She's a friend of mine. I served with her in the General Assembly," White said. "Her health is not well. She's a woman of character and she's done much for the state of Illinois. It'd be a shame if the only woman in this race would not be successful in getting on the ballot."

Severns called White a "dear friend and man of integrity."

The enemy of my enemy is my friend. An ad hoc tag team was formed. For the next month, White would publicly back Severns's struggle to stay on the ballot. But in his comment to AP reporter Conrad, White hinted at a larger problem that loomed over the McCarthy campaign: *Her health is not well.*

Indeed, Penny Severns was critically ill. She and her campaign were fighting to keep secret her declining health. But those who had known her before the campaign for secretary of state sensed that the cancer was slowly stealing her life.

In fact, Severns had entered the hospital in November, just two weeks before she filed her petitions of candidacy. In the midst of the most critical first stage of any political campaign, the phase during which the *T*s need to be crossed and the *I*s should be dotted, when names on petitions must be written and not printed, when the people circulating those petitions must be loyal and true, Penny Severns got sick. She got very, very sick.

Mutchler remembers:

"We were going to spend Thanksgiving at my sister's house in Indiana. But Penny got sick. That's when they found the tumor on her skull. It's clear now, as I look back, that the cancer had metastasized."

It was after she'd returned home from the hospital that Severns called a campaign aide in Springfield to ask why all of the petitions had not been bound and prepared for filing.

"I know there were a lot of petitions left over," Mutchler says. "I don't remember exactly where they were, but I recall they were somewhere outside of Springfield. I believe at the time we had 12,000 signatures."

Attorney John R. Keith, too, remembers there was a surplus.

"It was related to me that she had been sitting on several thousand signatures, but that staff told her not to worry about it. She was concerned about getting those petitions filed in Springfield, but she was told they had plenty already and that there would be no problem."

But it was too late. Penny Severns couldn't roll back the clock and the clock was running. Time was running out.

Above Jesse White's parents, Julia Mae and Jesse C. White Sr., both felt the sting of the South's Jim Crow era.

SLIDES IN VAIN FOR SCHURZ

Earl Gorden of Schurz is out at third when Jesse White of Waller tags him on force play from Pitcher Vince Giuffre. Schurz won City league game in Kilbourne park, 7 to 3. (TRIBUNE Photo)

(Story on page 2)

Left This *Chicago Tribune* photo captures Jesse White in one of his rare appearances as an infielder, this time for Waller High School.

Left Although virtually all of his college statistics have vanished, Jesse White was widely recognized as a basketball and baseball star at Alabama State College. His athletic prowess earned him induction into the Southwestern Athletic Conference Hall of Fame.

Right As a center fielder for the Salt Lake City Bees, Jesse White played alongside Glenn Beckert, who later starred for the Chicago Cubs. Beckert today wonders if the 1969 Cubs might have won a pennant with White in centerfield.

Left As a 101st Airborne paratrooper, Jesse White completed 35 jumps during his Army career.

Chiefs
AL WINTERS STUDIO
Lewis Bishop, Bill Miller, Jerry Palma, Bobby Adams, Dick Burwell, Jesse White
Morhardt, Calvin Koonce, Walter Bales, Spencer Scott, Ken Hubbs, Pete Desilvia, Mel
Jim Hansen, Wayne Carlander, Phil Borders, Tony Balsamo, Stewart Bowers, Art

Above At Class B Wenatchee, White played with Kenny Hubbs, who was killed in an airplane crash just two years after he was brought up to the Cubs. White is shown in the first row, far right. Hubbs is in the second row, fifth from left.

Above Today, Jesse White's tumblers receive a stipend for their performances. In the early days, however, the team survived on whatever White could afford from his teacher's salary and money he earned as a Chicago Park District physical instructor. This is an early photo of the team, founded in 1959.

Above Although he's now a septuagenarian, Jesse White takes pride in maintaining good physical health. During tumbling team performances he is likely to do headstands as tumblers vault between his legs.

Right Founded on a shoestring, today's Jesse White Tumblers receive a stipend for their performances. This was one of his performing troupes in 2004.

Left Former reporter Charles N. Wheeler III says, "One of the hallmarks of Jesse as a legislative committee chairman is that he was very considerate, very respectful of the average citizen." Here White presides over a House Human Services Committee hearing in Springfield.

Right An avid fisherman, White has often used angling as a way to teach life lessons to kids. And sometimes he just fishes for the fun of it.

Above Surrounded by loved ones, Jesse White for the second time takes the oath of office as Illinois' first African American secretary of state.

Right As secretary of state, Jesse White has championed the cause of organ donation and transplantation. His popularity transcends the baseball politics of Chicago, too. Here, former Cubs farmhand White stands with (from left) former White Sox pitcher Bob Howry, Sox broadcaster Ed Farmer and 2005 World Series hero Paul Konerko. Farmer, a former big league hurler, several years ago received a life-saving kidney transplant from his brother.

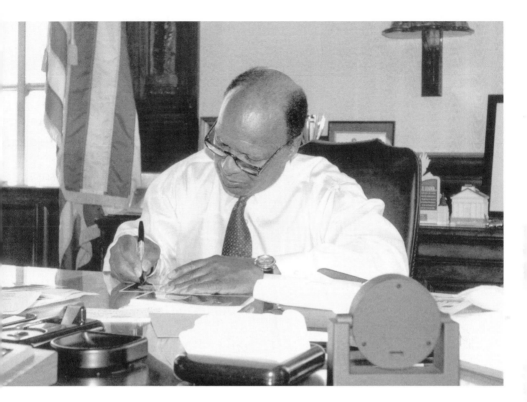

bove At his desk in the state capitol in Springfield, Jesse White carries out his duties as
:cretary of state.

ight Longtime friend
ıd supporter Ed Kelly
ıew Jesse White was a
inner, he just wasn't
ınvinced that winning
e 1998 Democratic
imary was a sure thing.

Right Jesse White is unabashed in his admiration for former Cook County Board President George Dunne, the man he calls "godfather."

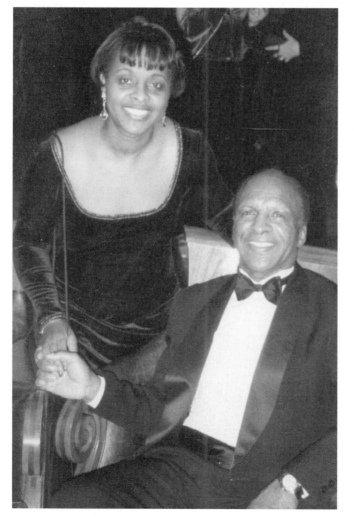

Left At a formal event with daughter, Glenna White Jones, who says, "There are times when I have to pull him aside and say, 'Hey, it's time for you to relax. Take off your shoes, put your feet up and watch the basketball game. Just enjoy some time together with your family.'"

If McCarthy was going to beat Jesse White, he was going to have to beat him downstate, and anything that Penny Severns got would have been votes taken away from him

— Paul Green,
professor of political science,
Roosevelt University

Chapter Thirty There's an old axiom in baseball that says pitching and defense win ballgames.

In ice hockey, even if a goaltender is perfect, the best his team can do is muster a tie unless his teammates find a way to dent the opposing net.

The 1985 Super Bowl Champion Chicago Bears may have had the best pure defense in the history of the National Football League, but without a little help from Walter Payton, Jim McMahon and Willie Gault, the championship trophy would rest in Boston.

In sports, playing defense rarely puts points on the board. The same goes for politics. If your opponent lands a powerful right to your jaw and you can't counter with a right cross of your own, you'll eventually suffer a knockout or lose on a decision. After the McCarthy campaign began firing its offensive volleys at the Severns campaign, the game would be over unless Severns fired back. Successful political campaigns are the ones that respond to attacks with counterattacks. Rapid response is critical when the opponent is on the attack. If you don't knock your opponent back on his heels, rarely do you win. Political defense doesn't score points.

On January 14, 1998, Severns made an attempt to do just that. In an impressive display of fraternity, the Illinois Senate Democratic Caucus, led by its leader Senator Emil Jones Jr., formally asked McCarthy to withdraw his challenge to Severns's petitions. In a letter signed by Jones and twenty-four Senate Democratic colleagues, McCarthy was urged to drop his complaint "in the interest of party unity." Jones's letter sought to capitalize on questions that McCarthy was not, in fact, a Democrat and that his use of a Republican attorney would turn off traditional Democratic voters. In part, the senate Democrats' letter read:

Your attorney, who is on retainer with Republican Senate President Pate Philip, has a long track record of working against Senate Democrats and has used many of the same tactics and characterizations now being employed against Penny Severns in previous maneuvers against Senate Democrats.

In November it is imperative that the Democratic Party present to voters its strongest candidate for the Office of Secretary of State ... You can assist our party in this endeavor by allowing this strong field of candidates to go forward.

Indeed, McCarthy was the only one of the three Democratic candidates for secretary of state who had never been tested at the ballot box. Jesse White had won eight elections to the Illinois House of Representatives and twice had been elected as the Cook County recorder of deeds. Penny Severns in 1972 had been the youngest person ever elected as a delegate to a Democratic National Convention and had established a track record as a tenaciously partisan legislator and party official.

But the Orland Park police chief had no such party credentials. In fact, there had been chatter in 1997 that McCarthy would run for statewide office in Illinois, but that he would do so under the Republican Party banner.

Tim McAnarney, McCarthy's director of downstate operations in the 1998 primary, said any notion that McCarthy was not a Democratic was unfounded.

"Tim was independent, certainly not part of the Chicago Democratic machine," McAnarney recalls. "He was a Democrat, but we were selling him as someone who was different, as opposed to Jesse, who was a Cook County machine candidate.

"The Republicans came to McCarthy and asked him to run on the Republican ticket. In fact, Mrs. (Ronald) Reagan called him and asked Tim if he would run as a Republican for secretary of state, treasurer. They basically offered him anything he wanted. Her quote to him was, 'Tim, when did you leave our team?'

"And Tim said, 'Mrs. Reagan, I respect you, I respect your husband, but I was never on your team. My father was a Chicago police officer. I was born and raised a Democrat. I was never a Republican. I liked your husband, but my job was to protect the presidency. So I'm a Democrat. Thank you, but I'll be running as a Democrat.' She was very surprised."

The Severns camp was making a game effort to knock McCarthy back on his heels. Only a day earlier, McCarthy attorney Burt Odelson, who Senator Jones had characterized as a GOP operative, had issued a scathing statement alleging that Severns's supporters were guilty of fraudulently submitting flawed petitions. In a terse, sixty-nine-word news release, the McCarthy campaign said:

Burt Odelson, the attorney handling the Penny Severns' petition challenge, has called for an investigation by the U.S. Attorney into petition fraud concerning Severns' petitions. Quotes Odelson, "I have been practicing election law for more than 20 years and in all my investigations, I have never come across such blatant fraud. All pertinent documents have been delivered to the proper authorities and I expect that appropriate action will be taken."

Most political campaigns begin with pledges of cleanliness and a publicly stated hope that the candidates will focus on the issues of the office sought. Most political campaigns end with candidates lobbing grenades, firebombs and spitballs at each other as the issues dribble into the gutter.

The 1998 Democratic primary campaign for secretary of state was following such a traditional blueprint. But as the frigid days of January disappeared from the calendar, the campaign wasn't just getting dirty, it was becoming bizarre.

On or about the same day Severns's senate colleagues were asking McCarthy to drop his petition challenge in a spirit of party unity, someone allegedly was knocking on the front door of Julia Phillips. Mrs. Phillips, who lived in Chicago, was the mother of Dick Mell, the powerful alderman of Chicago's 33rd Ward. In later years, Mell would earn the reputation for putting a son-in-law in the Governor's Mansion in Springfield. But in the winter of 1998, he was just a Chicago powerbroker who happened to have spearheaded a good chunk of Penny Severns's petition effort.

In a column dated January 22, 1998, *Springfield State Journal-Register* reporter Bernard Schoenburg summarized the latest twist in the campaign for secretary of state:

McCarthy, Severns Camps Exchange Nasty Blows

The pre-primary battle between state Senator Penny Severns, D-Decatur, and Orland Park Police Chief Tim McCarthy is taking weird and ugly turns.

McCarthy, Severns and Cook County Recorder of Deeds Jesse White all want to be the Democratic nominee for secretary of state.

McCarthy has said fraud is rampant on the petitions circulated to get Severns on the March 17 primary ballot. Severns has said McCarthy showed "true cowardice" in his petition challenge to remove her from the ballot.

Enter Chicago Alderman Dick Mell's mother.

In addition to being a powerful alderman, Mell is Democratic committeeman in Chicago's 33rd Ward and the father-in-law of U.S. Representative Rod Blagojevich, D-Chicago. Mell also is a "100 percent" Severns supporter.

Mell said Wednesday that two men apparently working on behalf of McCarthy paid a visit to Julia Phillips, Mell's mom.

"They came and pounded on her door at like 11 o'clock at night," Mell said in a telephone interview. He said the incident, which he thinks happened January 14, involved "Gestapo-like tactics."

The men wanted to know if Phillips had signed a Severns petition, Mell said. Phillips said she had and signed an affidavit to that effect.

"They went up and down the whole block, pounding (and) saying 'Open up, police,'" Mell said.

"One of our younger women on the street went and kicked their ass off the block," Mell added.

Oh, and the license plate on their van showed it belonged to Burt Odelson, the Evergreen Park lawyer handling McCarthy's challenge, Mell said.

As Alice said while gazing down the rabbit hole, things are getting curiouser and curiouser. Maybe being an afterthought in a three-way catfight wasn't so bad after all. Maybe Jesse White's seat in the bleachers was a safe place to be in this game, depending on who was in the batter's box.

Schoenburg's column continued:

Odelson said his office van has been used by one of his firm's paralegals, who is working with people checking signatures. But he said they have "specific dictates" not to go to homes after 9 p.m.

Almost before the ink was dry on Schoenburg's piece, a Chicago city worker publicly complained he was threatened with the loss of his job if he didn't sign a statement saying that the petitions he circulated were flawed.

In stories published January 24 in both the *Chicago Sun-Times* and the *Chicago Tribune,* Chicago city worker Mark Lengyel said he was pressured into signing a statement that he was not present when the Severns petitions he circulated were notarized.

Under a *Sun-Times* headline that read, *Volunteer for Severns Complains of Intimidation,* Lengyel, identified in subsequent newspaper accounts as an operating engineer for the City of Chicago, said he was threatened with his job:

Lengyel said the incident took place January 11 at his workplace at 5801 N. Pulaski, read the story in the January 24 editions of the Sun-Times. *"These guys said, 'You better sign this or you'll be subpoenaed and might lose your job.'" Lengyel said. "I told them that wouldn't be right, but I got scared for my livelihood."*

Lengyel said he was able to remember the Illinois license plate of the car the men were driving. According to state records, the plate belongs to a black 1993 Chevrolet Caprice registered to the Chicago Police Department.

The White campaign saw an opportunity to run to daylight in this latest controversy and sprinted through the hole. Without conferring with the Severns camp, White's campaign issued a news release calling for McCarthy to withdraw from the secretary of state's race.

In part, the release read:

Jesse White, Democratic candidate for Illinois secretary of state, today called for opponent Tim McCarthy to withdraw his candidacy for secretary of state.

Simultaneously, White requested a Justice Department investigation into allegations that two McCarthy supporters driving a Chicago Police Department vehicle earlier this week tried to intimidate supporters of another candidate for secretary of state.

In a letter to U.S. Attorney Scott Lassar, White called for a probe to determine if there have been any civil rights violations connected with rival Tim McCarthy's challenge of fellow Democrat Penny Severns' nominating petitions.

Did White actually think McCarthy would acquiesce and withdraw from the race? Of course not. But McCarthy had been fighting this fight on the balls of his feet and he might have been scoring points. It was time to knock the Orland Park police chief back on his heels.

Independently and without conferring with White's supporters, Severns's spokeswoman Terry Mutchler issued a statement that was picked up in an Associated Press account published January 25 by the *Springfield State Journal-Register* under the headline, *McCarthy Urged to Quit Race After Claims of Coercion:*

(Severns) Spokeswoman Terry Mutchler says the Severns campaign has evidence to prove who was behind the incident and has filed a complaint with the Illinois State Board of Elections asking for an investigation.

The AP story also quoted White, who called the incident a "shameful display of thuggery and intimidation. For a political campaign to reach such depths of harassment is disgraceful and represents a violation of all shreds of human decency."

McCarthy was clearly being double-teamed, but from where he stood he needed to cast doubt on Jesse White's gallantry toward their common opponent. Until then, McCarthy had been engaged in a one-front assault. The White campaign's decision to attack the Orland Park police chief forced McCarthy to pay attention to the statements being issued by the coach and founder of the Jesse White Tumbling Team.

"McCarthy is the only candidate talking about the issues people care about," said McCarthy spokeswoman Kitty Kurth to the Associated Press. "If (White) wants McCarthy to drop out of the race, he should call McCarthy and ask him instead of using the media as his messenger."

But White kept up the pressure. When asked for evidence that McCarthy's campaign may have been behind the Lengyel incident, a White campaign spokesman replied:

"Who challenged the petitions? Who has reasons to have her off the ballot? Tim McCarthy does, not Jesse White. We were against the petition challenge from the beginning."

As the petition fight percolated into the mainstream media, the Severns and White camps were privately discussing a strategy to take with them into negotiations about the three-way Democratic candidate debate. Scheduled for March 11 in Chicago, the debate was to feature McCarthy, White and Severns in a thirty-minute forum to be videotaped at the WLS-TV studios, 190 N. State Street.

Of the three, Severns was the most polished public speaker. Of the three, McCarthy was clearly the most physically imposing. The White debate negotiators understood what Vice President Richard M. Nixon learned thirty-eight years earlier when Penny Severns was watching his debate against Senator John F. Kennedy: It's not necessarily what you say, it's how you look when you say it. White's people called Severns's people. It was time to do some talking.

In a call to Severns's debate representative, former senate staffer Linda Kingman, a White campaign aide floated a suggestion: the candidates should sit behind a table and resist any suggestions that they stand. After all, Kingman's candidate was suffering from health problems and White didn't need for McCarthy to tower over him. There should be no notes. Severns was an accomplished public speaker and, if nothing else, White had taught elementary school for thirty-three years and was accustomed to performing with a group of gymnasts. McCarthy, meanwhile, may have saved Ronald Reagan's life, but he didn't win any awards for elocution in talking about it afterward.

In his last conversation with Senator Severns a few days before the January 23 debate meeting at WLS-TV studios, a White campaign aide explained the strategy to the Decatur lawmaker. Severns and the White staffer were friends from their days as fellow employees in the Illinois Comptroller's Office. The White staffer was on a cell phone to Severns at her home.

"Penny, there's no reason to give this guy any advantage," the campaign official told her over the phone. "McCarthy's a big guy, and you and Jesse don't need to look small next to him. So we suggest that the three of you sit. You've been through this thing a dozen times before and so has Jesse, so we don't think you two need any notes.

"You're going to have to trust me on this one, Senator. This format will work for both of us."

"I understand," Severns replied. "Make sure Linda Kingman knows."

The enemy of my enemy is my friend.

Battle lines often blur in the heat of a party primary. After all, a political primary is no different from a fight among family members. After the family has aired its differences, there's the hope that the bleeding stops and that uncles and aunts, nephews, cousins, brothers and sisters can patch their differences and regroup in the shade of the family tree.

And like a quarrel within a family, this fight featured subterranean combatants who knew each other from previous campaigns. Just as Jesse White and Penny Severns were buddies before they decided to chase the same brass ring, so, too, were many of the staff, consultants and advisers known to one another and, in some cases, brothers and sisters in previous campaigns.

The White-Severns friendship was legitimate. For Jesse White, to be elected as the secretary of state of Illinois would be the crown jewel in a career of public service. For Penny Severns, a term or two as secretary of state could provide that penultimate rung on the ladder to the governor's office. Timing is everything in politics, and both White and Severns figured the time was right. Two-term incumbent George H. Ryan was running for governor after eight years as secretary of state and, for the first time since 1982, there would be no Republican statewide officeholder making a charge at the office.

The Republicans had a family spat of their own brewing, with former state Representative Al Salvi and Representative Robert Churchill throwing pots and pans at each other next door. For the first time since Alan J. Dixon resigned from the office in 1981 following his election to the United States Senate, the Democrats had an excellent chance to wrest back the office of nearly 4,000 employees – second in jobs only to the governor.

At 64, this was probably Jesse White's only real shot at secretary of state. His window of opportunity was too small for all but the most diminutive of cat burglars. Both Ryan and Jim Edgar before him were reelected to the office. There was reason to believe the winner of the 1998 sweepstakes would seek reelection, meaning that 2006 would provide the next possible open-office election for secretary of state. At that point Jesse

White would be 72. This was 1998. This was it, his only chance to ascend to the office.

At 46, Severns was in the prime of her political life as she pondered her second statewide run. But she was reading the same tea leaves that White was. If she could win two terms as secretary, she would be 54 and a candidate for governor in 2006. She'd already made history in 1994 when she and Dawn Clark Netsch won their respective primary races for lieutenant governor and governor. It marked the first time in American history that women won a major party nomination and ran as a team for governor and lieutenant governor.

John R. Keith, Severns's attorney, believes White and Severns battled inner conflicts as they forced themselves to run against one another.

"I think it was a true friendship they had for one another," Keith says. "The perception I had is that each of them felt this was a once-in-a-lifetime opportunity to be secretary of state and that running for another office was not what he or she wanted at the time."

Keith uses a baseball analogy to score his point.

"Let's look at it this way: Wally Pipp didn't play one day. If Lou Gehrig hadn't stepped in that day, who knows what career, if any, he would have had? Politicians perceive in their own minds when the time is right for them to run or not." They made a movie about Gehrig, named a disease after him and tagged Pipp with an asterisk for being the guy who gave way to the pride of the Yankees.

"In her case, she's 45 (when she made the decision to run). If she doesn't run, she has to look a couple years down the road and wonder what might happen to her senate district in reapportionment. In fact, Decatur's now represented by a Republican. Did she think that might happen, that there might be a shift in demographics and everything that would jeopardize her senate seat?

"A lot of people criticized Alan Dixon for running for the U.S. Senate when he did." In fact, Dixon was the last Democrat in the secretary of state's office and he surrendered the office when he won the U.S. Senate seat in 1980. "But that was the time to run. That's what I mean by a once-in-a-lifetime chance."

Caught in the cross fire of a friendship between White, the former state representative, and Severns, the incumbent state senator, was a career law enforcement officer who thought his dossier was perfect for the office of secretary of state.

Now, probably more than a few McCarthy backers had higher office stars in their eyes. But campaign spokeswoman Kurth believes McCarthy had no designs on governor or United States senator. At least not in 1998.

"There may have been other people in the campaign who saw him as a candidate for governor or whatever, but it's not something that Tim ever wanted," Kurth insists. "Tim liked secretary of state because he saw it as a natural extension of his law enforcement and his law enforcement management background.

"At other points of his career he looked at the Cook County sheriff's race for the same reason. He knows what he knows how to do. The idea of him running for governor might have been in somebody's mind, but I don't think it was necessarily in the forefront of his mind."

McAnarney, the Springfield native who spearheaded the downstate effort, said McCarthy was a diamond in the rough.

"He'd never run before," says McAnarney. "Didn't know anything about campaigning. That's a huge jump, never running for office to running for one of the most powerful offices in the state. But he was a very quick study. He took to the campaign well. And don't forget, he already had a reputation as a person of substance. He did have a record as a Secret Service agent."

Again and again, "that record" of Tim McCarthy's Secret Service experience was the one political issue that gnawed at Jesse White. After almost forty years of pulling ghetto kids out of the projects, after eight terms as a member of the Illinois General Assembly, after two successful campaigns for Cook County recorder of deeds, "that record," that day when Tim McCarthy stopped a bullet intended for Ronald Reagan, "that record" really bothered Jesse White.

It was Tim McCarthy's serendipitous appointment with a .38 caliber slug that threw Jesse White off the track. Normally soft-spoken, Jesse White's demeanor often is misinterpreted as lacking the killer instincts of a successful politician.

In fact, Jesse White may well be the nicest man ever elected to public office. But mention Tim McCarthy to him in January of 1998, suggest that McCarthy saved a nation from a state funeral and a potentially chaotic transition of power in the most powerful nation on the planet, well, nice guys can get pissed off, too.

"That's exactly right," White admits today. "Sometimes people mistake kindness and gentleness for weakness. I could not have won that election if I had been a weak person. I'm the kind of guy who is a quiet storm. You can push me, but once you push me to the boiling point, then you have to watch out. Nothing will stop me.

"I had spent time saving lives, too. Consider that right now, we've had 10,000 kids come through my program in forty-six years and no one ever referred to me as a hero. Yet, here's a guy who's paid to do a job and he's considered a hero. I got a little carried away in that campaign and I said that. Truthfully, I probably should not have said that. So I may have struck out in an improper manner at that time. Probably, if I had to do it over again, I would take another tack.

"But that's not to say that I wouldn't fight as hard as I fought."

In fact, ask Jesse White today what the tipping point was, what it was that made him pull the trigger and decide once and for all to run for secretary of state.

And he'll tell you. He'll tell you that he went to several of his friends in the Democratic Party, some of the most powerful people in Illinois politics. And he'll tell you that he asked his friends for their blessings, for a wink, a nod a handshake – an endorsement – so that he could run for secretary of state knowing he had his friends' support.

"Why did I decide to run?" White repeats the question.

"Let me tell you why. I was told that I couldn't have it. I was told that I shouldn't run. Don't waste your time, don't waste anyone else's time. Don't spend your money, don't spend anyone else's money. They told me that Tim McCarthy was going to be the next secretary of state."

And what did Jesse White say?

"I said, 'Have a good day. I'll see you on the campaign trail.'"

If you can't stand the heat, get out of the kitchen

— Harry S Truman

Chapter Thirty-One Serious candidates for public office run because they believe they are the best-qualified people for office. To be sure, there are more than a fair share of Lar Dalys and Lyndon LaRouches who muster enough support to get their names printed on ballots all across the republic. But they populate the margins. If they make any impact at all – and rarely they do – it's as a spoiler in a razor-thin finish. They might deny victory, but seldom do they partake in its feast.

It is the serious candidates who take their candidacies seriously. More often than not, the solemnity of a campaign is the root cause for the nastiness that bubbles to the forefront in the closing weeks of a political fight. If you have no ego, no self-esteem, find another calling. Politics requires at least enough ego to place your name on the firing line for anyone with an opinion, a camera or a word processor.

Mix together a cup of serious determination and a spoonful of ego, add a dash of spicy rhetoric, and the result is a tasty political news story.

Make no mistake, all three Democratic candidates for Illinois secretary of state in 1998 were dead-on earnest about their efforts and their dreams of holding the office.

For Jesse White, that determination may well have caused him to say publicly what he had only harbored privately until the first week of February. In an interview with the *St. Louis Post-Dispatch,* White suggested that opponent Tim McCarthy was little more than an escort when he was gunned down by John W. Hinckley Jr. in front of the Washington Hilton. White, a member of Cook County's Democratic organization for four decades, saw McCarthy as an outsider whose time was still in the distant future. At least Severns was battle tested. In White's mind, McCarthy was a guy who peeked through the fence while everyone else planted the seeds, harvested the wheat, kneaded the dough and baked the bread. And now that the air was filled with a mouth-watering aroma, McCarthy was pulling up a seat and tying a napkin around his neck.

In the interview with the *Post-Dispatch,* Jesse White allowed his emotion and tongue to get the best of him. He said McCarthy was simply doing the job for which he was paid during the Reagan assassination attempt. Nothing less, nothing more. To Jesse White, a store clerk who saves a baby from a fire is a hero. A fire fighter who saves a baby from a fire may have been brave to do so, but that's what he gets paid to do.

In a letter published February 6 in the *Chicago Sun-Times,* which had picked up the story out of St. Louis, White attempted to calm the political tempest created by his own hand:

In a story published recently in the St. Louis Post-Dispatch, *I was paraphrased as saying that one of my opponents, Tim McCarthy, was merely a bystander in his role as one of President Ronald Reagan's bodyguards the day Reagan and McCarthy were wounded in 1981. I did not say that McCarthy was a "bystander," and the reporter who wrote the story has verified that I did not say he was a bystander.*

But more important, the heat of a campaign has caused this issue to spin out of control and to become a focus of the Sun-Times …

If I left any impression that I do not appreciate and admire the work of the Secret Service, or any other law enforcement agency in America, then I offer my sincere apologies. Any person who dedicates his life to protecting the lives of our citizens is a hero.

That, too, has been my life's philosophy.

Jesse White, Democratic Candidate for Secretary of State

"I may have struck out in an improper manner," White says seven years later. "As part of my campaign strategies over the years, I've never been negative. I have so much I can talk about that's positive and about what I'd like to do that I don't have to try to go after someone else. Every one of us, at one time or another, has to go back into our own community and we want to go there with our head held high.

"As I look back on that campaign, I can see that I was awfully uncomfortable because I really didn't like that I had to fight in a Democratic primary. I felt a lot more comfortable in the fall, running against Salvi, then I ever did running against McCarthy because we had the 'family' divided.

"But sometimes that's the way campaigns get. You become so focused on what you're trying to achieve that sometimes emotions get the best of you. I was determined to win that office.

"I don't think I even knew what the salary for that office was until the week before the election, and the only way I found out was that someone brought it up at the debate. I wanted to win that office even if it paid only $10,000 a year. I was that driven."

Even heroes can let their hearts get in the way of what their minds know they should be doing. In Jesse White's case, the Tim McCarthy-as-Bystander story could have been devastating. Given the opportunity, the McCarthy campaign could have continued to pound White as being soft in supporting law enforcement officers. But the Bystander Story didn't have legs. Ironically, it was an act of the McCarthy camp that inadvertently cut the legs right out from under the Bystander Story. Three days after the *Chicago Sun-Times* published Jesse White's letter under the headline, *White Clarifies Remark on McCarthy as a Hero,* the entire definition of hero would come to the table for dissection.

On February 9, Carl R. Draper would sign his name into a footnote in Illinois political history. Draper, the hearing officer appointed by the Illinois State Board of Elections, had been working feverishly to complete his report and recommendation to the board. With the March 17 primary just thirty-six days away, it was critical that the board determine – one way or another – if Penny Severns's name should appear on the Democratic primary ballot. There was no luxury of time and deliberation. Hundreds of thousands of ballots had to be printed and certified by election officials in each of the state's 102 counties.

Between 3:27 p.m. on December 22, when an elections clerk time-stamped the complaint signed by Imogene Bosak and Patricia M. O'Sullivan, and February 9, attorneys for both sides scrambled to accentuate their respective versions of truth.

Hearing officers presided over 1,300 pages of transcribed hearings. Another 1,000-plus pages of affidavits, records and other exhibits had been presented to the board for official review. Over the course of seven weeks, the two sides had exhausted every conceivable strategy in an effort to sustain their arguments. Forty-eight days after O'Sullivan and Bosak v. Severns became a petition challenge, the moment of consequence had arrived. It would be left to politicians and historians to argue whether the moment of consequence was a moment of truth.

In his report to the State Board of Elections, hearing officer Draper concluded, in part:

The ultimate issue in this cause is very simple. Does candidate Penny Severns have at least 5,000 valid signatures on her nominating petition? While the issue or factual question is simple, the sheer volume of information that had to be reviewed in order to conclude the analysis was extraordinary ...

Based on the results ... the hearing officer finds and recommends that the board conclude that candidate Penny Severns has a total of 4,824 valid signatures and 3,140 invalid signatures on her nominating petition (total 7,964) ...

The results contained in this decision are believed by the hearing officer to represent a fair and accurate determination of the issues. It is therefore the recommendation of the hearing officer that the objection to the nominating petition of candidate Penny Severns be sustained.

Dated this 9th day of February
Carl R. Draper, Hearing Officer

All that remained was an official adoption of the recommendation by the six members of the State Board of Elections. Unanimously the six – three Democrats and three Republicans – voted to uphold Draper's recommendation.

On February 11, Penny Severns's name was removed from the March 17 primary election ballot.

You know the nearer your destination, the more you're slip-slidin' away

— Paul Simon

Chapter Thirty-Two In retrospect, the decision by the Illinois State Board of Elections marked the end of Penny Severns's political life. Within ten days of that decision, she reached the end of life itself.

Before the case could officially be laid to rest, Severns had to decide if she would appeal. But the day after the board of elections voted to disqualify her nominating petitions, Senator Severns began to experience difficulty breathing.

Terry Mutchler, her press secretary and confidante, remembers the circumstances surrounding the hospitalization:

"They took her to the hospital in a car, not an ambulance. I just thought it was going to be an overnight stay. The day she got admitted was a Thursday. I remember telling the press that she was watching *Seinfeld* when she started having difficulty breathing and *Seinfeld* was on Thursdays."

During Severns's stay at Memorial Medical Center in Springfield, attorney Keith stopped in to discuss the possibility of an appeal.

"We discussed the business (of the challenge) as a lawyer and a client," Keith says. "I provided her with my opinion and observations from a legal point of view."

Because of the privacy involved in his attorney-client relationship with Severns, Keith will not discuss the details of their discussion. He does admit, however, that the 3,140 signatures found invalid was "a lot."

"I had a feeling when I left the hospital that she was not going to go ahead" with an appeal. "She had not confirmed that to me. After that was done I asked her how she was doing. I told her, 'Hang in there. A lot of people love you and no matter what you do, you're a winner.'

"I told her good-bye and I had a feeling it was *good-bye.* I took her a rose, as a friend, and gave it to her. I kissed her on the forehead and I left."

Mutchler, who lived with Severns in their Decatur home, says she believes that neither she nor her friend knew that she was dying.

"First, I think it was personal denial," Mutchler says. "And then, I also think it was because both Penny and I had a very deep faith. She would often say, 'This is just a bump in the road.' Now, I knew it was more than just a bump in the road, but the truth is, the honest-to-God, go-to-the-grave truth is, that I didn't know that she was going to die. And yet somehow, somewhere, I must have. Somehow, somewhere, I think she knew.

"Part of me was relieved when she decided not to challenge (the state board of elections decision) to kick her off the ballot. But I truly did not know that she was going to die when she did. I thought we had forever. I thought we had a lot longer than we had."

Mutchler is more than just wistful at the recollection of her friend. Since that 1998 campaign, Mutchler has earned her law degree from John Marshall Law School in Chicago. Today, she is an assistant attorney general in the administration of one of Illinois' most promising young politicians, Lisa Madigan. Still, seven years after Penny Severns' death, sadness seeps through Terry Mutchler's eyes.

"Can you know? Can anybody know? I don't think people die without knowing it somewhere, unless they're in a car accident or something unexpected like that. I think people have premonitions. I think somehow they know. I think somehow she knew."

On Wednesday, February 18, Severns called Mutchler and asked her to drive to Springfield and take her home to Decatur.

"She said, 'Hey, I'm getting out today and I want to wait for you to come and get me.' She loved that car of hers. It was a Volvo and she had handpicked this thing. I picked Penny up and we went home.

"I remember her saying to me then, 'Isn't this going to be great? We're past this stuff, I'll be feeling stronger.' And I actually believed that in my heart."

After they arrived home, Mutchler and Severns spent the evening crafting the announcement that her campaign for secretary of state was over. The announcement would come in the form of an open letter, and they would release it the following day, Thursday, February 19.

"We worked on the statement all night."

Mutchler took the statement to the Blue Room, the news conference center in the press room of the Illinois state capitol. To the assembled journalists, their recorders and their cameras, Mutchler read the statement, printed on Severns's senate letterhead:

To my Constituents in the 51st District, colleagues and the many supporters around the state:

Friends, I believe that I have enough signatures to remain on the ballot for the March 17th Democratic Primary. I believe that I am in a solid legal position to move forward with an appeal to the Circuit Court. I believe that I would be successful in pursuing a remedy through the court system and know that I and my supporters would be vindicated.

I believe with all my heart that I am right and that the challenge to my petitions was an underhanded effort to deny the voters of Illinois a choice to support me for the office of Secretary of State.

As a matter of principle, I would like to move forward in the legal system to remain on the ballot. As a matter of practicality, that is not something that I am able to do at this time. Even though I believe it was a wrong decision, I will not appeal the decision made last week by the State Board of Elections.

After conferring with my family, close friends and my doctor, I have made this difficult decision for two reasons: financially, it would be a tremendous burden to mount an appeal in addition to the already tens of thousands of dollars in legal bills. Medically, I am not in a position to pursue an appeal.

As you know, I have been battling breast cancer since 1994. With your love, support and prayers, I have been able to remain active. However, over the last few weeks my medical condition has worsened and I will not be able to undergo a third round of chemotherapy. Right now, I need to exert all the energy I have on getting healthy. For now, I will remain in my home and, for the near future, will not make any public appearances. I continue to remain in touch with my office on a daily basis by telephone, several times a day, as I have done even from the hospital. Know that I will continue to meet your needs and address your concerns.

Words cannot express the deep gratitude that I and my family have for the countless cards, letters, prayers and calls of support. Those acts of love have meant more to me than I could ever express and, quite honestly, they have helped keep my spirits very, very high.

While my faith is not something I wear on my sleeve, I have an unshakeable belief in a Living God who can restore me to full health. My family and I hang on to that promise. As St. Augustine once said, "Understanding is the reward of faith. Therefore, let us seek not to understand that we may believe, but believe that we may understand." Friends, believing is the most important part. I know that you stand with me and my family in that hope.

Thank you so much for your patience and kindness to my family and to myself. I have long said, quoting Yeats, "Think where one's glory most begins and ends, and say that my glory is that I have such friends."

I look forward to seeing you all very soon.

Your friend and Senator,
Penny Severns

That same day, the McCarthy campaign released an impressive list of endorsements under a news release headline that read:

Tim McCarthy Endorsed in His Bid for Secretary of State
By Dozens of Elected Officials from Across Illinois

The news release did not mention the fact the field of candidates had been narrowed from three to two.

In a rear-view mirror column published two weeks later, *Springfield State Journal-Register* columnist Bernard Schoenburg questioned the wisdom of McCarthy's announcement that day:

Just hours (after Mutchler's emotionally-charged announcement), McCarthy and a roomful of supporters had a news conference of their own in the same room at the state Capitol. They wished her well, but continued with the conference. McCarthy said people came from far and wide to attend the conference, so he couldn't cancel. He was wrong about that.

Thus, the fallout began to rain down on the McCarthy camp. In winning the battle to knock Penny Severns off the ballot, McCarthy was losing all hope of controlling the war of public relations and goodwill. Although neither the White nor the McCarthy campaigns had enough money to conduct scientific polling, political veterans could feel a pall settling over the campaign. Soon that pall would explode into a backlash.

In Chicago, Jesse White's campaign unveiled a key endorsement designed to pick up support among women following Severns's dismissal from the ticket. Although McCarthy's endorsements were plentiful and included such political notables as Chicago Congressman William Lipinski and House Speaker Michael J. Madigan, White's campaign took a decidedly different tack.

Politics is nothing if it's not about counting. The most successful politicians learn how to count at an early age. Use your fingers, use your toes, use an abacus, use whatever means necessary to come up with one more vote than the other candidate. Dawn Clark Netsch, Severns's erstwhile running mate, knows better than most the power of the female vote in Illinois. She watched it blossom in 1992 when Carol Moseley Braun upended incumbent U.S. Senator Alan J. Dixon in the wake of Dixon's support of Supreme Court nominee Clarence Thomas. Thomas was trashed throughout senate confirmation hearings on the strength of allegations by law professor Anita Hill that he had sexually harassed her.

"It was the dumbest thing McCarthy could have done," Netsch candidly volunteers. "I said it then and I remember saying, 'Cripes, why would you do that?'

"I think public opinion changed against Clarence Thomas because of a deep-seated feeling that many women believed they had been taken advantage of for a long time. During the time of the Clarence Thomas-Anita Hill thing, I was giving talks all around the state. And I can remember several instances downstate, and I'm talking about middle-aged women, not raging feminists.

"When I would refer to the Clarence Thomas affair, I could sense that there were many of them who had felt the sting of sexual harassment and that ran much deeper than people may have thought at the time.

"There's no way McCarthy was going to be helped by challenging her petitions. You look like a bully. You look like a mobster. Nobody ever knows why elections are won or lost, but I assume that played a major role in his defeat, don't you think? I think it was absolutely stupid. I can't imagine anything that would be more designed to arouse the wrath and energy of a lot of people, particularly women.

"It looks like the same old system where the boys can't stand to be upstaged by a female."

The Jesse White campaign sensed there was a substantial female backlash bubbling beneath the surface of the Democratic primary. If you study political math in the modern era, one lesson you will learn is that more women than men vote in Democratic primary elections. A good fisherman fishes where the fish are, and a good politician politicks where the votes are.

In a news conference in White's campaign office in Greek Town, Lorna Brett, president of the Chicago Chapter of the National Organization for Women (NOW), blistered McCarthy. Brett accused McCarthy of a "callous and cavalier attitude toward women in government" and made an appeal to Democratic women to shift their allegiance from Severns to White.

Deviating from her prepared remarks, Brett told reporters, "Tim McCarthy didn't make Penny Severns sick. Tim McCarthy makes me sick."

Mutchler's appearance before the Springfield press corps gave reporters their first real indication that Severns's health may have been worse than had been reported. And Penny had a statewide following in the media, not only from her years as a lawmaker, but also from her campaign for lieutenant governor four years earlier. McCarthy was in for a rough ride. Just how rough, however, not even the media yet knew.

In the early morning hours of February 21, surrounded by family and loved ones, Penny Severns died in her Decatur home. Less than forty-eight hours after her best friend announced that Severns would not appeal the election board's decision, the 46-year-old state senator, a hero to thousands of women across the state of Illinois, succumbed to complications from cancer.

The McCarthy camp was stunned.

"I was horrified," says McCarthy campaign spokeswoman Kitty Kurth. "We were all horrified. Especially after going through cancer with Paul Tsongas, I was really shocked that Senator Severns would have, through her campaign committee, not been completely honest with her supporters about her health."

To this day, Kurth and others affiliated with McCarthy maintain that Severns's campaign was responsible for hiding the gravity of her illness.

"I always thought that she was very ethical and very upright about everything and we were honestly believing her press releases and we were believing what her campaign was saying to her supporters. When I found out that, clearly, they had not been straight with anybody, I was shocked.

"Looking back, though, part of our shock was that I didn't know anyone in her campaign. I didn't have the kind of back-channel information that a lot of times you do, especially in primaries." In that regard, the McCarthy people might not have known what White's campaign suspected about Severns's health.

Tim McAnarney echoed Kurth's claim that no one in the McCarthy camp had understood the severity of Severns's illness.

"I'm sure we upset some people. Had we known Penny was that ill, obviously, we wouldn't have challenged the petitions," McAnarney contends. "She looked healthy, and we did not anticipate her being that sick. I don't think Penny knew she was that ill. I don't think she would have gotten into the race if she had known she was that ill."

Schoenburg, in the same column that questioned McCarthy's decision not to cancel his February 19 news conference, also chided the Severns camp for being somewhat furtive about her illness:

Severns was also at fault because she played a public relations game in addition to fighting the challenge ... Severns was a great fighter whose courage in the face of a deadly disease was inspiring. But to be running a statewide race while as sick as she was is something to be questioned. And her public statements didn't let on how bad things were.

Chicago Tribune writer Christi Parsons shed some insight on Severns's mettle, a theory that might explain some of the mixed signals being received in the political community. Parsons recalls covering the Severns campaign for lieutenant governor in 1994 after the Decatur senator was diagnosed with breast cancer.

"She had a sense of invincibility," Parsons remembers.

"Chemotherapy was something that had to be worked into her schedule, and chemotherapy didn't bother her one bit.

"One of the visions of her that stays with me to this day is her taking a chemotherapy treatment while eating a peanut butter and jelly sandwich."

Parsons conducted the last one-on-one interview with Severns just a few short weeks before her death.

"It had not yet occurred to her that this was the end, that she was going to die, that she might die. She was still wearing that armor of invincibility."

In fact, Parsons believes Severns viewed their interview as an opportunity for the ever-conscious politician to set the table for the next political challenge.

"I think it was the same thing that caused her to file in the first place, even after the diagnosis that the cancer had reappeared," Parsons surmises. "She was ambitious and, in her mind, invincible. And I mean ambitious in a positive sense. She lived for her political career."

And she died caressing it.

For his part, Jesse White began wearing a pink lapel ribbon to recognize the fight against breast cancer. His decision to wear the lapel pin did not escape the wrath of columnist Schoenburg:

White's motives to immortalize a woman who was running against him and champion a health care cause smack of politics.

In fact, the suggestion that he wear the pin actually came from Severns's attorney, John R. Keith, passed through a consultant to the White campaign. That fact has not been made public until now.

Meanwhile, White's campaign scrambled to capture those Severns supporters who, even before her death, had been left without a candidate. Both White's and McCarthy's camps suspended political operations until after Severns's funeral, held on a cold, but sunny, morning at St. Patrick's Catholic Church in Decatur. An overflow crowd was ushered into a room adjacent to the church, where the service was channeled through a closed-circuit audio system. White attended the service; McCarthy did not.

As soon as the campaign resumed on February 25, the White campaign began to marshal the endorsements of Severns's supporters. In a packed news conference in the capitol press room, a cluster of elected officials, led by senate colleagues Emil Jones Jr. and Assistant Senate Minority Leader Vince Demuzio, used the opportunity to endorse White as a means to blast McCarthy. In the February 26 editions of the *Chicago Sun-Times,* Springfield correspondent Dave McKinney filed this story under the headline, *Severns' Supporters Back White; McCarthy Ripped for Petition Fight:*

SPRINGFIELD – A day after mourning state Senator Penny Severns, supporters of her secretary of state campaign joined forces with Democrat Jesse White and lashed out at opponent Tim McCarthy for making "her last days and hours on earth hell."

Demuzio, who himself succumbed to cancer in 2004, turned to White during the news conference:

"I'll say to you, Jesse, she never considered you anything except no. 2. But since she's not here, I'm quite sure she'd consider you no. 1 now."

Seven years later, Mutchler says Severns would have endorsed White's campaign had she lived long enough.

"There was never any public question that she was going to endorse Jesse after she was taken off the ballot," Mutchler says matter-of-factly. "That's how she felt. At the end of the day, at the end of a very long day, I know that Penny liked Jesse and that she wanted to give him an endorsement. She just ran out of time."

The campaign **took a hero**

and turned him into

a politician.

— Kitty Kurth

White

Chapter Thirty-Three In the end, Jesse White cruised to victory.

As he stood under the bright television lights in the grand ballroom of Chicago's Palmer House Hilton, White hugged one of his first and staunchest supporters, Cook County Board Commissioner John Daley. It was a snapshot that confirmed the support that most suspected but could never really confirm until the votes from Chicago's 11th Ward poured in.

White beat Tim McCarthy by more than 100,000 votes, 484,798 to 384,603, largely on the strength of his support in Chicago and the suburbs. White carried forty-one of the city's fifty wards. Downstate, McCarthy was very impressive, beating White in all but seven counties outside Cook. Among those seven counties White won were Penny Severns's home county of Macon and neighboring Sangamon County, the seat of state government and a place where politics is religious and religion is political.

Roosevelt University political science professor Paul Green believes White would have beaten McCarthy one-on-one even without the Severns controversy.

"Given the numbers and the fact that Jesse White defeated McCarthy in the suburban townships by 22,000 votes, there was little McCarthy could have done," Green ventures. "Let's go in reverse. White wins the primary by 100,000 votes. The only way McCarthy beats him is if there's a suburban anti-Chicago run and then McCarthy gets as much of the Chicago vote as he could get.

"But McCarthy was not running against a regular Chicago Democrat. He was running against Jesse White, a man with a resume. It was a battle of resumes, that's what I think I called it at the time. It was an election for White to lose. There's no way you could win a contested (Democratic) primary against a man like Jesse White, who has so much cross-racial appeal.

"People don't realize that because they like to go back to the 'shirts and skins' racial politics of the 1980s. The candidate means something. Jesse White has a resume that matches up with anyone, including McCarthy, who had a great resume and was a good guy."

In fact, McCarthy still is a good guy. He still is police chief of Orland Park and still goes home each night to a family that loves and respects him. And he'll always be remembered as a man who saved the life of a president. Not many men can say that. In fact, Tim McCarthy rarely does.

Kitty Kurth, who more than earned her consultant fee during that wild primary campaign of 1998, says McCarthy painstakingly avoids references to that day in 1981 when he saved Ronald Reagan's life.

"To this day he will rarely talk about the Reagan shooting. And if he does, he'll ask for contributions to his high school. If he talks to reporters about it, he'll ask for money but the money is for his high school."

McCarthy's alma mater, Leo High School, once an all-white school operated by the Christian Brothers of Ireland, now has an enrollment that is exclusively African American. It's clear that McCarthy's loyalty, such an important chamber in a politician's heart, is color-blind.

Wistfully, Kurth laments the outcome of Tim McCarthy's only run for public office.

"He's an incredibly decent guy," she says. "He was just thrown into the wrong situation at the wrong time. I have to tell you, we really and truly had no idea how sick Penny was.

"But at some point what happened was … the campaign took a hero and turned him into a politician. And that's exactly what happened."

Today Jesse White speaks glowingly of McCarthy's public service as a law enforcement officer.

"Any time I have asked him to provide assistance on legislation or input on an issue, Tim McCarthy has been there for us," White says. "He's testified on behalf of my bills before the General Assembly. I consider Tim McCarthy to be not only a quality lawman, but also a friend.

"That campaign was a very tough campaign, especially for someone coming out of the box for the first time. I would hope that Tim McCarthy lets time heal wounds and someday comes back into politics. He has an awful lot to offer."

Friends, in political campaigns, are often difficult to identify. Murray Kempton, the late Newsday columnist, once described editorial writers as *partisan fighters who come down from the hills after the battle and shoot the wounded.* Likewise, savvy politicians charge to the battlefield after the fight and embrace the survivor. In other words, victory has a thousand fathers while defeat is an orphan.

One legitimate father of the Jesse White victory was John Daley, son of a legendary mayor of Chicago and brother of another legendary mayor of Chicago. John Daley learned life's lessons from the last big city political boss, Richard J. Daley. As former University of Illinois Chicago professor Milton Rakove advised in his book about the first Mayor Daley, *Don't make no waves, don't back no losers.* It's an axiom successful politicians follow.

But John Daley never gave a second thought to the maxim. He backed Jesse White's candidacy from its infancy right through White's election. Because of the nature of politics in the family and because the White campaign never had enough money to poll likely Democratic primary voters, all Jesse had was John Daley's word.

"I had a feeling throughout the campaign that he was going to win," Daley says. In fact, Daley sees similarities between White's 1998 primary fight and brother Richard M. Daley's own Democratic primary race for Cook County state's attorney in 1980.

"It reminded me almost of 1980 with Rich because Jesse was under tremendous pressure to get out of the race. When Rich ran for state's attorney, he had very little support from the leaders in the party. In fact, a vast majority of them opposed him. But Rich didn't care.

"Same way. Jesse said he just didn't care, that he was going to do it anyway. And I remember telling him, 'Jesse, if you're going to do it, do it all the way.'

"In the beginning he got pressure to withdraw and he told me, 'I'm not dropping out. I'm going ahead.' And I kept encouraging him, telling him that he was going to win this thing."

John Daley has been witness to a sea change in Chicago politics, from the record-breaking tenure of his father to his brother's assault on their father's record. Between them, John Daley's father and brother have occupied the big desk on the fifth floor of Chicago's City Hall for more than thirty-seven years since 1955.

In Chicago, buildings got bigger, some people moved out, some other people moved back in, and the Union Stockyards died a bloodless death. The south side steel mills boomed and then rusted. And the African American population began to flex its considerable muscle in the political community of Illinois.

By 1998, Chicago had seen two African American mayors in Harold Washington and Eugene Sawyer. Roland W. Burris, who in 1978 broke the color barrier in statewide Illinois politics, had risen by 1990 to become the state's attorney general. Two years later, Carol Moseley Braun became the first African American woman to win a seat in the United States Senate.

Still, there were more than just whispers that the statewide Democratic ticket in 1998 was a little too dark. Burris was waging a hard-fought campaign for governor in the primary. Braun was gearing up for a nasty reelection challenge from Republican Peter Fitzgerald. John Stroger was seeking reelection as Cook County Board president and the right to oversee the nation's nineteenth largest government unit. And, of course, there was that tumbling man who used to play in the Chicago Cubs organization. Four of the top-of-the-ticket office seekers were black.

"Quite honestly," Commissioner Daley says, "there was talk out there that Jesse would not win because he was a minority. That was being pushed out there. And that made me support him even more.

"I think Jesse resented it. I picked up the whisper campaign early on and the talk grew stronger as Jesse's chances improved. That strong talk bothered me very much. They tried to play it quietly, but it became more and more vocal as we got closer to the (primary) election. Some people tried to make it sound like the whole ticket would go down."

When John Daley was a boy growing up in Bridgeport, the neighborhood was populated predominantly by the sons and daughters of Irish immigrants. With a few Italians and Poles sprinkled around, the Bridgeport community was very white even though the neighborhoods adjacent to the east and south were exploding with the growth of African Americans. Richard J. Daley presided as Chicago's mayor during the turbulent 1960s and 1970s. He was the city's mayor when John F. Kennedy was assassinated. He was mayor when Robert F. Kennedy was assassinated. And Richard J. Daley was mayor of Chicago when, on April 4, 1968, the assassination of civil rights leader Reverend Martin Luther King Jr. triggered violence and rioting on the city's West Side.

Around the dinner table each evening, Richard J. Daley and his family discussed the news of the day. By either a convergence of the planets or a violent growth spurt in American politics, the news of those days was spectacular.

"We would discuss every topic that would affect the city because my dad encouraged discussion at the table," John Daley remembers. "Race was one of them. Education was one, the disparity and problems in education. We discussed the Vietnam War.

"As much as President Kennedy's death bothered my dad, King's death affected him tremendously. Forget how the city burned afterward. My dad was just stunned that this young man was shot and killed at such a young age and at the violence that was occurring in the country at the time. The violence was claiming the lives of political and religious leaders."

Daley remembers the bitter fight when Harold Washington defeated brother Rich and eventually became the first African American mayor of Chicago. After Washington defeated the younger Daley and incumbent Jane Byrne in the primary, racial politics reached a boiling point in Chicago. John Daley says he felt some of the same, ugly racial undertones as Braun, Burris, Stroger and White approached the 1998 Democratic primary.

"It wasn't as racial as when Harold ran for mayor, but it was close and that bothered me tremendously."

Daley wasn't the only Democrat who felt some pressure. It was a family fight and the family wasn't united. Pressure seemed to permeate the ranks of powerful Democrats during the campaign for secretary of state.

Edmund Kelly, who once commanded 5,000 jobs as the immensely powerful committeeman from the 47th Ward, backed White from the beginning but says the pressure to back off was immense.

"I got a lot of pressure for not being with McCarthy," Kelly recalls. "I was slate-making chairman and I had a lot to do with Jesse up here on the North Side. I know Tim McCarthy, but I got a lot of pressure from the South Side. Unbelievable. But I wouldn't budge."

Kelly says that, unlike John Daley, he had his doubts that White could win.

"We felt he would do well in the African American wards, but in the white wards I figured he would have major problems. *Major* problems."

Who knows when a campaign turns to the advantage of one of the candidates? Would Jesse White have won with Penny Severns included in a three-way race? We'll never know. Would Jesse White have won had Tim McCarthy not suffered blowback following Severns' death? We'll never know.

McCarthy downstate campaign coordinator Tim McAnarney talks somewhat wistfully about the final days of that campaign, seven years after the fact.

"We felt very good about our position," McAnarney explains. "We didn't have any money for polling, but we felt good about our chances going into the last week of the campaign.

"Then – bang – I knew the weekend before the election that we had lost. I was in Chicago, having lunch with a friend. The conversation went like this:

"Tim, it's too bad. You just lost."

"What do you mean we just lost? I feel pretty good."

"I was just in the 32nd Ward offices, and while I was there they were wheeling Jesse's brochures in and wheeling McCarthy's out to the garbage. They said they'd just gotten the word: They're going with Jesse."

Indeed, the 32nd Ward carried Jesse White 3,411 to 1,730.

Vision in the rearview mirror is crystal clear. In a political campaign, though, while rumors abound and tales grow out of chance meetings between backroom deal-makers, it's never over until, well, you know, until the last man is out.

Not until the results from John Daley's 11th Ward were delivered to White's election night conclave did one of the consultants believe that Daley's word was his bond. Until the results trickled into the Palmer House that night, there still was doubt by at least one Jesse White campaign consultant that the tumbling team coach and founder could be sold out. That's when Brian Hopkins, one of Daley's top advisers, rushed into the Palmer House Grand Ballroom around 10 p.m. on March 17.

"You guys are going to win," Hopkins gushed. "You carried Bridgeport 2-1."

Bridgeport, the boyhood home of Mayor Richard M. Daley and his younger brother John, delivered the day for White. The final vote canvass showed White thumping McCarthy 6,263 to 3,784 in the 11th Ward, from where the legendary Richard J. Daley once ruled Chicago.

John Daley was right all along. John Daley was true to his word. And he didn't back no loser.

Al Salvi was a very
disliked Republican.

I more or less thought
Jesse White
would be **the**
front-runner in that race.

— Susan Kuczka, Chicago Tribune reporter

Chapter Thirty-Four The November general election was boring.

Then again, after the bizarre series of events that highlighted the Democratic primary, an Ali-Frazier fight was an exercise in tedium.

Al Salvi, who lost badly to then-Congressman Richard J. Durbin in the 1996 campaign for the United States Senate, was beaten the day he won the right to square off against Jesse White. In defeating Republican Representative Bob Churchill, Salvi continued to rankle the moderate wing of the Illinois Republican Party. As bitter as the campaign was on the Democratic side, Jesse White's party was able to regroup and rally behind its nominee for secretary of state.

If there was a rift between White and the likes of state party chairman and House Speaker Mike Madigan, they cemented that crack the day after the primary votes were counted. Even without McCarthy on the Democratic ticket to serve as a magnet for supporters of Madigan's south suburban house candidates, the Democrats would increase their majority in the House of Representatives.

Before the 1998 elections, Madigan presided over a razor-thin, no-room-for-error 60-58 majority in the house. Following the 1998 election his majority increased to 62-56.

"We were friends before that campaign," Jesse White asserts, "and we are friends now. We both did what we believed we had to do during that campaign, and Mike Madigan continues to work in the best interests of his constituents and the state as a whole. We simply found ourselves on opposite sides during some differences in family opinion."

"In fairness to Mike Madigan," Commissioner John Daley recollects, "he thought McCarthy would help in electing state senators and state representatives and no one knows Illinois politics better than Mike Madigan.

"As speaker, he was looking from his perspective as to what was best for the party. Could he gain five or six more seats in the house so we could keep a majority?"

On the Republican side, Salvi was a wealthy personal injury lawyer from Lake County. He provided a harsh contrast to the affable Jesse White, former schoolteacher and mentor to inner-city kids. Salvi had served in the Illinois House of Representatives from 1993 to 1997. At 38, he was a politician starving for an office and the Illinois media sensed his ambition was somewhat blind.

In her story about the secretary of state debate, published September 24, 1998, *Tribune* writer Susan Kuczka wrote this under the headline, *Ambitions Setting Salvi, White Apart in Secretary of State Race:*

Beyond the topics discussed at the debate, the race for secretary of state may come down to how voters react to Salvi, whose politically ambitious nature and conservative ideology were scorned by the state's leading Republicans in the 1996 and 1998 primaries.

Two years ago, a lackluster campaign by former Lieutenant Governor Bob Kustra, combined with Salvi's appeal from the right, made him the GOP nominee for U.S. Senate against the eventual winner, Richard Durbin.

In March, Salvi defeated veteran state Representative Robert Churchill (R-Lake Villa) for the secretary of state nomination. While Churchill was little known and under-funded, the closeness of the primary race indicated lingering dissatisfaction among some Republicans for Salvi.

While Salvi gained statewide name recognition from his U.S. Senate run, his Democratic opponent is best known outside of Cook County for his work in founding a tumbling team 29 years ago for poor inner-city youths.

Unlike Salvi, who is looking to expand the office into nontraditional areas such as education through a special license plate with a surcharge dedicated to local schools, White is focusing his campaign on asking voters to consider who is more qualified to hold the office – an old-fashioned campaign theme from an old-fashioned kind of politician.

Voters in the 1998 Illinois general election favored old-fashioned politicians. George H. Ryan, a gruff but well-known gentleman from the hardscrabble town of Kankakee, was leaving his post as secretary of state to run for governor.

He was an old-fashioned politician. And despite a scandal that would dog his days during his one term as governor, Ryan would win in 1998.

So old-fashioned was Ryan that he provided some of the only fireworks in the race for the office he was vacating. George Ryan was as loyal a Republican as the good Lord has ever planted on American soil. He rose through the ranks of the Kankakee County Board in 1972 to win election as state representative. He rose through the ranks of the House Republican Caucus to win election as its minority leader in 1977. When the Republicans wrested control of the House of Representatives in the 1980 Reagan landslide in Illinois, George Ryan rose to the rank of speaker of the house.

Most political insiders believed Ryan would be Governor James R. Thompson's pick to succeed Alan J. Dixon as secretary of state when Dixon left for Washington. Yet, when Thompson selected the lesser-known and lightly-tested Jim Edgar instead, George Ryan pursed his lips and marched to the beat of his party's drum.

A year later, when Jim Thompson needed a running mate, George Ryan was his guy. Patience and loyalty paid political dividends to George H. Ryan.

Ryan's steady and methodical rise through Illinois politics and the Republican Party was an exercise in patience and party loyalty. When the time came in 1990 for the GOP to slate its candidate for secretary of state, George Ryan again answered the call. Many believed Ryan had finally climbed to where he always belonged. Nurtured in the patronage-rich enclave of Kankakee County, where public employees once coughed up predetermined percentages of their salaries to the local Republican Party, Ryan was ready to take over the patronage-rich secretary of state's office in 1990. He was born to command a patronage army in Illinois as much as George S. Patton was born to command the Third Army in France.

While serving in the General Assembly, Ryan developed a working relationship with dozens of Democrats. First elected just two years apart from districts strikingly different, yet remarkably similar, George Ryan and Jesse White were products of an old and abandoned system of electing state representatives. Under the system that was thrown out by a voter initiative in 1982, each of the fifty-nine legislative districts was represented by three members of the house. In 1982, voters approved a constitutional change that cut the house membership by a third and created 118 single-member districts. The new makeup of the House of Representatives in effect eradicated minority party representation in each of the old house districts.

One of George Ryan's loyal opponents in the General Assembly was Jesse White, the man who represented the house district that ran "from the Gold Coast to the Soul Coast" on Chicago's near north side. Ryan and White were fraternity brothers from their days in the General Assembly.

Their constituencies were strikingly different in many ways: Ryan's was Republican and generally rural; White's was Democratic and unequivocally urban. But both men came from old political systems where party loyalty was rewarded with jobs and party loyalists kept the jobs in the political family.

Al Salvi, on the other hand, was one of several Young Turk Republicans who liked to turn over tables and preach the gospel of his party's emerging hard-line conservatism. He was determined to push the system's envelope and rush to the front of the Republican Party pack. After serving just four years in the General Assembly, Salvi leaped into the U.S. Senate race against Richard J. Durbin. In the mind of an old-fashioned politician like George Ryan, Al Salvi not only had not paid his dues, he was guilty of disrespecting the system.

Politics is a rough enough business when your friends are on your side. It becomes almost intolerable when you can count your friends among your enemies. Make no mistake. If Al Salvi had only suspected that his party was not 100 percent behind him, the secretary of state race would confirm his suspicions.

Salvi smelled blood in the water as Ryan ground out his campaign for governor in 1998 against Democrat Glenn Poshard. During his second four-year term as secretary of state, Ryan was forced to fend off investigations into the deaths of six children who were killed when the van in which they were riding crashed and burst into flames. The van struck a piece of tractor-trailer equipment dropped from a rig driven by a driver who, it would later be proven, illegally obtained his commercial driver's license under Ryan's watch.

Salvi was forced to make a choice: run with a candidate for governor who might well be indicted down the road or run against him. It was an unenviable choice, especially for a candidate who was relatively unknown among the general public and generally disliked by so many old-timers in his own party.

By September, Ryan was fighting off allegations that his campaign was using official secretary of state resources for political purposes. In its editions of September 26, 1998, the *Springfield State Journal-Register* ran side-by-side skyline stories atop page 1 under the headline, *Ryan Campaign Work Probed.*

State Journal-Register capitol bureau reporter Doug Finke's story read, in part:

A special prosecutor is reviewing Illinois State Police findings on whether Republican gubernatorial candidate George Ryan's campaign illegally used state resources.

Attorneys in the Illinois appellate prosecutor's office will review the material at the request of Sangamon County State's Attorney Pat Kelley, who bowed out of the investigation because he is a Ryan supporter.

State police investigators turned over more than 1,000 pages of interviews and other documents to the appellate prosecutor's office for review. The office will determine if charges should be filed.

A day earlier, Ryan had caught wind of a comment made by Salvi to a journalist on the campaign trail. Salvi had said corruption in Ryan's secretary of state office was "widespread." Ryan fumed.

"The next time a reporter sticks a microphone in my face," Ryan told a friend, "I'm going to say something nice about Jesse White."

True to his word, Ryan the next day told journalists that Jesse White was better prepared than Salvi to serve as secretary of state. The comment shocked political observers across Illinois. It's one thing to bad-mouth a fellow party member in a caucus or behind closed doors. It's unheard of to bash a running mate in print.

"Well, Mr. Salvi's not that familiar with what goes on in that office," Ryan told reporters at a campaign stop in Chicago. "Obviously, I think Jesse White's probably got a better grasp of what goes on in the office than Al Salvi. I think (Jesse White has) probably spent a little more time in state government.

"He was in the General Assembly and has what I think (is) a better idea about how the secretary of state's office functions. I think Al just doesn't know what he's talking about in this case."

For his part, Jesse White did his best to stay out of the family feud next door. He wasn't about to get between Salvi and Ryan. At the same time, he was not about to send back the gift that George Ryan sent his way.

And for his part, Salvi couldn't catch a break. Even when Jesse White mistakenly labeled Salvi as the biggest drunk-driving defense attorney in his home of Lake County, the Salvi campaign failed to capitalize.

There appeared to be a general mistrust of Salvi's political motives. In numerous editorial board sessions, Jesse White was asked if he had designs on running for higher office. In each editorial boardroom White responded with the same response: I will not use the office of secretary of state as a springboard to higher office.

At age 64, he had the credibility to back up the promise.

Salvi, meanwhile, had just come off a race for the U.S. Senate and looked like a man who was dying to win an election, any election. So when his campaign on June 25 mailed numbered fund-raising tickets to secretary of state employees, the media were ready, willing and more than able to pounce on Salvi.

In envelopes handwritten and addressed to employees of the office he was seeking, Salvi enclosed tickets to "A Special Event with Al Salvi" to be held July 8 at the Illinois Building at the Illinois State Fairgrounds. The tickets, priced at $50 per person, were sequentially numbered.

In other words, the intimation was, *We know who you are and we know where you work. Oh, and we know where you live, too.*

The press beat Salvi to a pulp.

In a Sunday story of the July 12 editions of the *Chicago Tribune,* political writer Rick Pearson skewered the GOP's candidate for secretary of state. The story was headlined, *Salvi Raises $50,000 and a Furor.*

Al Salvi likes to know who his friends are, Pearson led.

On Wednesday night, at the Illinois State Fairgrounds in Springfield, an estimated 1,200 people showed up for a $50-a-head fundraising event for Salvi, the Republican candidate for secretary of state.

Hundreds of them were state employees, which came as no surprise. Salvi's campaign sent numbered tickets, soliciting $50 contributions, to Springfield-area workers in the secretary of state's office, using a state-generated list of employees obtained by a state lawmaker who is Salvi's law partner and who also serves as Salvi's campaign chairman.

Enclosed in each letter was a numbered ticket to the event, which would allow the Salvi campaign to track who coughed up for the tickets and who did not.

In essence, Salvi asked the people whose careers he would control should he win the election, to give him some help.

... The solicitation has some office employees fuming.

Pearson's story even quotes incumbent Ryan's staff as saying Ryan enacted policies prohibiting such solicitations from his own employees.

"This is classic political prostitution with a twist," said Jim Howard, executive director of Common Cause of Illinois. "The message to state employees is, 'Pay up.'"

Salvi asked Secretary of State George Ryan's office for its employee list but was turned down, Ryan aides said.

Although Pearson's story did not quote White's campaign staff, White campaign manager Thomas N. Benigno issued a directive to the campaign's fund-raisers: there would be no solicitations of contributions from employees of the secretary of state's office. The edict was an extension of White's policies within the Cook County recorder of deeds office. If an employee voluntarily stepped up and contributed to the White campaign, the contribution would be accepted, no strings attached. If an employee chose not to contribute, there would be no retribution. The bottom line was, the White campaign would not knowingly solicit a campaign contribution from the office he was seeking.

In subsequent statewide elections, numerous candidates have adopted variations of White's no-solicitation policy.

The issue of raising campaign money from state employees was moot. Unlike the primary, when Jesse White was forced to take out a personal loan of $60,000 so his campaign could purchase radio advertising during the last week of the campaign, money poured in for his race against Salvi.

Even the Jesse White Tumbling Team benefited from the whiplash Salvi suffered at the hands of his Republican brethren.

Salvi's opponent in the 1996 GOP primary for the U.S. Senate was Lieutenant Governor Robert Kustra, whose term as Illinois' no. 2 man was set to expire in January 1999. Kustra had accepted the position of president of Eastern Kentucky University and spent the last months of 1998 liquidating his Illinois political account. One of the beneficiaries of Kustra's *going-out-of-business* generosity was the Jesse White Tumbling Team.

"The challenges and opportunities created by the tumbling team have kept thousands of at-risk kids on the 'straight and narrow' and allowed them to become productive members of our society," Kustra said in announcing the gift.

"I am pleased that I can help Jesse's kids continue their education beyond high school."

Illinois Issues, a monthly magazine published by the University of Illinois at Springfield, explained how Kustra may have laughed the last laugh at nemesis Salvi:

With about $100,000 in political donations burning a hole in his pocket, Lieutenant Governor Bob Kustra has found some worthy recipients, including his former political rival's current campaign opponent.

Kustra, a Republican, donated $20,000 to the Jesse White Tumblers. White, the Cook County recorder of deeds, is the Democratic secretary of state candidate running against Republican Al Salvi. Salvi beat the favored Kustra in a surprise trouncing in the 1996 U.S. Senate primary. Salvi then went on to lose to Springfield Democrat Dick Durbin.

While Kustra and White dismissed the donation as political (sic), Salvi's staff criticized White for mixing money from his tumbling team with that of his campaign. White criticized Salvi for raising "an old issue." He says the attorney general found no wrongdoing.

Before leaving next month to be president of Eastern Kentucky University, Kustra will empty his campaign kitty, giving to, among others, the Illinois Senate Republicans and the Illinois Campaign for Political Reform, which he co-chairs with former U.S. Senator Paul Simon.

Ronald P. Cooley was a campaign aide to White in 1998 and remembers the day Kustra announced the gift to the tumblers.

"We were leaving the Blue Room at the capitol after Kustra announced the contribution to the tumbling team." Cooley recalls. "In the time it took to walk down from the second floor to the car, my cell phone started to ring. Salvi had already called reporters in Chicago and they wanted to know if the contribution was political."

It wasn't, and the allegation backfired on Salvi after Kustra showed journalists the money was donated directly to the tax-exempt, charitable foundation that operates the Jesse White Tumbling Team.

"Lieutenant Governor Kustra did not give $20,000 to Cook County Recorder of Deeds Jesse White," responded Christopher L. Allen, Kustra's press secretary. "The contribution was to the not-for-profit Jesse White Tumbling Team in an effort to establish a higher education fund for the tumblers.

"It was a contribution to help kids go on to college."

In the end, the comparatively boring race turned into a November 3 rout. Astute political observers knew from the turnout in key wards that Jesse White would win going away. Although Carol Moseley Braun ultimately lost her fight for reelection to the U.S. Senate, the African American community poured out in huge numbers that were compared to the turnout when Harold Washington led his people to victory in 1983.

Jesse White thumped Al Salvi by 437,206 votes – 1,874,626 to 1,437,420. This time he carried 29 of the state's 102 counties and crushed Salvi where it counted most: Cook County voters favored Jesse White by a 957,565 to 384,207 margin.

The kid from Dogtown in Alton, — the one who rode the same buses as Rosa Parks and who saw the same ugly racism that thrust his college minister to the forefront of the modern civil rights movement in America, — he won the big race of his life.

Once too old to graduate to the major leagues of baseball and now thought by some to be too old to go far in politics, this was the man who became the first African American elected to the office of Illinois Secretary of State.

A giant leap for most politicians, but a small step for a man who teaches kids how to fly.

The minds of some
of our statesmen,
like the pupil of the human eye, contract
themselves the more,
the stronger light
there is shed upon them.

— Thomas Moore

Chapter Thirty-Five When Jesse White took the oath in January 1999 as the thirty-seventh secretary of state in Illinois history, the office was mired in scandal. The officeholder is constitutionally designated as third in line of succession to the governor and commands the largest secretary of state office in the nation. The primary function of the office is the regulation of drivers and motor vehicles. It's not sexy stuff, but it's hands-on, public contact business. If the office runs well, the officeholder has a lease that's virtually unbreakable at election time.

But goodwill cannot overcome scandal. And when six kids die in a fiery crash and the media take an interest and the driver who caused the crash got his trucking license illegally, look out.

During the 1998 campaign, Republican incumbent Secretary of State George H. Ryan's ship began to take on water. Ryan, who was the GOP's candidate for governor and who would ultimately prevail over Democrat Glenn Poshard, a congressman from southern Illinois, was under fire for allegations of corruption and malfeasance during his eight years as secretary of state.

Ryan, a former lieutenant governor and speaker of the Illinois House of Representatives, repeatedly denied charges that his office was rife with corrupt administrative employees. The news media began in 1998 to report that Ryan's inspector general, Dean R. Bauer, helped thwart an internal investigation into the deaths of six children. The children of Duane and Janet Willis were killed four years earlier in a fiery traffic accident involving a truck driver who obtained his driver's license illegally through the Illinois secretary of state's office.

By the time Ryan was sworn in as the state's new governor, the United States Attorney's Office was on Ryan like ants on a discarded watermelon rind at a Fourth of July picnic.

During his campaign to succeed Ryan as secretary of state, Jesse White recognized a glaring need for an independent internal affairs department within the office. The only way the Office of Secretary of State could once again gain the public's trust was to allow a harsh light to shine on its internal machinery. In a news release dated September 3, 1998, the Jesse White campaign called for radical reform within the office:

White Calls for Professional, Non-Political Internal Affairs Chief

Jesse White, Democratic candidate for Illinois secretary of state, today said he will conduct a nationwide search for a law enforcement professional who will serve as the next inspector general and weed out corruption in the secretary of state's office.

White's proposal follows allegations that some current employees may have been involved in selling commercial driver's licenses to unqualified drivers.

A key to White's proposal will prohibit the next inspector general from participating in partisan politics while serving the secretary of state as its internal affairs chief.

Prohibiting the next inspector general from any involvement in politics allows him/her to be independent in rooting out corruption. An example of such independent law enforcement is the director of the Federal Bureau of Investigation. White said he may consider a term appointment for the position to further remove the inspector general from internal interference ...

"The next inspector general will have one concern and one concern only," said White. "That person will root out any hint of wrongdoing within the Secretary of State's Office and will be free to do so without any strings or consideration.

"My primary goal is to restore whatever integrity may have been lost because of the actions of some unscrupulous employees."

Bauer was a longtime Ryan lackey and had served as police chief in the administration of Ryan's mayoral brother of Kankakee. His loyalty to his boss was unqualified and unquestioned.

During editorial board sessions with newspapers throughout the 1998 campaign for secretary of state, the topic of political corruption dominated discussions. Although Ryan and his top aides succeeded in avoiding indictment during the 1998 campaign for governor, the ax fell swiftly and often after he ascended into the governor's mansion. On February 1, 2000, thirteen months after Ryan's term as secretary of state ended, former Inspector General Bauer, the man hired to root out corruption from the Office of Secretary of State, was indicted by a federal grand jury in Chicago. The situation was summarized by a July 2000 story out of the Associated Press Springfield Bureau:

The indictment last Tuesday was actually a revised indictment of Dean Bauer, Ryan's longtime friend and his inspector general during Ryan's two terms as secretary of state. Bauer is charged with covering up evidence of corruption to protect Ryan's political interests.

It alleges that Bauer met with a whistleblower and falsely promised to investigate her claims that secretary of state employees were illegally issuing truck driver's licenses in exchange for bribes.

Prosecutors say Ryan arranged the meeting after the whistleblower— an unidentified employee of the DeKalb driver's licensing center — went on television with her face obscured and complained about corruption.

The investigation, dubbed "Operation Safe Road," was launched in the aftermath of a 1994 highway accident in Wisconsin that killed six children and involved a driver accused of illicitly obtaining his license in Illinois.

Illinois officials have since warned other states that unqualified truck drivers may have traded tainted Illinois licenses for licenses elsewhere. Hundreds of licenses have been revoked in Illinois and Florida, and New York officials have ordered new tests for about 100 truckers from Illinois.

Bauer was among the first of Ryan's top-level aides to be imprisoned after he pleaded guilty January 17, 2001, to federal charges of obstruction of justice. Bauer was sentenced to 366 days in prison and ordered to pay a $10,000 fine for his role in covering up the illegal sale of commercial driver's licenses by employees of the secretary of state.

Clearly the integrity of the office was in the crosshairs of public opinion. By December of 2003, Ryan himself became the sixty-sixth person indicted in the U.S. Attorney's Operation Safe Road probe of corruption within the Office of Secretary of State. In a news release announcing Ryan's indictment, U.S. Attorney General John Ashcroft zeroed in on the erosion of the public's trust in Ryan's former office.

"On the stone walls of the Justice Department in Washington," Ashcroft said, "are chiseled the words: 'No free government can survive that is not based on the integrity of the law.' When a public official abuses his office, he drains the reservoir of public trust on which our democratic institutions rely. In bringing these indictments, the Justice Department is seeking to protect the faith the American people must have in their government."

Indeed, the challenge of restoring faith to the Illinois Office of Secretary of State stared square in the eye of the Jesse White administration as he took office in 1999. This was the first Democratic secretary of state to walk through the doors since 1981. Moreover, Jesse White would be the first product of the Chicago regular Democratic organization to serve as secretary of state since Michael J. Howlett left the office in 1977. The times and the temperatures of public opinion had changed dramatically in the twenty-two years between Chicago Democratic organization secretaries of state. Change whistled through the capitol as lawmakers began to boast about, rather than avoid, government reform.

Jesse White had demonstrated his understanding of the problem when he promised during the campaign in September that an internal affairs officer, completely independent of the front office administration, was necessary to cleanse the office. Not only was it imperative that the new secretary of state address the reality of corruption, he understood full well that he needed also to attack the perception that the public trust was at auction to the highest bidder.

White's first inspector general, Don Strom, left for a post at Washington University in St. Louis one year into the administration. His second appointment, David Grossman, became bogged down in a fledgling administration's senior staff conflict. Finding the right person to fill the bill from the government's point of view as well as the public's was not coming easy to the newly elected secretary of state. It was time for a political Mulligan after Grossman resigned the position less than a year after he was appointed. More than ever, it became critical that Jesse White select a no-nonsense internal watchdog to restore public trust to the office.

The new secretary of state turned to a former federal prosecutor to shake the bugs out of the carpet. Enter James B. Burns.

Burns, who was appointed in 1993 by President Bill Clinton to serve as the U.S. attorney for the Northern District of Illinois, was no stranger to politics. He left the U.S. Attorney's Office in 1997 to launch an unsuccessful campaign for the Democratic nomination for governor of Illinois.

Seven years earlier, Democratic gubernatorial nominee Neil F. Hartigan selected Burns as his running mate. A native of McLeansboro in southern Illinois, Burns was a Big Ten basketball star at Northwestern University and had a cup of coffee with the Chicago Bulls before finishing his professional basketball career with the Dallas Chapparels of the NBA's rival American Basketball League. His geographic balance and fresh face was a complement to Hartigan's two decades on the Illinois political scene. Hartigan and Burns lost that 1990 race to the Republican tandem of Jim Edgar and Bob Kustra.

With Jim Burns, White saw an opportunity to send a strong signal to the people who elected him as secretary of state. Burns's reputation as an independent federal prosecutor brought White and his office instant credibility.

"There were a couple of phone calls from some people inquiring whether I had any interest in talking with Jesse about the job," Burns says. "Frankly, I always liked the public side better and it sounded kind of intriguing, although I had a couple of people tell me they thought I'd be nuts to come over here. I think the term one of them used was 'quicksand' because of the history this office has had. But to me it was kind of intriguing and it was dependent on what Jesse had to say."

Burns and White talked over the possibilities and the ground rules Burns figured he'd need to be an effective internal affairs officer.

"Some of the obvious things were that I needed independence. I wanted to do my own hiring and moving and promoting. In other words, what I was subtly saying was that there would be no patronage, no nothing. It was understood that I would not only do my own hiring, but if the people I was inheriting didn't work out, that I could move them out."

Jesse White agreed to Burns's terms. Why not? They were similar to the terms he'd outlined during the campaign in 1998.

"And they've lived up to that 100 percent," Burns continues. "We've come to an arrangement – and a lot of guys in his position would have egos too big to permit this – he's really on a need-to-know basis. Once we've reached the point in an investigation and he needs to know, then we do that."

Burns also insisted on placing the inspector general's employees under the personnel code, where they would not be subject to arbitrary dismissal, even upon the eventuality that administrations change.

"I have to go through that arcane personnel process to get people hired," Burns explains. "But it's worth doing that because that's a further indication that our people are independent. You go around to a lot of IGs' offices around the country and everyone is exempt (from personnel codes and serves at the desire of the elected official). What's that tell you?

"But if somebody comes in when Jesse and I leave, it's going to be real hard for them to monkey with the office."

"Bringing Jim Burns in as inspector general was the best thing that Jesse White could possibly have done," says U.S. Senator Richard J. Durbin. "Everyone who knows Jim Burns knows that he is above reproach. It was the signal Jesse needed to give that he was not going to tolerate the old policies of the previous administration."

Durbin's sentiments are echoed by Gene Callahan, former journalist and longtime top aide and confidante to former Senator Alan J. Dixon.

"Hands down, the best thing Jesse White ever could have done," Callahan says.

Callahan understands good government as well as the importance of addressing public perception. He cut his government teeth in the office of the late Paul Simon, universally recognized as one of Illinois' more honorable politicians of the twentieth century.

Burns insists neither White nor his staff interfere with any aspect of the inspector general's office.

"The big credit to Jesse is that there's always been this sort of mind-set that we don't want any scandals, we don't want any noise," Burns explains. "The good thing is that things have been pretty quiet. When we get something, though, Jesse's just as excited as anybody. He's like the new sheriff in town and his office is the one ferreting it out, finding the problems and dealing with them. We may only do six, seven, eight criminal cases a year, but you know what? That's enough."

It's enough to send the message that the "culture of corruption" that permeated the office when Jesse White was elected would not be tolerated. Burns remembers that when he took over as inspector general, "morale was horrible and the public's attitude toward the office was pretty low.

"The secretary of state's office has had such a storied history of scandal over the years. It's been viewed as a patronage office and a fund-raising office. Some people have used it as a steppingstone to run for governor or higher office."

Had Jesse White harbored ambitions for higher office, he would have had ample opportunity to trumpet his success and innovation. With the license-for-bribes specter haunting the previous administration, White focused on sanitizing a corrupted commercial driver's licensing program. To honor his late friend and sister-in-arms, he created the Penny Severns Literacy Program to promote reading and education among young people. And he redoubled his efforts to raise Illinois' consciousness of organ donation and transplantation.

But Burns believes the Jesse White era will be viewed as the one that brought a sense of order and respect back to the Office of Secretary of State.

"My discussions with Jesse were simple. I told him, 'Jesse, you could shorten the lines at the driver's facilities dramatically. You could change some of the business practices dramatically for the better. But that's not what people will remember you for. Your real legacy and the real opportunity you have here is to change the culture and clean it up.'

"And that's the kind of legacy that will be lasting. And I think that's going to be his legacy and he deserves it. The so-called culture of corruption, it takes a while to build it. It doesn't just happen overnight. And it takes a while to unwind it."

You can fly!

You can fly!

You can fly!

— Peter Pan

Chapter Thirty-Six Four years after his election as secretary of state, Jesse White put together a campaign that most politicians can only dream about. In 2002, he crushed Republican Kris Cohn, 2,390,181 to 1,051,672, for 69.4 percent of the vote. His 1,338,509-vote plurality was one of the largest in state history. Moreover, he became the first African American candidate in Illinois history to win each of the state's 102 counties.

It was a remarkable achievement, considering that only twenty-four years earlier, Illinois voters elected the first African American statewide constitutional officer in state history.

Dick Durbin, senior senator from Illinois and second-ranking Democrat in the U.S. Senate, was the unsuccessful candidate for lieutenant governor in 1978 when Illinois elected its first black statewide official. That year, Roland W. Burris, a former bank examiner from downstate Centralia, defeated John Castle of DeKalb, becoming the first African American in Illinois history to win a constitutional office.

Since then, black candidates Carol Moseley Braun, Barack Obama and Jesse White have followed Burris and have won statewide elections in Illinois.

Durbin said he believes people like White, Burris, Braun and Obama have put to rest racial considerations for public office in Illinois.

"I really think our state has come so far," Durbin ventures. "When you stop to think that the two most popular vote-getters in Illinois are Barack Obama and Jesse White, man, I feel good about that. I'm glad that happened in my lifetime. I can remember the days when blacks were just (made to) run as a matter of symbolism.

"But it's a new day and it's a great day. I feel great about our state, that race is no longer a problem. I really don't believe it is a factor anymore. I can't imagine anyone would think twice about slating anyone because of concerns over reactions to race. And that's a great feeling. It not only means the state has come a long way, but the people who guided it along that path, who've been elected, had a lot to prove.

"They had to prove they were up to the job and that the public confidence that had been given to them was well placed. You have to give them credit along the way. People like Jesse White have laid the foundation for future generations to have a chance."

For future generations to have a chance.

Chances in and of themselves are not necessarily gifts. But without a chance there are millions of kids who can never show what kind of natural gifts they've been given.

The chances that Jesse White gives have been part of a million miracles in his life. Paving the way for young African Americans to *have a chance* to win elective office in their native land is just one of them.

Some might say it would be a miracle for a human to fly. But Jesse White has already been a part of that miracle-in-the-making. If you've ever seen the Jesse White Tumblers perform, you know that people do fly. The key is in the takeoff and in the landing. Jesse White sees to it that they learn how to take off and as they do, he teaches their spirit how to fly, too.

And when they land, they should land softly and to the roar of the crowd. But if they land hard, if there's a flaw in their finish, there's always that chance for redemption from the man who performs redemptive miracles every day in the mean streets of Chicago.

Santa Claus may have a hard time working the projects in Chicago, but then again, no one calls Santa, *Mister Claus.*

Santa Claus may take a detour around The Greens, but the man they call Mister keeps coming right back at 'em. The bad guys don't mess with him; they don't mess with his kids. Figuring a way down the chimney is pretty spectacular. Getting back up is miraculous. Leaving something under the tree is what Santa Claus is all about. Leaving behind the example of love, respect and understanding is priceless when the gift is self.

And if a chance is a gift, Jesse White is Santa Claus 365 days a year.

That's Jesse to your mother. *Mister* White to you.

INDEX

They Call Heroes Mister . . .